Film Figures

Film Figures

An Organological Approach

Warwick Mules

BLOOMSBURY ACADEMIC
NEW YORK • LONDON • OXFORD • NEW DELHI • SYDNEY

BLOOMSBURY ACADEMIC

Bloomsbury Publishing Inc, 1359 Broadway, New York, NY 10018, USA
Bloomsbury Publishing Plc, 50 Bedford Square, London, WC1B 3DP, UK
Bloomsbury Publishing Ireland, 29 Earlsfort Terrace, Dublin 2, D02 AY28, Ireland

BLOOMSBURY, BLOOMSBURY ACADEMIC and the Diana logo are trademarks
of Bloomsbury Publishing Plc

First published in the United States of America 2024
Paperback edition published 2025

Copyright © Warwick Mules, 2024

For legal purposes the Acknowledgments on p. xi constitute an extension of this copyright page.

Cover design: Eleanor Rose
Cover image: still from *Der letzte Mann (The Last Laugh)*,
1924, dir. F.W Murnau © Photo 12 / Alamy

All rights reserved. No part of this publication may be: i) reproduced or transmitted in any form, electronic or mechanical, including photocopying, recording or by means of any information storage or retrieval system without prior permission in writing from the publishers; or ii) used or reproduced in any way for the training, development or operation of artificial intelligence (AI) technologies, including generative AI technologies. The rights holders expressly reserve this publication from the text and data mining exception as per Article 4(3) of the Digital Single Market Directive (EU) 2019/790.

Bloomsbury Publishing Inc does not have any control over, or responsibility for, any third-party websites referred to or in this book. All internet addresses given in this book were correct at the time of going to press. The author and publisher regret any inconvenience caused if addresses have changed or sites have ceased to exist, but can accept no responsibility for any such changes.

A catalog record for this book is available from the Library of Congress.

Library of Congress Cataloging-in-Publication Data

Names: Mules, Warwick, author.
Title: Film figures : an organological approach / Warwick Mules.
Description: New York : Bloomsbury Academic, 2024. | Includes bibliographical references and index. | Summary: "Develops a program for undertaking figural analysis of narrative film by drawing on the work of three philosophers: Walter Benjamin, Jacques Lacan and Gilles Deleuze"– Provided by publisher.
Identifiers: LCCN 2023030901 (print) | LCCN 2023030902 (ebook) | ISBN 9781501361210 (hardback) | ISBN 9798765112465 (paperback) | ISBN 9781501361234 (epub) | ISBN 9781501361227 (pdf) | ISBN 9781501361241
Subjects: LCSH: Motion pictures–Philosophy. | Characters and characteristics in motion pictures.
Classification: LCC PN1995 .M735 2024 (print) | LCC PN1995 (ebook) | DDC 791.4301–dc23/eng/20231023
LC record available at https://lccn.loc.gov/2023030901
LC ebook record available at https://lccn.loc.gov/2023030902

ISBN: HB: 978-1-5013-6121-0
PB: 979-8-7651-1246-5
ePDF: 978-1-5013-6122-7
eBook: 978-1-5013-6123-4

Typeset by RefineCatch Limited, Bungay, Suffolk

For product safety related questions contact productsafety@bloomsbury.com.

To find out more about our authors and books visit www.bloomsbury.com
and sign up for our newsletters.

For Helen

Contents

List of figures	viii
Preface	ix
Acknowledgements	xi
Introduction	1
1 Organology	33
2 Hermeneutics	53
3 Dreaming	77
4 Cinematic time	99
5 Spherology	123
Conclusion	155
Notes	159
Bibliography	165
Index	175

Figures

0.1	*L'Eclisse*, dir. Michelangelo Antonioni (1961)	2
0.2	*L'Eclisse*, dir. Michelangelo Antonioni (1961)	4
0.3	*The Third Man*, dir. Carol Reed (1949)	18
1.1	*Rear Window*, dir. Alfred Hitchcock (1954)	43
1.2	*Rear Window*, dir. Alfred Hitchcock (1954)	44
2.1	*The Last Laugh*, dir. F.W. Murnau (1924)	67
2.2	*The Last Laugh*, dir. F.W. Murnau (1924)	69
3.1	*The Lady from Shanghai*, dir. Orson Welles (1947)	95
3.2	*The Lady from Shanghai*, dir. Orson Welles (1947)	96
4.1	*L'Eclisse*, dir. Michelangelo Antonioni (1961)	103
4.2	*L'Eclisse*, dir. Michelangelo Antonioni (1961)	107
4.3	*L'Eclisse*, dir. Michelangelo Antonioni (1961)	108
4.4	*Une Femme Douce*, dir. Robert Bresson (1969)	114
4.5	*Une Femme Douce*, dir. Robert Bresson (1969)	115
4.6	*Une Femme Douce*, dir. Robert Bresson (1969)	115
5.1	*The Father*, dir. Florian Zeller (2020)	138
5.2	*The Father*, dir. Florian Zeller (2020)	143
5.3	*The Father*, dir. Florian Zeller (2020)	150
5.4	*The Father*, dir. Florian Zeller (2020)	153

Preface

The existential threat facing humans today is their inability to care for the future in view of catastrophes to come. Locked into what philosopher Peter Sloterdijk calls cynical reason, humans are preparing themselves for the future but in a self-defeating way, where what gets done merely reproduces the conditions under which catastrophes come instead of transforming them into new life. The problem lies in the kind of doing that gets things done, which, for humans, is the technical achievement of a certain kind of relation they have with machines to extend their control of time and space at the expense of the non-human world and ultimately at their own expense as well. Guided by the capitalist profit motive, the human-machine relation is locked into the drive of technical efficiency threatening unchecked creative destruction and system collapse sustaining all planetary life.

In what way do film figures relate to catastrophes to come and in what sense are they concerned with taking proper care for the future? Following the work of Bernard Stiegler, whose organology of the human-machine relation informs the argument of this book, an answer can be found in the cinematic way contemporary humans recognize each other in terms of problems besetting their lives. The question of recognition together with the question of moral right concerning sufficiencies of reason required for doing things – why we *ought* to do them – is built into the way we see *cinematically*; that is, through moving images projected onto a screen in which the desire for stories is acted out. This book shows how the relation between the human and the technology humans employ for projecting their desires into the future is bound into the problem of creative destruction endemic to the drive of capitalism as told to us in the fabulation of films, posing the question of how we might avoid its vitiating effects.

The problem of creative destruction resolves into a question of who the human thinks it is in relation to *techne* – artificial intelligence – and in what sense this *who* is deluded in its thinking. Deluded thinking thinks the relation to *techne* in terms of means–end efficiency for the good of humans by presupposing what good is, thereby turning it into a dogmatic good unable to think otherwise: a pathological form of *anthropy* leading to psychic rigidity, social ossification and ultimately spiritual death in the rage thus produced. Means–end thinking is deluded in the sense that, in today's hyper-industrialized, globalized capitalist free market world, the profit motive has phase-shifted means–end efficiency into black box calculative rationality, placing acquiescing humans under the control of algorithmic governance, the effect of which is to strip them of their capacity to imagine otherwise and thus of the ability to think with sufficient care for the future in knowing other ways and means of doing so.

Through an examination of the cinematic conditions of film story-telling, *Film Figures* shows how the means–end logic of the technical drive is also a counter-drive, which Stiegler calls *neganthropy*: the resistivity of humans to negentropy – the tendency toward disorder – as a saving power. By reversing means–end logic in neganthropic resistance, we find ourselves with the counter-drive in its refusal of the entropic tendency towards disorder, thereby freeing up possibility in 'other pathways' thinking – other ways in which the film, in our relation to it, could be. We begin our inquiry by opening ourselves to the counter-drive of films in which the *who* we are seeking can be found as *figures of resistance* there on the screen gesturing otherwise to the means–end efficiencies of action in film story-telling.

Selected films are examined in developing an organology of film figures: an inquiry into the *resistive potential* of films as concretized memory structures in which the counter-wise projection of the *figural* operates to open up possibility for the telling of a future other than the one fated to be. In the face of out-of-control creative destruction, we can turn from within the film archive – the residue of our desires stored in films – to rediscover the *who* we have surrendered to the means–end logic of efficiency-seeking in the drive of capitalist production/consumption, thereby reclaiming our noetic freedom to think and project ourselves otherwise. In doing so, we will have taken a first step towards another future through the saving power of neganthropy: the resistivity of human existence to the automation of machine intelligence as *right reason* for shaping new life.

Acknowledgements

This book could not have been written without the help of a number of people. In particular, I would like to thank Daniel Ross for his efforts in translating many of Stiegler's publications. I also wish to express my deep gratitude to Helen Miller for her untiring support through the long gestation of the book and her insights into the films analysed as well as her ideas on film in general. I would also like to thank Erika Kerruish for reading chapter drafts as well as our many discussions on issues pertaining to visual technology. I would like to thank Grayson Cooke for our lively discussions on the function of the digital in the creative arts which have helped me formulate the planetarium perspective adopted in the book, David Baker for our many conversations of everything in general, and Grace Garnett for her helpful insights into films.

Introduction

The *figural*

The title of this book says two things about itself. It says this book is concerned with something called 'film figures' and at the same time it says that this something is a doing: film *figures* in the transitive sense of an act of figuring, for instance, when someone says 'I am figuring it out', in the sense of working through a problem, giving it shape in one's mind and by putting pen to paper or on a computer screen. In hermeneutic terms, to figure is to give 'shape' to a future possibility – something that *could* happen out of all the possibilities of its happening.[1] The book *Film Figures* does what it says in its title: it figures the future out, makes it come forth as a promised event taking shape in the figuring process itself. The key to film figures lies in their self-reflexive doing: an activity working through itself in self-questioning, overflowing into other acts of self-questioning, including this book.

As part of the event of the *figural*, I will open up self-questioning with a first hypothesis:

> The *figural* is *feeling for the future* in which a film questions its *telos* – its aim or purpose – by calling the viewer into self-questioning to figure it out.

By calling the viewer into self-questioning, her fate becomes entangled in the fate of the *dramatis personae* – the characters – whose inner feelings are acted out as figures appearing and disappearing on the screen. Here, we need to think of feeling in both senses of the word: as *care* for what we feel and as *reaching out* for what we care about – the future in its promise, not as time already known and calculated in advance but as a '*to-come* that nothing could foreclose' (Derrida 2017: 49). By questioning the means–end logic of teleological progress, figures feel – care for by reaching out – for the future *otherwise*, seeking what they could have been as having happened but *not yet*. Figural thinking invokes the *stranger* in me in the telling of stories, the non-I of my self as double: the other me-in-me had I taken a different path in life's pathways. In my figural thinking, figures become overreaches of my desire to imagine myself otherwise, to *be* the stranger in me: the desired other who is also feared in the death-that-awaits which is the cessation of life to which I would be fated *had not this other future been imaginable.*

In theatrical terms, film figures are re-performances of my fearful desire for the future performed in the film's memorizing – its staging of past events – which is the outward expression of inner conflict in the struggle of life to *go on* by resisting death-that-awaits unfolding on the screen. Figural analysis of film is concerned with how this inner struggle is acted out, leading to an emancipation of the spirit by calling viewers into questioning situations. Let us now presume that the retroactive experience of figuring is already happening when I watch a film, calling me into it. While the action of the film progresses through *desire* – what is wanted in life – it simultaneously regresses in *drive*: the blind seeking of the automation probing for the future in the film's sealed-in pathway towards ending in which what is wanted is being tested for its worth *had a different path been taken.*

To feel the *weight* of the counter-force of drive – its resistive force – let us place ourselves inside a film-in-question. The film I have in mind is Michelangelo Antonioni's *L'Eclisse* (1961) when we see a young stockbroker Piero seated in his

Figure 0.1 Piero driving his car backwards. *L'Eclisse*, dir. Michelangelo Antonioni (1961).

sports car in the street outside his Rome office suddenly drive backwards at breakneck speed. In its sheer excessiveness, Piero's unexpected action raises a question: why did he feel the need to drive his car in such a reckless manner? In answer, we may note that, just before he hits the accelerator, a smile comes across his face; having jilted his date moments before, another plan of action has come to mind – to chance his luck with someone else, Vittoria – the woman he had met that afternoon in the stock exchange. However, plot detail does not explain why the director has seen fit to put such a gratuitous action in the film. If we are to comprehend the significance of this resistive action we should look not to motivations of plot but to the character's gestures – his bodily 'doings' – in what they are telling us: that this happened and that in happening it did not need to happen.

By placing Piero's action of driving backwards under question, we have opened our perceptual awareness to the *figural* – a comportment to the future in which characters are switched from their psychological mode of being as individuals vested with autoaffective life, to a gestural mode of performativity, transforming them into figures appearing and disappearing on the screen. The gesture of driving backwards *figures* other gestures of backward motion spreading through the film which, in thermodynamic terms, is the amplification of *negentropic force* – the resistivity of life in the tendency towards death in organic systems. From the switched perspective of the *figural* we are beginning to realize that what motivates all the characters' actions is an underlying resistivity towards ending carried by the gestural economy of images, a *neganthropic potential*[2] – the resistive potential of the human – becoming real on the screen as the cinematic life of the film. The character Piero *becomes* the very gesture he is enacting in driving his car backwards as a *figure of resistance*: a counter-movement moving against the plot's forward progress, opening the film to another time, not ahead of him but rearward, in the future of another path to be probed for and tested as one of the many ways in which the film is figuring itself out.

In hermeneutic terms, the fulfilment of a figured reality is the movement of time back across itself: an interpretive event of the future's promise in which what must have happened in the past is carried into the future retroactively – from the immediacy of its effects projected backwards to its cause posited after the fact as a fictionalized 'quasi-cause' (Deleuze 1990: 6, 33). The hermeneutic scholar Erich Auerbach calls the time-shifting of figures *figura*: 'the idea of something that is new and appears for the first time, of something that creates change in things that normally resist change' (2014: 66). As cinematic *figura*, film figures *bear* the future with them by 'resisting the resistance' of the *telos* of the story told – refusing its negentropic tendency in coming to an end. In their *forbearance* (in the sense of 'bearing up against', 'enduring'),³ film figures point otherwise to create change in things that resist change – resisting the forward progress of action in the completion of ends – generating 'something that is new'. The something new generated in this doubling of resistance on itself is another future in what the figure seeks had a different path been taken.

Let us now apply these ideas to the actions we have placed under question in *L'Eclisse*. In the sheer potential of its happening, the backward motion of the car which did not need to happen points otherwise by phase-shifting out of the time within it – its chronological means–end potential – into the a-chronology of the moment falling out of sync with itself, transforming the car and its driver into blind figures seeking for a future they cannot see ahead of them, repeated elsewhere, for instance when we see Vittoria wandering through a deserted plaza start walking backwards as if she too were resisting time within her. As she retreats, the camera cuts to what lies before her: a line of flag poles bending as if moved by some mysterious force, and an imposing statue staring down at her as if she had stumbled upon a strange void of inhuman nothingness.

Given the parallelism between these two moments – Piero's reversal of his car and Vittoria's walking backwards – in which there is no localized cause to explain

Figure 0.2 Vittoria walks backwards facing the void. *L'Eclisse*, dir. Michelangelo Antonioni (1961).

the connection between them, we find ourselves calling upon ideas, for instance the quantum thought of non-local interactivity in which two discrete entities are said to be 'entangled' in each other's being, where, in Vicky Kirby's words, 'the very ontology of the entities emerges through relationality; the entities do not preexist their involvement' (2011: 76).[4] Applying the idea of quantum superposition as ontological inconsistency to ascertain the conditions under which the two moments of backward motion can be linked, I propose a second hypothesis:

> The superposition of two moments of non-local affectivity in cinematic storytelling is an event of the *figural* in which the moments are in a relation of *paraconsistency*.

What is paraconsistency? How does a paraconsistent relation work in the quantum thought of superposition understood as entangled being? These will be our questions for the next section.

Paraconsistency

The problem we are seeking to solve is the parallelism of non-local interactivity in film in which actions are superposed on one another, thereby generating paradoxical situations, the logic of which we are attempting to explain through the employment of quantum thought. As the physicists tell us, we cannot observe superposition directly but only its consequences (Rovelli 2021: 46). To overcome this limitation, superposition must be *hypothesized* – fictionalized – to make sense of the paradoxical state-of-being precipitated by its effects; that is, to 'think of the metaphysical condition which allows for our relation to objects and our representation of the world – a condition that cannot be actually experienced but that could be rationally conceived' (Longo 2015: 31). Such metaphysical thinking is routinely employed by scientists, including quantum physicists, in developing their models; for instance, Schrödinger's well-known thought experiment to demonstrate that quantum effects are not limited to the microscopic scale of atomic physics but demonstrable at the macroscopic scale of human experience as well. To make his point, he imagines a cat inside a black box apparatus, exposed to a dose of poison released randomly, to describe the quantum wave function where the ontological reality of the cat as either dead or alive is actualized when someone opens the box (Rovelli 2021: 52). Here, it is important to keep in mind that the scientist's imagination is not all 'in the head' but communicated through writing things down and having them published, where what was imagined becomes subject to the judgement of peers. Fictionalizing thus has a communicative function to ensure the worth of what is imagined, without which nothing could be *said* to be imagined as sufficient to the truth of what is said. The downside of fictionalizing is that it generates ontological ambiguity between the act of fictionalizing and what is being fictionalized, an interpretive gesture which *is itself* an act of superposing, triggering a tautological succession of positings at risk of infinite regress in what logicians call an 'explosion' of meaning, where anything can mean anything at all (Priest 2000: 308). Is there a solution to this problem?

Following the non-philosophical thought of François Laruelle, film-philosopher John Ó Maoilearca has argued that non-Euclidian, non-dialectical 'paraconsistent' logic can be employed to make sense of the saying of superposition without succumbing to regress in logical explosiveness, 'where *everything* said is true' (2015: 128). To make his case, Ó Maoilearca distinguishes between two modes of being of any given substance: being coherent and being consistent in which the former refers to the unity of form, whereas the latter relates to the paraconsistency of substance: the way the substance 'holds itself together – its thickness or viscosity. Cinema too has a variable consistency, how it edits together ("stands still, together")' (128), holding itself together in the immanence of its own affectivity. In its *fictionalizing* of the world of objects and action, cinema 'edits together' heterogeneous elements by superposing the act of fictionalizing onto the fictional event, thereby generating ontological ambiguity between them, *rendered paraconsistent by the editing process itself*. In logical-analytical terms, film editing is understood to be an exercise of practical reason (praxis) predicated on the assumption of consistency in filmic 'substance' – the metastasis of its image flow – rather than the coherence of its form. In applying these insights to the hypothesized state of superposition which we have identified in *L'Eclisse*, we can say that the two moments in superposition – when Piero drives backwards and when Vittoria walks backwards – *leap* into each other's reality, rendered paraconsistent – 'edit[ed] together' – with the binding capacity of negentropic force: the force of resistivity holding the film together in its slide into entropic disorder.

To account for the identity relation between Piero and Vittoria in terms of paraconsistency, we will invoke Laruelle's notion of the *dyad couple* as 'cloning' in which two relate to one another through a One – a non-assimilable Real – as two 'in-One', a radical idea of superposed identity derived from Fichte's notion of the self-positing of I = I as the originary duplicity of the split subject 'aris[ing] in the power of the imagination itself' (Fichte 1988: 288, Laruelle 2013: 140).[5] Applying this idea to *L'Eclisse*, we can say that the dyad couple Piero-Vittoria is placed together-apart in a superposed relation, entangled in each other's 'being there at this place and time' which is also 'being there at this place and time', both of which – *because* of their non-locality – become compossibly affective through the retarding effect of negentropic force drawing them together in their apartness as two in-One spreading across the surface of the film's image flow. Through the paraconsistent logic of their non-local interaction – how the non-assimilable Real is binding them together-apart – the film is telling us that the paths of these two characters will meet in quantum terms in which their union as One – the happy couple – will have happened in its not happening: a condition of ontological indeterminacy pointing directly to the film's failure to coincide with its own memory – a catastrophic falling out of sync with itself in which both characters will be erased.

The force of resistance

In demonstrating the hypothesis of quantum superposition as an *event of the figural* we have triggered a switch in our perception, from seeing *with* the force of time drawing actions to their ends, to seeing *against* the force of time in the film's negative momentum (negentropy). The switch in our perception *is itself* an event of the *figural*, opening itself otherwise in a dimension of the film unseen from the means–end 'seeing with' position. From the perspective gained by seeing from within this unseen dimension, we uncover the *irreality* of the *figural*: its status as ambiguously either/or, a condition of undecidability Jacques Derrida calls *life death* in which life and death are superposed in self-erasing alterity, leaving a remainder 'that is no longer either *posited* or *opposed* and that would no longer be something in the sense of a position' (2020: 2). Like a gestalt switch whereby a figure of a vase suddenly flicks to a figure of human profiles in which the vase disappears – flicking back again when we make an effort to see the figure otherwise – *life death* oscillates between the face of life and the face of death, the appearance of one face erasing the appearance of the other, the remainder of which is the lingering of the images as autoaffecting appearances flickering across the screen. In cinematic story-telling, figural switching of *life death* opens up an *ontological gap* between life and death as a *gap that refuses to close* in which characters-as-figures resist the death-that-awaits in life gained in the film's falling out of sync with itself as the counter-force of *neganthropy*.

What is neganthropy? Neganthropy is proposed by philosopher of technics Bernard Stiegler to account for the accomplishment of what quantum physicist Erwin Schrödinger calls 'negative entropy' (1967: 71): the resistive force of life in entropic decay as being-towards-death 'in a specifically human and artificial mode' (Stiegler 2021: 58). What role does resistance play in Stiegler's thinking? Throughout his writings, Stiegler argues that we should reject the notion of resistance in favour of inventiveness (2016: 61–2). The argument runs something like this: in our efforts to avoid death in the slide of entropy, resistance resists, rendering a resistive attitude to life incapable of doing whatever is needed to re-invent ourselves in new projects, to affirm life against death. However, we will argue the reverse: resistance is required as a *necessary condition* for Stiegler's project of reconstitutive technics, without which inventiveness risks capture in the death drive of the automated systems of industrial life in which the creativity of humans is at risk of being eclipsed by the intelligence of machines. In its most primary sense, resistance relates to the will, which, as Stiegler himself proposes, is neganthropic struggle against the control of automated systems (2018: 48) – in effect, a resistive affirmation of the will *against itself*. It turns out that Stiegler's project requires resistance after all – resistance that affirms as it resists. In terms of film, affirmative resistance is the inventiveness of filmmaking praxis (localized tactics of direction) understood as a *dispositif* – a game played by the film with-against its own mechanism, its own rules (Martin 2014: 179) – the key tactic whereby films are continually figuring themselves out.

The *life death* struggle of neganthropic resistance – anthropic life struggling with-against the systems in which it is artificially entwined – is acted out in the *agon* of story-telling. In the *act* of telling a story, the film concretizes memory stored in the system into an image flow organized into discrete elements by the workings of a 'figure-matrix' (Lyotard 2011: 244) – a dynamic array of figure-images falling in and out of sync with themselves in the gap that refuses to close, for example the dyad couple Piero-Vittoria in *L'Eclisse* whose desire for each other is constantly thwarted by out-of-sync cinematic motion (to be discussed more fully in Chapter 4). Movement across the gap generates 'flicker[ing] of the figure' (Massumi 2011: 94), an excess of piezo-electrical light-life switching between the face of life and the face of death. As it flickers across the screen, light-life *figures* the irreality of life death struggle in which the threat of memory erasure is ever-present, foreshadowed by the *eclipse* – the quantum moment when the dead past and the living future cross back-over each other – as potentially catastrophic (the threat of chaos in a collapsed time frame reality). Figural analysis is an attempt to work out how this dynamic matrix of *life death* struggle operates in film story-telling when we take into account the viewing experience itself.

Drive

The drive of film is its retardation: the counter-force that keeps images flowing on the screen carrying onscreen action with it, without which the film could not hold itself together and all of its elements would disperse in entropic drift. Drive should not be confused with the progress of action in the fulfilment of ends; rather, drive is the *thwarting* of progress in delays, deferrals, detours and wanderings necessary to allow time for the *telling* of a story – accounting for action as worthy of recall – by testing it in questioning situations. As thwarted progress, drive becomes 'negative entropy' or negentropy – resistance to entropic drift – the sliding tendency towards cessation (death time), kept at bay in the film's duration, its sheer persistence on the screen and in the viewer's perception (without which there would be no film to see since any attempt to begin will have already been eclipsed by its cessation at degree zero).

Take, for instance, the state of near cessation reached in Antonioni's *L'Eclisse*, in which Piero's and Vittoria's lives seem strangely affected by an inhibiting force such that their every action seems to be resisting itself in entropic drifting, moving closer and closer to *memory death* in which all trace of them will be erased. In its ending, the film survives at their expense when the camera ceases to make them appear in what remains on the screen; in the final shots of the film, what we see are empty streets flooded with an eerie artificial twilight foreboding inhuman nothingness in catastrophic loss. In the restlessness of their incompleted lives, Vittoria and Piero are figures of neganthropic resistance: forms of cinematic life continually at risk of memory death – permanent erasure by the drive in its efficiency-seeking wanderings.

In his book *Time Driven: Metapsychology and the Splitting of the Drive* (2005), Adrian Johnston uncovers the dynamics of Freudian drive in the libidinal system '"somewhere between soma and psyche"' (xxxi) as a 'self-sabotaging mechanism, or, one could say, a perpetual frustration machine' (xxxii). Picking up on

Johnston's Freudian notion of the complex processes of the drive as 'an implacable conflict between two incompatible temporal orders' (xxxi) in-between soma (externalized body) and psyche (internalized self-reflexivity), I propose drive to be a pre-conscious impulse seeking blindly for conditions of repetition in a thermodynamic system of energy exchange. In its impulsiveness, drive probes blindly for a future with no foreknowledge to guide it as a 'perpetual frustration machine' split between soma and psyche, the operations of which must be thought, as Stiegler has proposed, in terms of 'tertiary retentions': the third memory of *mnemotechnesis* as technical support (2018: 48). The *figural* is feeling for the future in self-questioning as counter-action to the blind probing of drive carried by technical support: a seeking otherwise for release from the drive-impulse in its thwarted momentum moving towards stasis, at which point the mnemotechnical system by which the soma/psyche split is sustained would be equal to itself and all activity would cease.

The recursivity of drive opens a gap between what Johnston calls the 'axis of repetition' and the 'axis of alteration' (2005: xxxi), a scission in the becoming of time in which the past returns in a traumatic encounter with its ghostly afterlife. As mortal beings, we cannot go backwards in time, but we can feel its trace in an experience of 'afterwardsness' (*Nachträglichkeit*), for instance, when we look at a photograph of a deceased loved one, feeling the pangs of loss as a traumatic wound, reminding us that we too will some day die. In the camera reflex of Roland Barthes's '*punctum*' effect – the cut that splits time in two – in which 'he is dead and he is going to die' (Barthes 1993: 95), the loved one suddenly appears to us as a phantasmic other, the mysterious after-effect of a 'photographic rapture of time ... manifesting a unique connection between myself and my end' (Stiegler 2009: 17). In the rapture of time triggered by the cut, the loved one becomes transfigured into an impossible ideal – a figure of the future that will have been had she/he still been alive, testifying to the melancholic truth of mortality insofar as nothing living can survive its own death. Inscribing these issues in terms of cinema, the mystery of film – its 'filmicness' – resides in the cut of the *real* in which the resistance of drive is itself resisted by an enfiguring counter-tendency feeling for the future in anticipation of its loss as the very life of the film – its phantasmic otherness – which is something revealed on the screen in relation to what it hides from view: dead life that could have been lived in paths not taken. Film figures figure themselves out in the viewer's consciousness as the *real* of the film: the hallucinating after-effect of the past returning, the phantasmic otherness of which are these images I am seeing on the screen, hiding nothing but the void of what could have been.

The mystery of film

In an important publication on 'figural thinking', film theorist Adrian Martin undertakes a reading of Siegfried Kracauer's *History: The Last Things Before the Last*, a book with a decidedly apocalyptic tone influenced by Walter Benjamin's messianic hermeneutics in his attempt to reconcile the divine order of reality with the temporal reality of mortal life as theatrical performance (Martin 2012: 16). Moving towards a 'more Marxist, materialist knowledge system' (18) following Benjamin's lead, Kracauer 'conjures the existence of two spheres which exist in a deformed or inverted mirror relation: the sphere of humans, in their earthly society, and the 'superior realm' which, following Kierkegaard, Kracauer explicitly calls the 'religious' sphere' (19).

For Kracauer writing in Benjamin's messianic tone, the *figural* points to a world to come, experienced in an ecstatic moment of self-transcendence to lift us out of the secular 'sphere of humans' and into the 'religious sphere', in an experience of the divine ideal 'which will attain an absolute human value' (Kracauer, cited in Martin 2012: 20), an idealist theory of the *figural* which Martin associates with Erich Auerbach's hermeneutic reading of ancient and classical texts (discussed briefly in the first section of this chapter and more fully in Chapter 2). However, Martin continues, Kracauer's thinking deflects from the idealist ascendant movement of its aim, towards that which it communicates: 'the transport system back and forth between the two spheres' (20), suggesting a collapse of the eternal ideal into the finite temporality of a horizontal process.

Having invoked the *figural* as a gesture that says something about itself and, in so doing, points to its own transcendence in the divine ideal, Kracauer, as Martin suggests, revokes it by showing its transcendental conditions of appearance as communicable in a 'transport system', binding the *figural* into a recursive movement, shuffling back and forth between the present and that which will have been as the future anterior to itself. This recursive movement back and forth between the present and the future that will have been is drive: the pulsional counter-force of direction in the fluidity of the film's memorizing. The *figural* – feeling for the future – is that which resists drive as anthropic counter-resistance to the negentropic force of time: a tragic/comic switching between the face of death and the face of life – 'he is dead and he is going to die' – flickering on the screen and in me as the *neganthropy* of cinematic life.

Martin's invocation of the *figural* as a reflexive activity collapsing the ascendant movement towards the divine ideal onto the material surface of the sphere in which the viewer perceives a moving something, suggests a secular approach to the perceptual experience of film in which figures lose their divine, other worldly character and become characteristics of an *incompletion* seeking completion and forever failing in the gap that refuses to close. Following this line of thinking, figural analysis becomes the setting out of the conditions under which transcendence fails in the 'transport system' keeping figures afloat in the mnemotechnical apparatus in and through which the organ of perception is carried from the dead past into the living future as an *organic machine*. In Martin's terms, it suggests a materialism of the *figural* for 'non-believers to understand and use a language of the sacred or the spiritual but without religion; to approach and celebrate mystery – especially poetic mystery ... but without the mystical. Figural thinking, is ... mixed up or crystallized in this challenge' (12). My own take on Martin's challenge to engage in a 'figural thinking' of film, is to develop what Stiegler calls an 'organology' (2018): a materialist account of the organ of perception as a 'quasi-machine' (Derrida 2002: 134); that is, an apparatus posited as necessary to explain the moving something under analysis, which, in terms of Martin's secularized figural thinking, is the 'mystery' of film without appealing to the 'religious'. In terms of the organology proposed in this book, the mystery of film is located in the effects of an actual apparatus – the cinematograph operating along the horizontal axis of finite temporality – as *mechanical creativity*.

Mechanical creativity

In materialist terms, mechanical creativity is the power of the imagination – the '*primordial source of protentions*' (Stiegler 2019: 47) – employed to project a future in the anterior of its having already happened inside an organic machine: a recursive operation of creative memorizing, which in the praxis of film, involves film directors 'slipping in' images in montage effects following the logic of the Kuleshov effect: an experience of the same image insinuating itself in the memory of the viewer *as if* she were seeing it each time in a different way (Stiegler 2011: 15). Proposed by the silent era Russian film director Lev Kuleshov, the Kuleshov effect involves an editing process in which an unchanged image of an actor's face is repeated but perceived by the audience to have changed its disposition according to the different circumstances in which it appears (hunger, grief, desire); even though the actor's facial expression does not change, the audience perceives its meaning to have changed, with novel consequences for the truth effects generated by the film. According to Stiegler, the Kuleshov effect induces a memory lapse in the same way that hearing a melody for a second and subsequent times involves a *'clearing away'* (19) of its previous memory without which 'nothing would have passed, nothing would have happened'.[6] This clearing away or *forgetting* (which is also a repression) prepares the viewer to receive memory-images from an arche-memory – the storehouse of memories of a *We*: an imagined group sharing a common past (88) – archived in the generalized past carried by tertiary retentions (mnemotechnics). Here, we encounter *anamnesis* – the remembering of a forgotten past – a past that 'will have' happened supplemented by *hypomnesis* (supervening technical support), as fiction becoming real on the screen through the power of imaginative projection to create something new. The Kuleshov effect is a symptom of arche-cinema – an originary cinematic trait – guiding and controlling human consciousness in the age of technological reproducibility in what Walter Benjamin describes as the shock of the new, which 'brings to light entirely new structures of matter' (Benjamin 2002: 117). The cinematic arche-trait compensates for the forgetting of the past in *anamnesis*, generating the return of the repressed forgotten in the clearing away as a phantasmic haunting of the film, where imagination carried by *hypomnesis* eclipses perception, which, for Stiegler, is 'the very principle of cinema' (2011: 15).

The montages formed through the Kuleshov effect constitute what Gilles Deleuze calls the 'power of the false' (1989: 126), the power to effect false movement in cinematic space predicated on the 'irrational cut' (213): the suturing of images in violation of the geometrical proportions of Euclidian space. While Deleuze's interest in the power of the false in cinematic vision relates to mathematical principles underlying spacetime reality, Stiegler's interest lies in the fictionalizing effects of cuts across the memorizing of films in responding to the 'desire for stories' (2011: 8). In the desire for stories, in which false images are emplaced in anamnesic memory (the inner lives of characters) carried by the *hypomnesis* of supervening technical support, the viewer experiences a life that is not her own by adopting the characters' time *as if* it were her own (10). Through this 'slipping in' of false images, a viewer sees-feels a future unfolding on the screen in a past she did not live but 'will have' lived as fiction becoming real *for her*. Slipping-in fictionalizes the future in the 'as-if' modality of story-telling, directed by the emplacement of false images in cinematic memorizing (the Kuleshov effect). The praxis of film story-telling

– how a teller 'tells' a tale through camera emplacement effecting cuts, irrational or otherwise – holds the key to grasping the recursive operation of creative memorizing: the *as-if* experience of viewing a film.

The act of story-telling begins from the future anterior position insofar as a telling is an *accounting* for something after the fact of its happening, re-enacting it otherwise in voices and images carried by a technics of memorizing (*mnemotechnesis*). The telling begins by working backwards into the tale told, feeling its way into a future that 'begins to have been always possible' (Bergson 2007: 82) in the retroaction of the telling *as if* it were actually happening. The 'as-if' retroactivity of viewing a film is the logical mode of belief in the world whereby the memory of the thing recorded is experienced as 'camera movement effect' (Bordwell 1977: 21): as if a camera were moving when what we actually see is apparent movement emanating from light reflected off the screen. What I see on the screen is the trace of what the camera has left behind, worked up by filmmakers into a telling of events retroacting themselves as quasi-automated re-performances through the actions of auto-affecting figures – figures flickering with *life death* – feeling for the future in images flowing across the screen. The creative aspect of this mechanism is the crafting of directorial interferences in which voices and images are slipped in, re-arranged, enhanced and distorted to create reality effects on the screen and in me as well as in others who – from the hermeneutic perspective of the future anterior – will have seen the film as I have, each in their own way. *We* will have become part of an *I–We*: a transindividuated collective of individuals whose perception of the passage of time is carried in the film's feeling for the future in its many screenings experienced in the social spheres of its viewers past, present and future as the spreading of cinematic consciousness (Stiegler 2011: 35 ff.). It all begins in the 'cutting room' of the studio and in the cinematograph-in-general (2014a), in which the slipping-in of voice-image connections proceeds in the praxis of filmmaking and in us as well as a generalized becoming-cinematic of the industrialized human's self-conscious noetic life.

The in-between

In his figural account of the process of film memorizing, Martin invokes the idea of the 'eternal inbetween' (2012: 20), ascribing it to Kracauer's reorientation of Benjamin's messianic thinking between 'the realms of the living and the dead', which, as I have argued, is a materialization of the idealization of the figure – its pointing to an ideal along a collapsed horizonal line of action as life death switching. What I am proposing in this book is an account of the conditions of possibility of the 'eternal inbetween' reduced to its materiality in the retroactivity of film figures in *life death* switching, a micro-process of image shaping across the surface of the screen (along the horizonal line of action) as feeling for the future, entwining macro-processes of ideation passing through a quantum field collapsed into one of its realities as *this* film – the one I am presently viewing. To grasp the temporal dimensions of the *figural* in this horizontalized hermeneutic manner, we need to think of the process of image shaping in thermodynamic terms as energy exchange in which memory is transferred from the dead past into the living future by means of a mnemotechnical apparatus – Martin's 'transport system' – which we have invoked as the cinematograph, understood in materialist terms as a quasi-machine for seeing moving images on a screen.

The term cinematograph was introduced into the nineteenth-century lexicon by the Lumière brothers as the name they gave to their camera-projector apparatus for recording and projecting moving photographic images onto a screen for exhibition to a viewing public eager for new experiences of a technical kind (Lumière 1936). The potential for such a device to pose questions concerning the technical mediation of the living future by the dead past was explored philosophically by Henri Bergson in his book *Creative Evolution* in which he proposed the cinematograph as the mechanical membrane of an organic machine (1911: 234–5): the *organon* of perception inside the cinematographic mechanism exteriorized out of the brain–body nexus and into a world refracted through a crystalline sphere in the becoming of life as prostheticized cinematic consciousness.

In this book, I will employ Bergson's thesis on an exteriorized world of perceptions or *views*, seen through the refracted reflections of the crystalline sphere: the *speculum* through which the world can be imagined otherwise in the image shaping praxis of filmmaking – *ad hoc* placements and directions making up its own rules according to the paraconsistent logic of a *dispositif* – understood as mechanical creativity working through the membrane of the cinematograph as the materialized in-between of film figures flickering with *life death* across the screen. By looking otherwise through the *speculum*, a world of views opens before us in their temporal aspects as paths taken in a new dimension of the *archival future* – the paradoxical condition of the dead past in the living future reawakening to a future already remembered but not yet.

Transcendental materialism?

I have proposed figural analysis in terms of Stiegler's organology as a materialist mode of philosophizing on the experience of industrialized memory as cinematic life, entailing a collapsed transcendence of the materiality of film in the failure to attain the ideal; in other words, a quasi-transcendental materialism. What is quasi-transcendental materialism? The Hegelian-Lacanian philosopher Adrian Johnston, whose Freudian drive concept we have employed in our development of film *mnemotechnesis*, defines transcendental materialism (without the quasi-) as 'an account of the emergence of self-determining, auto-reflexive transcendental subjectivity out of asubjective substance' (2014: 18). Transcendental materialism is concerned with an emergent process of phase-shifting in which a subject in-the-making seeks to determine its own being by shifting in and out of phase through asubjective substance. Transcendental materialism seeks this substance as the *ground* upon which the thinking machine functions as part-mechanical and part-organic: an *organic machine* vested with noetic reflexivity – the capacity to project otherwise than the machine in which a subject in-the-making *in-exists*[7] in free being. In its incompletion, the subject in-the-making is 'mixed up or crystallized' (Martin 2012: 12) in the machine as coming-to-be self-consciousness with a burgeoning capacity to see itself seeing otherwise than the way the machine allows it to see (i.e. as self-reflecting against the givenness of what is seen). In the film viewing experience, I find myself caught up in a process of phasing in and out of self-consciousness by seeing myself as other than what I see on the screen: the *real* of self-consciousness that cannot be avoided without surrendering my noetic freedom to project otherwise, which for Stiegler, is the capacity to dream, a key concept in his project of organological thinking (2019: 89–90).

To begin a transcendental materialist inquiry into the conditions of possibility of a self-reflecting subject, we need to acknowledge what Johnston calls the 'heft of actual existence' (2014: 18) – the weight or *force* of reality as it is experienced by an existent being reflecting on the process of its self-constitution, which, in screen experience, involves a perceptual rapport between what is *on the screen* and what is *in us* as the energy that binds the two together while keeping them apart as separate realities, without which the distance between them would collapse and I would *be* that which is on the screen – an absurdity no doubt. To keep this collapse from happening, there must be something in-between – a perception shared between onscreen and offscreen realities as the 'asubjective substance' through which my consciousness of what I see on the screen must pass in order to reflect on what I see as *not me*. In this way, we can say that Johnston's self-determining, auto-reflecting subject emerging out of asubjective substance is the viewer's self-consciousness *becoming cinematic* through the shared perception of what is on the screen and in me. Self-reflection must pass through the *organon* of perception – its auto-affectivity – in order to complete itself. In so doing, the viewer's self-consciousness phase-shifts into cinematic consciousness, where, as Stiegler has argued in *Technics and Time, 3*, 'I negate myself in making myself cinematic' (2011: 61), a paradoxical action of self-constitution in which the 'I' splits in two as a Fichtean–Laruellean originary *dyad* torn between a dead past and a living future (on the screen and in me).

Is Stiegler's philosophy of cinematic time a version of transcendental materialism as Johnston defines it? Throughout his *oeuvre*, Stiegler makes repeated reference to *noesis* and noetic freedom: concepts he derives from Plato and Aristotle and their search for a first principle upon which to base the rational pursuit of knowledge of the cosmos and the emplacement of *anthropos* (the human organism) in it – in the struggle to survive against the inhumanness of the non-human within us all (Stiegler 2018: 83). What is *noesis*? *Noesis* is the reflexivity required for consciousness to become self-conscious (i.e. subject to itself), which, in Aristotle's *De Anima*, is demonstrated in 'an actual exercise of a power of sense' (1941: 589, 429a) as a pre-subjective capacity for imaginative projection which does not involve 'a synthesis of concepts' (595, 432, 10). Aristotelian imaginative projection is a primary principle of noetic existence, adopted by Fichte in his response to Kant's transcendental unity of apperception where he (Kant) had overlooked it.[8] It follows that noetic freedom must have a transcendental field of the primary imagination (i.e. a field without a subject) in which its possibilities could be explored, proposed by Stiegler in the following terms: 'a transcendental field without a subject (which obviously does not mean that there is no *I* in this field ... but that *if there is* anything transcendental, it exceeds the subject, and does so as its default)' (2021a: 366).[9]

In this field, the (pre-subjective) *I* in-the-making finds itself placed under question: which path to take, given that any path open within the field could be either healthy or toxic to life as the transcendental condition of *life death*. Stiegler is here speaking about situations of self-questioning mediated by *écriture* (writing systems), whose doubled reality as both curative and toxic to living speech poses what Derrida calls a '*pharmakon*', where 'there is no such thing as a harmless remedy. The *pharmakon* can never be simply beneficial' (1981: 99). For

Stiegler, not only writing but all forms of symbolic communication pose themselves in pharmacological terms, opening up bifurcations in 'the pursuit of life by means other than life' (1998: 17). Bifurcations hold the key to this pursuit.

The ethical task

In responding to the life death *pharmakon* encountered in the transcendental field, I pose the following questions. What part does bifurcation play in the pursuit of a healthy life in cinematic terms? Is this path toxic or curative? In responding to these questions, we call forth the *idea* of the whole of time as all paths that could be taken projected in a single glance. In this condition of *self-transcendence* in the field of possible paths, the ethical task of having to choose the right path to lead a healthy noetic life – life capable of projecting otherwise freely – comes under the guidance of pharmacological thinking: all paths are right paths but they are also wrong paths; it is only in hindsight that we can we 'tell' the difference (account for their rightness or wrongness in a moral judgement).

Figure 0.3 Anna walks past Holly. *The Third Man*, dir. Carol Reed (1949).

For instance, consider the final scene in Carol Reed's *The Third Man* (1949), when we see Anna walking towards the camera as her would-be lover Holly waits by the side of the road. Will she turn towards him or walk straight past? Reflecting on paths that could be taken tells us that the right path to take is the latter. Why? Because we already know that she remains hopelessly in love with Harry Lime, the black marketeer whose criminal activities have led to the death and disfigurement of innocent children, an unforgiveable crime which taints Anna with its evil. Had she turned to Holly, the evil in her would in turn taint him, and they would all be affecting one another with the malevolence of Harry's actions. Holly's innocence is secured while Anna's guilt is confirmed by having her pass by as a tragic figure whose fate is to have been all-too-human in having fallen in love with the wrong man.

The film is providing us with a *sufficiency of reason* to judge the actions of its characters on moral grounds – what path should have been taken – ascertained in our glance otherwise at paths not taken in the path actually taken by the film (e.g. by having Anna walk past Holly rather than turn to him). The undecidability of possible paths is resolved through reflective thinking guided by an intuitive grasp of the *whole* of the paths that could be taken in which the path actually taken can be judged as right or wrong according to criteria arising from the situation itself as its *limiting condition* (*a posteriori* reasoning – reasoning after the fact in which an *a priori* truth must be found as its quasi-cause). All of these considerations are operating at a transcendental level to the viewer's subjective experience of the film, and without them we could not judge the worth of the film in its capacity for telling us about right and wrong action.

All films are *pharmakons* insofar as their narrative trajectories are constantly bifurcating, posing questions concerning the 'ought' of any given path taken, in which a sufficiency of reason needs to be found in story detail for the noetic viewer – the viewing consciousness 'switched' to its critical capacity for thinking otherwise – to make an assessment as to the *moral right* demonstrated in the film's telling of the story. Moral right – a concept drawn from German Idealism – is enacted in participation with others under conditions of undecidability generated by the aporetic relation between law and justice, which Derrida calls the 'force of law' or *moral obligation* (1990: 961). Moral obligation is the feeling that one should act in a certain way, where 'should' carries the force of an infinite judgement: a judgement based on the *a priori* principle of *right* as a good in itself; for instance, when we say that something to be done is 'the right thing to do' implying universal applicability – an infinite judgement restrained by what must be done in this situation; that is, according to its *limiting conditions*.[10] In our example of *The Third Man*, Anna is judged in an infinite judgement restrained by the film's limiting conditions in which her 'rightness' of action is assessed in terms of other paths that could have been taken. In Stiegler's terms, we need to develop a sense of 'moral consciousness' as the 'therapeutic' of the *pharmakon* in which the true and the false are in transition (2013: 23, 70–1); that is, undecidable in the Derridean sense of not having a rule by which to decide (Derrida 1990: 963). For Stiegler, the universality of moral right is demonstrated in a 'therapeutic capacity' to tell the true from the false in the undecidability of pharmacological situations: bifurcating path moments calling upon the moral consciousness of the subject – the viewer of the film 'switched' into critical capacity – in care relations with others as 'pharmacological arbitration (that is, the *therapeutic capacity*) [which] is the function of reason insofar it judges cognitively, sensibly and morally' (2018: 95).

Methexis

In this book, I propose pharmacological situations in terms of *methexis*, a term drawn from Plato's theory of ideas, meaning being-with or 'participation' (Gadamer 2007: 311). Following Hans-Georg Gadamer's 'fusional' hermeneutics – the fusion of time on a horizontal plane – *methexis* is a hermeneutic mode of self-reflection in which a reader-interpreter of cultural texts received from the past is *called* into problems of care for the future in terms of the undecidability of paths taken and not taken in 'the mediate moral sphere ... based on what ought to be' (1975: 189); that is, predicated in answer to the question 'What is the right path?' (2007: 398). Undecidability renders the determinacy of a path taken indeterminate, an obstacle calling the reader-interpreter to determine the indeterminacy to allow passage through. A *methexis* occurs when the reader-interpreter, having been called into self-questioning, steps back into a mediating position and interprets the indeterminacy on behalf of the future as communicable, thereby overcoming the obstacle in a 'fusion of horizons' in which the 'text disappears' (2007: 180); that is, withdraws in the clarity of a fused view.

Fusional hermeneutics is played out on a horizontal field of mutually embracing standpoints or *views* entering into communication such that they fuse – interpenetrate – thereby normalizing the disparities between them. Fusion is itself defused by the relativity of the *field of views* in which the *methexis* takes place, where all views are seen from the standpoint of other views (1975: 18). Gadamer's fusional hermeneutics is not enclosed in a circle but remains open in the indeterminacy of the *apeiron*[11] – an open horizon in which fusing and defusing tendencies interpenetrate: a dynamic field of views spiralling in and out of each other, fusing and defusing to embrace and be embraced by other views. Self-reflection takes the form of a *methexis* in which the I questions itself in relation to other views embracing it, '[not] limited to one particular sphere at a time [but] active in all directions'.

For Stiegler, methexical self-reflection triggered by the call constitutes participation in an *I–We* relation – a non-dialectical version of Hegel's dialectics of the 'life of the mind' (*Sittlichkeit*) as I–We set forth in section 177 of his *Phenomenology of Spirit* (Hegel 1977: 110–11, Stiegler 2018: 110). Adopting Hegel's I that is We and We that is I 'stepping out' of its situation to come back to itself in newly discovered self-consciousness, Stiegler proposes an *I–We* dyad in terms of a *pharmacological situation* in which the possibility of moral right is worked out in praxis without reducing it to a *state* fused in its own rationality; that is, as an incompletion seeking completion along an open temporal horizon (*apeiron*), forever failing to be 'at home in the world' as Hegel puts it (1991: 36). By employing Gadamer's methexical account of self-questioning together with Stiegler's non-dialectical or 'tragic' account of the pharmacological situation (2018: 110) (tragic because mortal in being-towards-death), we invoke a relativized field of views in which the becoming of an *I–We* tending towards fusion is defused by ongoing methexical self-questioning: the phasing in and out of self-consciousness of the *I* in relation to the *We* it is always already becoming across an open horizon 'active in all directions' (Gadamer 1975: 18).

For Stiegler, the questions posed to the *I* cast in a temporalized transcendental field – the *apeiron* or open horizon – relate to 'the *question of care*' (2021a: 366) in knowing the difference between right paths and wrong paths as a moral responsibility considered after the fact: one should have taken the right path in care for the future in 'the formation of a normativity of technical life' (2013: 65). From the perspective of the archival future, such care would be coming-to-know the *right* of the path that one should have taken as hermeneutic rationality related to questions of justice, law and moral responsibility, which Aristotle calls *phronesis* or practical wisdom (praxis), where 'good action itself is its end' (1941: 1025). In German Idealist terms, *right* (*Recht*) is the affirmation of myself in relation to others in a communality of mutually self-limiting free beings as a good in itself (Fichte 2000: 84–85, Hegel 1991: 96–7), an I–We relationality 'standing in relations of right' (Wood 2016: 256).

In Fichtean terms, right is not imposed *a priori* in the manner of the Kantian categorical imperative (i.e. through the enactment of a universal law); rather, we come to know what right is in practical life as the principle upon which a community standing in a relation of right *ought* to be; that is, through an educative process of learning *who* the human *must be* to stand in a relation of right. Both Fichtean right and its Hegelian derivative in institutionalized reason are predicated on the failure of the ideal of pure rationality to realize itself in a fully fused state of self-identification where I equals I in an absolute sense, which, if enacted politically, would result in control-based *anthropy*. In the struggle of the *I* with itself with respect to the practical tasks we set for ourselves as free beings thrown into existence, the right path 'will have' come to us as a path which could also be the wrong path. Working out which is which is the *I–We*'s guarantee of freedom in ongoing discussion, debate and free communication where the *principle of right* is operating in a practical way, which, if enacted politically, would be care-based *neganthropy*.

Stiegler's invocation of a temporalized 'transcendental field without a subject', which includes the *I* as inchoate potential in the viewer's receptivity to self-questioning in *life death* situations, accords with Johnston's transcendental materialism concerned with the emergence of subjectivity out of 'asubjective substance' (2014: 18), where asubjective substance is the temporal flux wherein the *I* finds itself under question, which, in Gilbert Simondon's terms, is a pre-individual field 'rich in potentials' (2020: 4). Yet, for Stiegler, the field is provisional ('*if there is* anything transcendental, it exceeds the subject and does so by default'), indicating the quasi- status of the field, insofar as a materialism, to avoid naivety about its own position, must account for ideations *including its own* as failed attempts to transcend their material limits. Accordingly, I consider Stiegler's position to be quasi-transcendental materialist; that is, concerned with the *failure* of transcendence, which, in filmic terms, means a speculative critical hermeneutic philosophizing on the conditions of possibility of cinematic life in processes of *mnemotechnesis* guided by the paraconsistent logic of practical reason in seeking ways through the limits of the transcendental gesture of I = I (in Simondon's terms, the phase-shift from pre-individual to individual existence) in pursuit of noetic freedom defined by a politics of neganthropic care, as acted out in the viewer's relation to the films themselves; that is, through *methexis*.

Care

The question of care relates to the entanglement of *life death* in a pharmacological situation as 'the point of departure for the formation of a healthy psychic apparatus' (Stiegler 2013: 3), where the health of the apparatus is understood propaedeutically: learning how to live well in 'the feeling that life is worth living'. In pharmacological terms, care is feeling for the future in discerning paths not taken in paths taken, a condition of moral self-consciousness turned out of itself and into the otherness of what I could be, defined here as *negative affectivity*. In the course of life's journey, whatever I might have gained in taking the path I did take comes at the cost of having not taken other paths in which the worth of one's life can be assessed in terms of loss-in-gain. Negative affectivity is the feeling of loss-in-gain I would no doubt feel when the right path comes to me in the sudden realization of not having taken it as the path I should have taken as *right*. In terms of moral right in films, the question of care relates to the negative affectivity of loss-in-gain in the viewer's experience of *this* film; for instance in questions of care for the future raised by Reed's *The Third Man*, in which the film is denied a happy ending (the path not taken) by having Anna walk past Holly (the path taken), thereby affirming the right path in a world restored to justice in which criminality is punished with the consequences of wrong actions revealed but at the expense of the wished for happy ending. Or, the feeling of loss in Antonioni's *L'Eclisse* in which Piero and Vittoria – the archetypal romantic couple – fail to live up to the promise of life in the shadow of annihilation felt in the meaningless void of a cinematically induced eclipse (the expense of not having taken the right path, the path expected of them, the one wished for in happy dreaming).

In film story-telling, care becomes feeling for the future otherwise had other paths been taken: a propaedeutics of *life death* as responsibility to the future exercised in the telling of stories as fables – cautionary tales – where lessons can be learnt in sharing the experience with others in the development of an *I–We* communality of individuated beings standing together 'in-One' in relations of *right*. By reading films pharmacologically – that is, as fables warning of dangers in taking or not taking paths in bifurcating path situations – possibilities of care yet to be lived are freed up and a new future gained in the loss of others, in the self-realization of *right* as a good in itself.

The limits of noetic freedom

In returning to the question of noetic freedom in its quasi-transcendental materialist mode, we need to get behind the subject and seek out its roots in Aristotle's analysis of *noesis* in Book VI of *Nichomachean Ethics*, as the capacity of the 'noetic soul' (as distinct from the sensible and the nutritive soul) to project otherwise in deliberating about the future with reference to past actions (1941: 1024), a requirement for the use of *public reason* in heeding lessons from the past as sufficient cause for future actions. For Stiegler, noetic freedom is the *capacity* of the noetic soul – the free self or *I* in its 'promise' (2018: 84) – to project itself otherwise (to dream of another way of being), as the necessary condition for 'the constituting of an epoch', without which such capacity *noesis* would sink into pre-individual drive, leading to regressive 'herd behaviour' (Ross and Ouyang 2021: 106), a condition of *anthropy* in which humans become toxic to themselves in 'runaway ... [self-] destruction' (Stiegler 2021: 82).

In the epoch of 'computational capitalism' (Stiegler 2021: 99), the consumer subject becomes divided from itself in dividuated being: a pre-individual tendency sustained by preference values gaining momentum in piezo-electro-communicational flows of 'data codes' (Colman et al. 2018: 9) interfacing between computerized screens and virtual realities accessed through vast memory banks interweaving themselves into the everyday lives of their users. Divided from itself in transdividuating tendencies controlled by algorithmic governance, the noetic soul finds itself caught up in desire feeding on itself in the identity formations of privately owned and managed internet sites under the rule of the profit motive, overflowing the public sphere with *dogma* – unreflected opinion – lacking sufficient care for the exercise of public reason as the precondition of free speech needed to act as a check against its tendency towards demagogy. In such circumstances, the decisional praxis of noetic individuals for transitioning into new life is short-circuited by the automation of machine intelligence in a deadlock of reason in which cynicism as 'enlightened false consciousness' rules (Sloterdijk 1987: 5). Under these conditions, the promise of noetic freedom – upon which the subject's decisional praxis to resist the control regimes of capitalist enterprise depends – is fulfilled by its very failure in ongoing incompletion as the never-ending task of moral being thrown into free existence to *go on* at all costs. In the current age of hyper-capitalism, an organological approach to film based on neganthropic care must begin from the failure of the promise of noetic freedom to project otherwise by turning to face the approaching catastrophe – runaway self-destruction against which *homo sapiens*, having surrendered noetic intelligence to the machine, will be defenceless – and from this place re-learn how to dream new dreams.

Stiegler's centring of his organological project on a defence of noetic freedom correlates with the pre-subjectivist concern of German Idealism, whose first principle was set out in an obscure fragment entitled 'The Oldest System Program of German Idealism' (*c.* 1796–97) written in Hegel's handwriting and co-authored by Schelling and Hölderlin, as 'the representation of *myself* as an absolutely free being. With the free self-conscious a whole world comes forth from nothing – the only true and thinkable *creation from nothing*' (Anon.: 3), a statement derived from Fichte's 1794 *Wissenschaftslehre* in which the self-positing of I = I is enabled by the retroactive projection of primary imagination as both creative and productive (Fichte 1982: 276). Stiegler's defence of noetic freedom can be traced back to the German Idealists' defence of the pre-subjective noetic soul capable of primary projection, initially proposed by Fichte as imaginative 'outreach' (193). Primary projection as imaginative outreach holds the key to the formation of imaginary worlds by the noetic soul (the human psyche), made real through Freudian 'reality testing' (Freud 1984: 440) – probing for the future in the figural domain of the entangled realities of our imaginative projections.

For Stiegler – whose thinking on the technologically 'enframed' subject begins with Heidegger's late philosophizing of the event of *Ereignis* – the turning of enframement (*Gestell*) out of itself, releasing noetic being into an abyss of its own making (Stiegler 1998: 7–8) – noetic freedom is understood as the release of free being out of technological ordering probing for the future in imaginative outreach (reality testing), which is the exercise of the noetic soul as a healthy *organon* capable of thinking, imagining and dreaming otherwise. The German Idealists' attempts to avoid entrapment in the Kantian correlationist circle is repeated in Stiegler's Heideggerian–Freudian efforts to think noetic freedom from inside the technical apparatus of hyper-industrialized capitalism as *Verneinung* – denial or 'repression of the spirit' (Stiegler 2018: 65) – in seeking release from the auto-efficiency of its drive, which, in terms set out in this book, is a question of *forbearance*: the backward-forward bearing of figures of resistance probing for the future as a way out – an exit point in what the future 'will have' been in a path not taken *had it been taken*. Stiegler's choice of apparatus to undertake this deconstituting of the industrially automatized subject is the cinematograph which, according to Bergson, is on the screen and 'inside us'

(1911: 235). By placing the noetic reflex inside the cinematographic apparatus, Stiegler's organology of film begins in the very movement of the subject's self-formation as a pre-subjective *I* with nothing more than a promise of free being projected otherwise within a temporalized transcendental field which is also a cosmic field of views: the archival future in which the experience of viewing films is always already immersed.

Becoming cinematic

Stiegler undertakes his project of deconstituting the modern technologically enframed subject in cinematic terms in *Technics and Time, 3*, in which he releases *himself* from technical enframement (Heideggerian *Gestell*) to claim free being in self-negation, announced in the following statement: 'I negate myself in making myself cinematic' (2011: 61). What does he mean by this? In the experience of viewing a film, there is something in me – a knowingness that I am *other* even though my time and my feelings may have become absorbed in its story-world in the 'desire for stories' (8). This sense of *knowingness* moves counter-wise within my *self* as a self-reflexive being forever failing to be who I am (my identity as I = I) as 'incomplete' (61), an 'inadequation at the heart of myself' without which I would be entirely cinematic and hence incapable of having an experience of film as my own. The statement 'I negate myself in making myself cinematic' entails the fundamental paradox of 'necessary freedom' in which to be free I must negate – repress – myself in who I claim to be as Freudian *Verneinung* (Freud 1984: 438).[12] In this way, the noetic *I* becomes a noetic *eye*: an I that can see itself otherwise 'only insofar as I am incomplete'.

The paradox of necessary freedom in the negation of the self by the self is the motivating factor of Fichte's response to Kant's transcendental unity of apperception, in which – as discussed previously with regard to the concept of *right* – he reveals that I = I must be a free act of self-positing restrained by other free acts as mutually self-limiting – a *necessary condition* of self-constitution (Fichte 1982: 189–95, 2000: 33). Fichte's free act of self-positing retroactivating itself into existence out of the nothingness of absolute freedom, which he calls *Tathandlung*, a performative act of self-overcoming as the eternal struggle of the self with itself (1992: 191–3), correlates with Stiegler's 'I negate myself in making myself cinematic' as the *I* seeking self-identification with other *I*s as the transindividuation of an *I–We* relation continually undoing itself in the act of its own 'doing'; that is, retroactivating itself into free existence in incessant incompletion. Here, Stiegler follows Simondon's transindividual-materialist analysis of pre-subjective being as 'syncrystallization' (2020: 168): the process of falling in and out of sync of an elemental crystallization of energetic flow drawing from the insubstantiality – the free nothingness – of pre-individual flux sustaining individuated life in a metastatic concretion such as a film, where 'life is *always* cinema' (Stiegler 2011: 16).

Becoming cinematic means having the capacity to exercise noetic freedom as part of the cinematic event: to project otherwise than the cinematographic apparatus understood in terms of Martin's 'transport system' shuffling memory back and forth between past and present/before and after in a disjunctive synthesis of disparated images flowing across the screen. When perceived by the noetic eye at micro-levels, synthesis unravels in the work of the figure-matrix holding things together in the duration of the film, which, when taken in their paraconsistencies (their 'entangled' connectivities), become micro-/macro-interweavings of what Stiegler calls an 'idiotext' (2021: 189): an open system composed of spiralling trace-data or discrete mnesic gestures concretized out of cosmic time in views from nowhere as *this* film. Trace-data passes through the film's memory in recursive loops, triggering phase-shifts of the viewer's consciousness in which repressed life repeatedly returns, where the *I* becomes cinematic in its forever failing to transcend itself in ongoing incomplete acts of quasi-transcendence in the desire for self-recognition: Fichte's I = I as the striving of self-transcendence and forever failing. Fichte has the last word here, insofar as his doctrine of *Anstoß* (1982: 189) – the check to the I's self-overcoming turning back into itself – constitutes the *split subject*, the bedrock of German Idealism through which we have passed in coming to conclusions here.

Facing the catastrophe

The aim of this book is to undertake an organology of film figures through a quasi-transcendental materialist account of film experience, proceeding from an initial definition of the *figural* as an activity of *feeling for the future* through the memory of film as the incompletion of a split subject forever failing to transcend its conditions of possibility in a completed act of self-unification, as developed in this introductory chapter. In general, the book is an inquiry into failed transcendence as the material reality of films – a *process* of memorizing forming itself into a concretion of time experienced through an organic machine: the cinematograph as an *organon* of perception installed in a mnemotechnical apparatus which humans have built for themselves to project their desires and fears through the apparatus as collective dreaming. As products of this machine, films have a built-in capacity to tell us about the conditions under which memorizing takes place in technologically mediated environments, which, in the current age of hyper-capitalism, are leading towards catastrophic immanence as memory death in which the capacity of *homo sapiens* to feel for the future is threatened with annihilation.

Under accelerated conditions of hyper-capitalism, the demand to consume in the exercise of free choice reaches globalizing proportions in an unrestricting of all restrictions, making it difficult, if not impossible, for individuals to project a future other than the one already projected by the data codes of mnemotechnical systems in which right is entailed in the exercise of *negative freedom* (my freedom from your restrictions on me). In hyper-capitalistic milieus, noetic freedom is willingly transferred to the phantasm that I am becoming in desire for an infinite future, driven by the impulse of creative destruction – the efficiency-seeking logic of hyper-capitalist enterprise ruthlessly deracinating existing connections to the past in the name of freedom to be myself as a universal good (the unrestricted *I*). Consequently, the capacity of humans as *noetic beings* to project a future for themselves in the exercise of *positive freedom* (our freedom in mutually self-limiting processes of an *I–We*) is in danger of being forgotten, leading to *anomie* of the life spirit and the collapse of the mnemotechnical systems sustaining it.

In catastrophic conditions of noetic crisis, we need a way to reframe our projects of critical reflection within the collapsing systems themselves, to take a 'step beyond' (Stiegler 2015: 118) by turning backwards into the archival future, in a *hermeneutic turn* in and through which reframing will have already begun. By turning into the past as already lived, the hermeneutic turn *unwills* the willingness of free choice in which the past is disavowed. By unwilling the will to choose, we invite the disavowed past back in a return of the repressed where I face the future otherwise in what it 'will have' become had other paths been taken, throwing the present path under a new light. In the hermeneutic turn, I do not step beyond the present into the future laid out in an array of possible paths; rather, in turning, I find that the step beyond has already been taken but *not yet*, in the future anterior of a past yet to pass through. My task is to take this path as the right path, to take it yet again as others might have but in a new frame of reference in which questions relating to current problems of care can be asked with a view to possibilities for another future, one conditioned by practical reason in relation to past actions in what they foretell. By turning backwards into the archival future, I am *already* reframing my questions and taking the right path, a path which could also be wrong.

The chapters

The following five chapters work through the key ideas of organology, hermeneutics, dreaming, cinematic time and spherology. Chapter 1 sets the groundwork for an organology of film in terms of the cinematograph: an abstract machine in and through which humans perceive temporal objects such as films in the transindividuated sense of *I–We*. Employing Stiegler's notion of *noesis* as self-reflective capacity, Derrida's idea of the archival future, Simondon's concept of transindividuation, Fichte's self-positing I = I as superposition, and Bergson's thesis on time as duration, the chapter works its way through the cinematograph to develop figural analysis from within an organological frame of reference. Applying Fichte's concept of *Anstoß* as a 'check' to perception when the I confronts – is superposed on – its non-I as strange and threatening, an analysis of Hitchcock's *Rear Window* is undertaken in terms of the struggle of *life death* enacted in the film in gendered terms in which the feminine is released from patriarchal control through Irigaray's notion of the *speculum* as a third view. Consideration is then given to how films as mnemotechnical objects are shaped and distributed through epochal change in the becoming cinematic of industrial life by employing Stiegler's notion of 'doubly epokhal redoubling' as a non-dialectical version of Hegelian *Sittlichkeit* (ethical life), through which the promise of technics might be fulfilled.

Chapter 2 begins with Gadamer's hermeneutic model of a field of views in which any given view sees and is seen through the *speculum* of spheres in which it is embraced and which it embraces in having a view relative to all other views, a cosmological-spherological model to which Stiegler's notion of neganthropy – the human–machine relation in resistance to entropic dissolution – is applied as key for thinking of hermeneutics from a quasi-transcendental materialist perspective. The idea of *methexis* as participation – drawn from Gadamer's reading of Plato – is introduced to account for the viewer's relation to characters in film story-telling as a mutually shared moral act in 'other pathways' thinking, where what is sought is the *right path*, while a Simondonian–Bergsonian crystalline flow concept is employed to show how the I functions as a prosthetic eye that can see otherwise in the flow, further developed into a thermodynamic model drawn from Lyotard in which the critical eye is inserted; the inserted eye sees otherwise in the flow of film images as the memory of what humans are becoming in their prosthetic relation to machines as non-inhuman potential. Drawing on Blanchot's idea of the distancing function of images, analysis of Murnau's *The Last Laugh* is undertaken to demonstrate the function of the critical eye in moments of shock caused by directorial interference to the 2D/3D structuring of the film's image flow, opening the film to its figural dimensions in which Auerbach's notion of *figura* and Derridean *life death* switching are applied to account for the film's tragicomic patterning of fate in the turning of fortune's wheel.

Chapter 3 deals with Stiegler's key idea of dreaming as the noetic imagination in its cinematic mode conditioned by Barthes's *punctum* effect when looking at photographic images as *life death* switching, developing a line of analysis from Capra's Hollywood melodrama, *It's a Wonderful Life*, in consideration of the quantum event of superposition opening up paths not taken, to modernist film through Lyotard's notion of acinema as anti-film. The key idea of *dispositif*, drawn from Martin, is introduced as the game played by the film against its generic conventions, which is the acinematic tendency of art film as sovereign to itself (i.e. as *right*). Films analysed include Welles's *The Lady from Shanghai* and Beckett's *Film*, while Stiegler's analysis of Fellini's *Intervista* is metacritiqued to demonstrate its tragicomic structure as acinematic.

Chapter 4 takes up the idea of the *dispositif* in modernist film (developed in the previous chapter) in which the analysis *itself* affirms the film's right to be (i.e. sovereign to itself). Working with Stiegler's critique of the current condition of malaise as enervation of the spirit in hypercapitalist milieus, requiring what I have called 'non-indecisive action' to break free from it, the chapter engages in figural analysis of Antonioni's *L'Eclisse* and Bresson's *Une Femme Douce*, employing Freud's blindness of the seeing eye, Benjamin's optical unconscious and Flusser's philosophical critique of the camera apparatus as acts of avoidance to develop the full measure of figural analysis.

Chapter 5 picks up all of these threads to re-work Stiegler's notion of the idiotext as the concretization of trace-data into mnemotechnical objects such as films in flows of cosmic light emplaced within a spherological model developed throughout the chapter. The question of *right* is re-posed in terms of the chamber film, apprehended within the cosmic field of views as a *Kammerspielfilm* (an experimental modelling of the artificial naturalness of a film's memory structure, the prototype of which was developed in the Weimar cinema) in which the *right of characters* – their rights claim on each other in situations in which their place in the world is put at risk of usurpation, requiring a sufficiency of reason supplied by the film's *dispositif* – is tested. Drawing from Balázs's notion of visual jointure, I undertake a series of passes through the memory chamber of Zeller's film *The Father* – a contemporary *Kammerspielfilm* – drawing conclusions concerning the fate of the human species at risk of self-annihilating memory death in the encroachment of artificial intelligence on everyday life, acted out in the fantasy of the film as Stieglerian arche-cinema.

1

Organology

The archival future

When did cinema begin? Philosopher of *mnemotechnesis* Bernard Stiegler has given us two dates – 1877 and 1895 – when recordings of sound and moving images stored in a mechanical device were experienced in public for the first time (2018: 157). The audiovision thus produced, albeit by different technical processes (phonographic and cinematographic), announces an epochal shift in the hominization of organic life: the exteriorization of *homo sapient* memory by machine prosthesis in the shaping of an *I–We* – a transindividuated network or group (2011: 88) – whose self-reflective capacity (*noesis*) is carried by the cinematograph, an apparatus for retaining and projecting screen memories as 'industrial life' (2014: 8). Industrial life is noetic life lived through *technics* (technical intelligence) in which a sense of the *new* is repeated as if for the first time. To be part of a cinematographically transindividuated We (a pluralized *I–We* relation) is to be opened to new dimensions of an *archival future* – a future already remembered *but not yet*.

The possibility of an archival future is proposed by Jacques Derrida in *Archive Fever* (1996) as the promise of technics; a 'pledge' or 'token' of the future:

> The archive has always been a pledge, and like every pledge, a token of the future. To put it more trivially: what is no longer archived in the same way is no longer lived in the same way. Archivable meaning is also and in advance codetermined by the structure that archives. It begins with the printer.

18

The *promise* of technics in the industrial age of reproducibility 'begin[ning] with the printer' (the prototype for the phonograph and cinematograph) is built into the capacity of technology to archive everything, thereby rendering the future archivably *real* – radically open to *all times* – as 'having passed' and as 'passing through' the archive in the emergence of the *new*. By entering the archival future *we alter the array of possibilities* lodged within it, opening new dimensions for living through the technical trace of industrial life as automated mnemotechnics or machine memory 'codetermin[ing]' its meaning as already determined (having passed) and in its possibilities for new experience (passing through).

In Stiegler's terms, the archival future is time materialized in the future anterior – the past that will have happened – as an 'idiotext' (2021: 189): an 'open system' composed of spiralling trace-data or mnesic gestures (idiosyncratic inflections from the past) binding into concretizations (technical objects such as films), while at the same time unbinding them in the *real* of a past that will have been possible – a future already remembered but not yet. The idiotext 'is a *memory that is a process of individuation: a memory that is written at the same time that it is read*, of which the writing is also the reading and vice versa' (1995: n.p.). Spiralling in and out of its own concretizations, the idiotext codetermines the meaning of the archival future – what the future will have been – the moment it is read, altering the frame of reference in which possibilities come into view.

From a film-hermeneutic perspective, what is at issue here is the *real* of the archival future: the potential of time stored within films open to possible meaning from within the archive in which they lie dormant as future memory not yet released. The idiotext is accessed by turning within the sphere in which the archive exists for me in relation to the cinematic consciousness of a '*We* in-the-making': an audience of transindividuated *I*s shaping themselves into a noetically informed *socious* – a society of self-questioning individuals binding themselves into a future through the experience of films and other objects of screen memory in the projection of industrial life as *ciné-mnemotechnesis* (cinematicized technical memory).

Throughout this book we will be pursuing the *real* of the archival future as simultaneously a limiting finitude and an unlimiting potential for new *I–We* relations of cinematic consciousness, calling for praxis (work to-be-made) to draw out this potential in films rediscovered in the archive, the newness of which lies in their capacity to *re-remember* the past in its 'having passed' as a future already remembered but not yet. By rediscovering films as archivably *real*, we turn to face the future as the past revived in new dimensions which, in their having passed into the dead past of what 'will have' been, are yet to be lived.

Transindividuation

I have coined the term 'We in-the-making' to define the pluralized sense of an audience transforming its grouped identity to sustain a metastable state as separably multiplying incompletions (an *I–We*). Drawing on Étienne Souriau's concept of instauration as the vitalization of an in-existent self – a pre-individual being – in 'work to-be-made' (2015: 220), a *We* in-the-making is a process of instauration: a non-teleological *passing through* in which an incompletion seeks completion in being together with other incompletions as 'Being-to-be-realized'. I propose the concept of *We* in-the-making as instaurative action to capture a stronger sense of the ongoing activity of *Bildung* – cultivated image shaping – in Simondonian transindividuation: a structuring activity emerging out of existing structures but *otherwise* in the way that a crystal liquidates the form in which it is seeded into an entirely new form: 'where one of the forms occupies the whole crystalline substance, and the other completely disappears' (Simondon 2020: 70).

Simondon proposes that, in any description of the transindividuating process, '[w]e must start with [pre-subjective] individuation, with the being grasped in its center according to spatiality and becoming, and not with the substantialized *individual* facing a world that is foreign to it' (2020: 11). I will argue, in line with Stiegler's critique of Simondonian transindividuation (Stiegler 2020: 9), that, for the forces to be kept in play, pre-subjective individuation – the exclamatory 'I' – must *itself* be called into question by something foreign to it (despite Simondon's rejection of this requirement): its *other* in the struggle-to-be, a condition of self-estrangement first proposed in post-Kantian philosophy by Fichte as the I of self-consciousness struggling with its phantasmic non-I as the stranger-in-me (1982: 189–95). In a following section of this chapter in which I analyse Alfred Hitchcock's *Rear Window*, I will turn to Fichte's proposal of the struggle-to-be in terms of an I confronting its non-I as the object to be overcome in a *free act* of self-positing as reciprocal self-limiting (*Tathandlung*),[1] correlating with Simondon's notion of a 'free act' of moral character in the formation of social groups (2020: 378). By considering Fichtean *Tathandlung* as the self-constituting act of a proto-Simondonian pre-subjective self split from itself in originary self-estrangement, which, in Stiegler's terms, is the human being's 'original duplicity' (1998: 196), I will be able to describe the process of transindividuation in the fantasy of film story-telling in terms of the struggle-to-be acted out by protagonists on the screen as part of the revitalized life of an *I–We* – a pluralized *socious* of transindividuated beings open to the future in the *finitude* of free existence.

A *We* in-the-making is a new identity formation 'syncrystallizing' out of an older form as the generative phase-shaping of being-as-becoming through crystalline amplification and self-propagation in the heterogeneity of pre-individual flux which Simondon calls 'transduction' (Simondon 2020: 13). From this organological-crystalline perspective, the generation of the film audience – the shaping of a higher order of psychic self-organization centred on the experience of film – is seen as a process of transduction/transindividuation falling out of sync with itself in which the *I* of an individual viewer (noetic self-consciousness) superposes with a *We* in-the-making as an incompletion attempting to complete itself and forever failing in the drive impulse. Were the act of incompletion to succeed, there would be no more work to-be-made and the *I–We* relation would close in on itself, rigidifying into a pure crystalline form purged of excess incompletion 'in the singularity of a perpetually recommencing *here* and *now*' (380), a condition I propose to call *hyper-syncrystallization*.

To uncover transindividuating processes of an *I–We* formation in cinematic milieus, we need look no further than films themselves as incomplete temporal objects attempting to complete themselves in which the process of self-transformation into individuated being takes place in the *agon* of story-telling, where protagonists *act out* the struggle to be. For Simondon, the struggle of self-transformation in a psychic self-organization (a Stieglerian *I–We*) is the collective 'calling itself into question . . . [in] an ongoing emotion that does not manage to resolve affectivity, an obstacle through which the individuated being explores its dimensions of being without the ability to surpass them' (2020: 11). As 'ongoing emotion', the struggle *is itself* the 'obstacle' through which the *I–We* explores its dimensions of being as a self-limiting process ('without the ability to surpass' its limits). We will take Simondon's notion of psychic individuation together with the Fichtean act of self-positing (*Tathandlung*) as mutually self-limiting in a transindividuating process of becoming free, to be axiomatic for onscreen struggles in which a protagonist faces an obstacle – an impediment to progress, blocking passage through – calling for its overcoming in a 'theatre of individuation' (Simondon 2020: 9), which Stiegler calls the 'passage into act . . . as *exclamatory*' (2013a: 191).

A *We* in-the-making is already shaping its future when the self-selecting *I* of a viewer (a noetic self-consciousness) 'adopts' the time of characters in a film as her time (Stiegler 2011: 10, 30–1), synchronizing her offscreen time with the temporal phasing and dephasing of the film: its re-remembering or *memorizing* of action through the retroaction of story-telling. The act of adoption correlates with Simondon's *free act*: the 'moral act ... that has enough reality to go beyond itself and encounter other acts' in the formation of a social network retro-activating itself in free existence (2020: 378). In the free act of adoption, the viewer *herself* participates in the struggles of the characters as the *agon* of the film – the shared suffering of life's ordeals – re-enacted onscreen. In the struggle-to-be, obstacles blocking 'passage into act' are overcome when the protagonist rises to the challenge of having to *go on*, which is also the collective 'calling itself into question' in the formation of self-identity 'through which the individuated being explores its dimensions'. By responding to the summons of *having to be*, the *I* acts in correlation with a *We* as an *I–We* relation shaping itself through 'the power of amplification' (396) into a democratized *socious* – a grouped identity of mutually self-limiting free beings as Fichtean 'finite sel[ves]' (Breazeale 1995: 102). Individual audience members are not solipsists locked into their own mental cocoons when viewing films but are already relating to a *We* in-the-making through the experience itself. To uncover transindividuating processes we need to access films as archivably *real* – as hermeneutically retrievable – in a questioning moment in which I am called to exercise my noetic freedom – my capacity to project otherwise in the struggle-to-be – as one of many such *I*s on and off the screen who could have and will have viewed this and other films past, present and future.

Bergson's thesis on duration

Let us now return to our beginning. Having declared the phono-cinematographic conditions for a cinematic *We* to have begun in 1877 and 1895, Stiegler adds: 'These dates ... constitute two immense turns in the *organological history of the power(s) to dream*' (2018: 157). What is organology? What is a dream? To answer these questions, I will turn to Henri Bergson's thesis on duration (*durée*), set forth in three books: *Time and Free Will* (2019), *Matter and Memory* (1988) and *Creative Evolution* (1911), constituting the framework of his philosophy of time consciousness: a reduction of our perception of the past to its organic operations (part/whole processes of time becoming space). The *epoché* of the reduction – its suspension in the critical moment of reflecting upon it – restores the 'true character of perception' as a 'system of nascent acts which plunges roots deep into the real [in which] the reality of things is no more constructed or reconstructed, but touched, penetrated, and lived' (1988: 69). For Bergson, the *real* of time is its arche-origin: a radical potential discoverable within us when we make an effort to resist our mental habits – our 'voluntary' attention to things in the world 'in the work of the mind' (101). By resisting our habit of acting on perceptions – by inducing a 'backward movement of the mind' – we open ourselves to the duration of time as *real*: the originary event when time's persistence is experienced both *for itself* and *for me*, which, in a counter-practical sense, releases the work of the mind from its habit of conceiving recollected time as a series of punctual nows in the mechanism of 'rectilinear progress' (104), making it receptive to the circuitry of memorizing transforming the whole of time into 'new circuits' as time passing through itself. The potential of the *real* is an openness to the *all* of time (time as absolute) in the finitude of duration (*durée*), without which time could not *pass through*.

In later work, Bergson clarified his thesis on time as a pluralism composed of multiple times – a 'coexistence of completely different rhythms' (Deleuze 1991: 78) – in response to Einstein's theory of relativity in which time was considered to be a fourth dimension of space and that its reality to us as past, present and future was nothing but an illusion (Murphy 1999: 70). As Murphy has argued, 'Bergson's critique of Einstein anticipates Bohm and Hiley's "ontological" interpretation of quantum mechanics ... which renews the confrontation with [Bergson's theory of] absolute time or independent time that Einstein successfully parried in 1922 [a reference to the public debate between Einstein and Bergson held in Paris in April of that year]'. In summary, Bergson's theory of durational time, although inconsistent with the determinism of Einsteinian relativity, anticipates the indeterminism of quantum mechanics and its invocation of absolute time as a *necessary condition* for reflective thinking of the experience of time as *flux* in which it is possible that something is capable of being in two places at the same time; that is, as paraconsistent with itself.[2] From a quantum physics perspective, a system predicated on non-local interaction must be thought strictly in atemporal terms as non-rectilinear vector lines traversing the entangled circuitry of Hilbert space, an abstract spacetime relation which, in *Matter and Memory*, Bergson had already hypothesized in terms of a memory cone depicted as a spool of verticalized memory (pure memory) unwinding on a horizontal plane (the plane of action); non-local interaction occurs at intersections of absolute or pure memory coinciding with the actuality of the recollected past when a choice is made 'from an infinite number of recollections'

(1988: 164) for the practical purpose of acting in a finite world (in quantum physics terms, a quantum event triggered by the collapsing of the quantum wave function into a particular ensemble of its elements when an observer's decisive act of observing interferes with the equipment under experimental conditions). For Bergson, the world is a crystalline sphere (1911: 22): a flow of images 'act[ing] and react[ing] upon one another' (1988: 17) in a 'material world' (19) incorporating the brain–body linkage as a perceptor–receptor function (24) inserting itself into the flow.

From a Bergsonian perspective informed by a generalized quantum effect, we will consider the duration of films in terms of a past that 'begins to have been always possible' (Bergson 2007: 82) in the gap between the past as having passed (the indefinite past) and the past in its passing (the recollected past), as images acting and reacting upon one another in the entangled realities of a crystalline sphere in which the perceiving eye sees itself seeing, the *speculum* of which is reflected in other views into which it is inserted as mirror images refracted through the material of the crystalline sphere (21). In this crystalline world of reflected images refracted through the sphere, we will consider what it is to *be* as a *free existent* (a noetic *I* which is also a noetic eye) affected by quantum difference: phase-shifting between the dead past and the living future through quantum leaps as *passing through*, where 'passing through' is the passage of time through itself experienced in the duration of films as simultaneously real and *irreal* – ontologically ambiguous as neither true nor false.[3]

To be inside a crystalline sphere is to *in-exist* (to not yet have being)[4] in preparation for action, when a choice is made from the heterogeneity of images passing across the surface of the sphere. Alternatively, to be outside the sphere is to *exist* (to have being) in the practicality of having to act as a matter of survival in the milieu in which the world of images 'syncrystallizes'; that is, becomes crystal clear in its meaning for me together with other *Is* as a *We* in-the-making, in Simondon's terms, a *socious* of moralized individuals existing freely in a self-limiting 'network of [free] acts' (2020: 379). Choosing *this* memory rather than any of the other memories passing across the sphere induces an inside/outside doubling effect, which, in quantum terms, is a superposition of the absolute past (collapsed) onto the relativized present in preparation for action. The in-existence of the *I* in the world of crystalline images becomes meaningful – shifts from non-being to being – when transformed into action by leaping across the circuitry of vector lines separating the past and the present as a quantum event in which the *I* both exists and in-exists in the paraconsistent logic of non-local interaction (in ontological terms, in the interpenetration of absolute and relative time). I am doubled on myself as *before* in the dead past and *after* in the living future, in the same way that a mirror image of myself is refracted through its own future in what I will have been in the just-past moment of perception.

The apparatus of self-reflection

In looking in a mirror, what I see is myself as both dead (left behind in the just past moment that can never be retrieved) and alive (reflected in the mirror image before my eyes); the mirror-apparatus delays the reflection by sending it through a refractive process in which the reflex of the delay generates a phantasm – the stranger in the mirror looking back at me – as an *imago* effect (it *is* and *is not* me; I am superposed on my *self* as both dead and alive). My purpose in invoking the mirror image as the apparatus needed to refract the reflection of me (the other me-in-me) is to demonstrate in a practical way how images do not simply reflect themselves *sui generis* but are themselves the effects of light having passed through a medium in which refractions appear as auto-affecting phantasms, the irreality of which requires paraconsistent correction to ensure perceptual clarity in the reception of the view perceived.

To account for paraconsistent correction in the *ontological difference* between the past as having passed and in its passing in the mirror reflection, I will invoke Fichte's concept of *Anstoß* (1982: 189): the 'check' in the experience of self-reflection when the I confronts its non-I – the stranger looking back at me as the phantasmic *other* me-in-me. Here, I follow Slavoj Žižek's account of Fichtean *Anstoß* (2012: 151–6), in which he makes a distinction between *not-I* and *non-I*. Not-I is that which is other than the absolute I: the empirical I of others out there in the world, whereas non-I is the absolute I's rejected *thing* standing in for the lack or absence of not-I as 'that which incites the I to endless positing' (152). For Žižek, the distinction between not-I and non-I can be explained by reference to the difference between a negation of a predicate ('he is not human') and an affirmation of a non-predicate ('he is inhuman'), where the former is 'external to humanity', while the latter is an infinite judgement 'marked by a terrifying excess … inherent to being human' (166). While not-I is observed in finite existence as the negated other of the I transcending it, the non-I is felt as *real* in the infinite possibility of being an I – a phantasmic self-estranging otherness. The experience of the check generates a retrojection – a 'coming back' or return of otherness – as disturbing non-I calling for correction to the I's self-positing development (*Tathandlung*) in the task of having to complete itself (i.e. as work to-be-made in Souriau's sense of this term), which, for Fichte, is endless struggle of the I with itself in ongoing incompletion through the projective 'power of *imagination*' (1982: 193). In sexual-generative terms, this incessant striving for self-completion may be understood as a masculinized version of the ego-ordeal of having to survive the trauma of the cut of the *real* as primary separation from the arche-origin of the feminine, a point to which I will return in following sections.

In practical terms, the *Anstoß* supplies us with a concept to account for perception as *interference* in the flow of cinematic images, when action reaches an obstacle blocking passage through, which, for Simondon as we have already seen, is the 'obstacle through which the individuated being explores its dimensions of being without the ability to surpass them' (2020: 11). Upon encountering *Anstoß*, the actor becomes 'conscious of being *externally summoned* to exercise one's freedom – more specifically, to exercise it through voluntarily *limiting it*' (Breazeale 1995: 97), which, in Simondon's terms as previously discussed, is the collective 'calling itself into question' as a self-limiting process in the retroactivity of 'free acts' of moral character in the formation of a *socious*. Responding to the summons of the *Anstoß* as the other me-in-me transforms the obstacle by passing through it so that the threat of the stranger (non-I) is pacified into self-reflecting otherness (not-I) retroacted as a self-limiting *quasi-cause*,[5] for instance when, in looking at the stranger in the mirror as the other me-in-me, I am moved to say in my mind's eye 'yes, that is me', thereby dissolving the initial strangeness of the stranger into the crystal clear certainty of self-identity (I = I) as the me I claim myself to be 'where the presented self is presented' (Fichte 1982: 195); that is, as having passed through the ordeal of *having to be*. In having passed through the ordeal of *Anstoß* in the impulse of having to be, I will have freed myself from the threat of the non-I (the stranger in me), which, in a retroactive sense, becomes a *free act* of self-positing in relation to other acts in a self-limiting process of 'free reciprocal efficacy' (Fichte 2000: 33), which, for Simondon with respect to his idea of transindividuation, is a 'free act' of moral character encountering other such acts in the formation of social networks or groups (2020: 378).

Self-identity *requires* a moment in which it is challenged by *Anstoß*, without which it would never pass through to be the self it claims to be, a process which remains incessantly incomplete. There must always be a remainder of *Anstoß* (the non-I as the other me-in-me) to ensure ongoing activity to allow the I to present itself to itself in relation to not-I as the otherness of the objective world outside me. As the irreducible excess of the equation I = I, *Anstoß* floats in-between the subjective and objective polarities of the I's in-existence. The check of *Anstoß* is the held back *real* of the 'productive imagination' (Fichte 1982: 201): the creative impulse enabling *passage through* in the face of impeding doubts plaguing me with uncertainty as the existent being that I am – free to act in the world 'in free recognition of other free individuals – a recognition accomplished by voluntary self-limitation of one's own freedom out of respect for the freedom of others' (Breazeale 1995: 96–7). It follows that, in any process of self-relation seeking passage through life's obstacles, there will always be *Anstoß* summoning me to be who I claim to be in terms of a primary struggle with the stranger in me projected by the productive imagination: a struggle between two hostile aspects of myself of which *I* am always and only one; active and passive/aggressive and suffering (Fichte 1982: 133) as an 'interplay of the self' (193), which, in meta-psychological terms, is the *psychomachia* of archetypal being projected in the creative imagination as the traumatype of a soul struggling with itself in the 'theatre of individuation' (Simondon 2020: 9), seeking release in an 'endlessly outreaching activity' (Fichte 1982: 194).

Rear Window

A clear example of the *Anstoß* process can be found in Alfred Hitchcock's *Rear Window* (1954), a modern *Kammerspielfilm*[6] in which a male photojournalist recuperating with a broken leg in his New York apartment on a hot summer's day thinks he sees a man murder his wife in the apartment opposite – a refracted reflection of his own situation in which he quarrels with his fiancé over their differences in life's expectations, in which he, the man of action, compares himself to her disadvantage as a woman devoted to appearances and fashion. In what follows I will analyse the positions of watching and being watched which, for the sake of clarity I will define in terms of the characters' names: I will call the man who thinks he sees the murder taking place *Jeff* (the watching man) and the man whom Jeff imagines has murdered his wife *Thorwald* (the watched man); also, I will call the woman who acts on the watching man's behalf *Lisa* (the watching man's accomplice/fiancé).

What at first glance seem to Jeff to be everyday activities begin to look more like foul play and his initial suspicion turns into a firm conviction that Thorwald has indeed murdered his wife. An initial 'check' to Jeff's perception when he notices blinds drawn when they should be open creates a blind spot in the film which is then filled in by his imagination into the shape of a monstrous other: a ruthless killer who has murdered his wife (a projection of Jeff's uncomfortable feelings towards his fiancé Lisa). Jeff's perception has *interfered* with what he sees, distorting it into the phantasmic *real* – a hallucinating image – of an absent other calling back at him, reaching a climax when Thorwald realizes that he is being watched and looks directly across at Jeff as the man watching him: an act of mutual self-recognition that draws the man Jeff thinks he sees (reflected as not-I) and the man Jeff imagines he sees (refracted as non-I) together as hostile to each other.

Intruding into Jeff's apartment, Thorwald asks 'what do you want from me?' as if *he* were the one being summoned. Upon this, Thorwald moves menacingly towards Jeff rendered helpless in his wheelchair who, in a futile attempt to save himself, fends his attacker off with camera flashes, buying himself enough time for rescuers to come to his rescue. As the two men struggle – in a Fichtean 'clash of ... opposites' between active and passive/aggressive and suffering principles of the split subject struggling with itself (Fichte 1982: 191–5) – Jeff is thrown over the balcony to the death-that-awaits but with his fall broken by rescuers arriving just in time to save him.

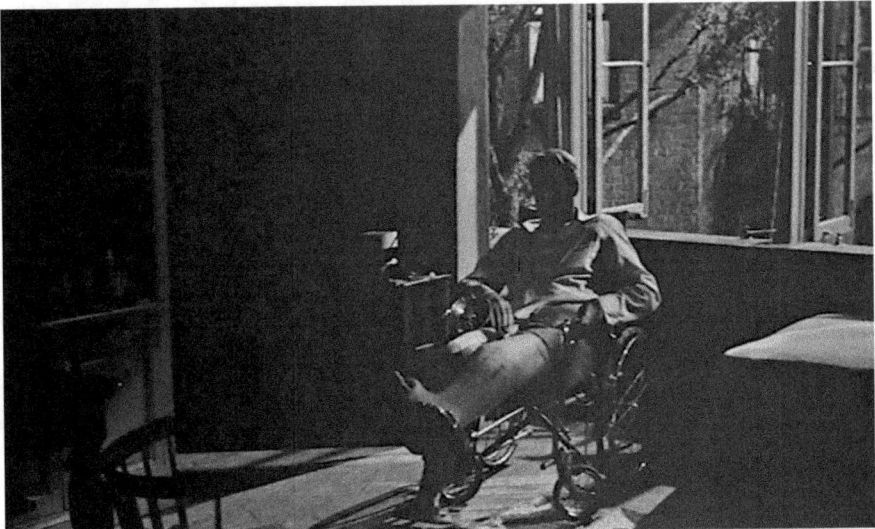

Figure 1.1 Jeff withdraws into the safety of the shadows. *Rear Window*, dir. Alfred Hitchcock (1954).

Figure 1.2 Thorwald caught in the camera flash. *Rear Window*, dir. Alfred Hitchcock (1954).

Let us now return to the beginning of the film and run through the events again: in having suffered the loss of his capacity to act in the world (he has a broken leg), Jeff succumbs to a *fantasy* stimulated by his voyeuristic pleasure in watching others, in which he is confronted by the phantasm of the non-I – the *other* me-in-me hovering over the small details of everyday life – which, as *Anstoß* appearing in the form of a monstrous wife murderer, becomes the obstacle invoked by his restless seeking for relief from physical limitation (confined to his apartment in a wheelchair), bearing potential for its dissolution when the watched man Thorwald looks back. The returned look reverses the trajectory of the gaze, drawing the non-I back into the body of the perceiving I, where 'they annul one another' (Fichte 1982: 124) in a struggle to the death which resolves *Anstoß* in the return of normal perception in which the *right* perspective is found as view X missing from the overall picture.[7]

As Jeff regains composure in having been rescued from certain death, he is told that Thorwald has been arrested and has confessed to having murdered his wife. The threat to the archetypal male ego struggling with itself is pacified in routine police procedure and everything in the world is set right in the restitution of the *comic continuity* of life (Langer 1953: 363), when all of the characters watched by Jeff, depicted as leading alienated, miserable lives isolated in their apartments, find their true partners in each other in a renewal of life's spirit, discovering between them the communal link that had been missing.

With the help of our noetic eye (the eye that sees otherwise), we can draw some conclusions with regard to the film's moral vision. As the *other* me-in-me, the *Anstoß* calls me to rise to its challenge to test my worthiness as the being I take myself to be, which is an obligation *to myself* as part of a *socious* of other Is threatened with the alienating tendencies of modern life as a cinematically transindividuated *I–We*. The struggle-to-be acted out by the characters resolves all tensions and contradictions, restoring the order of the world in the comic continuity of life. Criminals are punished and everyone is satisfied including me, my moral sense of self worth having been fulfilled in theirs. Everything is set *right*, and all's well with the world in a Hollywood happy ending. However, there still remains the possibility of further *Anstoß* as the ontological condition of an incomplete I = I calling for work to-be-made in the endless struggle of life, without which psychic life – life projected inwardly as self-reflection – would cease in the I = I's drive of self-destruction (Fichte 1982: 187), collapsing the happy ending into a nightmare of unending alienation.

The necessity of ongoing *Anstoß* is affirmed in *Rear Window* when we consider that the struggle of the man with himself includes a third: Lisa, who, in seeking to emulate Jeff's masculine traits to gain his approval, becomes more than he is to himself as the rescuer needed to overcome the threat to him by turning it onto herself. It is *she* who undertakes the dangerous task of rescuing *him* by flushing the murderer out of his apartment, proving to her fiancé that she is worthy of his respect, thus affirming her gendered position in the heterosexualized 'sexuate difference' of 1950s gender politics: the being-together of 'man' and 'woman' participating jointly in a moralized *socious* 'formed by two' (Irigaray 2013: 131): she receives her nature from him as his supplemental other in the social hierarchization of life. In an ironic twist at the end of the film Jeff finds himself even more dependent on Lisa, having broken his other leg in the life and death struggle of the two aspects of himself, the hostile relation between them having been corrected by the intervention of a third aspect: the feminine point of view in which view X has been gendered as the new normalized view of things. Having fallen from the masculine world of action, Jeff now finds himself inactive in Lisa's feminized world of image-shaping (fashion) in which he nevertheless derives secret pleasure. Through the process of mutual self-limitation in the subjectification of sexuate difference, Jeff and Lisa are called to be free together as the natural couple of the Hollywood dream in post-World

War II American capitalistic society in which women were accorded an ambiguous status as both objects of male desire and as practical agents of their own free being, itself restricted to naturalized maternal care towards family as the *summum bonum* of the 'imagined community' – how a *socious* ought to be.

My analysis of *Anstoß* in *Rear Window* is incomplete. It has not accounted for the fact that what the viewer sees is not the real action of actors but their memory traced across the screen in which images are slipped in, sometimes for disruptive purposes, for instance when we see Thorwald leaving his apartment in the company of a woman who may or may not be his wife after the moment in which we become convinced that he has indeed murdered her, an image that Jeff does not see as a complicating view from nowhere. These slipped-in images are what Hitchcock calls MacGuffins: a *special kind* of false image designed to foil the viewer's recollection of events and further complicate the thwarted progress of the plot towards a satisfying ending. In a general sense, the presence of slipped-in images – constituting the whole of the image array including images that characters can and cannot see – tells us in a *specific way* that the memory we experience is not the characters' memory but rather the film's memorizing of the characters' memory filling out a clear view of the scene and then foiling it with incongruous detail.

In Stiegler's terms, what the viewer experiences in watching a film is *hypomnesis* (technical memory) supervening – changing, disrupting – *anamnesis* (the memory of characters' inner feelings and expressions) as the visual projection of the whole of what we see in a 'corrected' state. In an organological account of the perception of film images, we need to consider the mirror model of self-reflection in terms of the memorizing of films in which reflections are refracted through a mnemotechnical apparatus to correct them, a correction which, in the experience of the viewer, has already happened (had the correction not already happened, there would be no clear image to see, in the same way that we do not see the refractions of light in our retinas when we see the world before our eyes). Images are reflected after the fact of their having been refracted, metastabilizing into clear vision in the image flow in our eyes and on the screen *into which the apparatus retreats*. Our pursuit of the *real* of the archival future is conditioned by a recessed technical apparatus in which the I's self-consciousness is shaped by the film's memorizing reflected through the refractions of the medium through which they must pass – the cinematograph – in which already corrected images seem to be auto-affecting themselves in the way they appear to us on the screen.

My employment of Fichtean *Anstoß* as the summoning of the self to act on behalf of itself in self-completion raises the question of whether *Anstoß* as *Tathandlung* – the retro-performative act of self-positing – can effect a break with current *I–We* relations that may have become toxic to noetic life, for instance in my analysis of *Rear Window* when we realize that the gendering of hetero-sexuate difference is limited to a masculine frame of reference, thus short-circuiting any possibility of self-affirming feminine freedom by making it pass through the masculine ordeal of primary struggle with itself. Can the *Anstoß* be applied in such a way that it runs counter to the hegemony of viewpoints prevailing in a milieu which tends towards hyper-syncrystallization of masculinity as the unstated norm? What we would be seeking from this resistive understanding of *Anstoß* is the possibility of inducing a new dimension within the archival future as a pathway not yet taken in the open horizon (*apeiron*) excluded by subjectification of the female view to an unstated and hence normalized male perspective. There are always other views to see.

In the foregoing analysis of *Rear Window*, I claim that a new a dimension can be seen in what feminist philosopher Luce Irigaray calls the 'speculum' (1985: 136): the 'polished mirror' of speculation in which it becomes possible to see the *other woman* (the woman that Lisa could be other than as a dutiful helpmeet to Jeff employing 'feminine' ruses to outwit male authority), through an arche-feminized viewpoint. The *speculum* is the mirror doubled on itself so that the viewer sees herself seeing, generating a reflex action in which she becomes self-aware of the possibility of seeing with different eyes. By looking through the *speculum* with a feminine eye, the story of primary struggle of sexuate being in which Lisa can only be seen in a supplemental role as Jeff's accomplice shifts its point of focus, where the obstacle to be confronted is not Thorwald's threat to Jeff but Jeff's threat to Lisa insofar as he sees her as nothing but appearance and fashion. Through the feminized *speculum*, it is not *she* but *he* who becomes *Anstoß*: the obstacle that must be worked through in order to reclaim feminine identity acting on behalf of herself in the difference between the masculine and feminine tendencies of the struggle to be. Looking through the polished mirror of a feminized *speculum*, she becomes *She*: the one to lead us out of the masculinized 'closure of the world' and into the 'open horizon' of a feminized *apeiron* – the boundless becoming of pre-existent life (Irigaray 2013: 11).

The *speculum*

Experience tells us that the mirror apparatus hides itself in the image reflected (i.e. we do not see the refraction *as such* but only what remains of it in the mirror image). What we see in a reflected image is the *trace* of a withdrawn apparatus hiding itself in the void of a *blank screen*. What we also see revealed in the void is the *real* of the apparatus – its potential for reflection stripped back to degree zero in which a future awaits. By looking through what we see into the blankness of the screen, we release our view of what we see into the unknown of view X – the future that awaits.

For Irigaray, the blank screen is not a flat mirror but the concavity of a 'specular surface' in which we find 'not the [masculine] void of nothingness but the [feminine] dazzle of multifaceted speleology. A scintillating and incandescent concavity' (1985: 143). Irigaray calls this specular surface the *speculum* of self-reflection refracting the *apeiron* of cosmic becoming, an open horizon of free being 'between-us', undoing the mirrored self-on-self relations of the masculine ordering of the world where 'subjects move on the chessboard of a closed whole' (2013: 11). Irigaray adopts the *speculum* of the recessed apparatus as an 'instrument' for speculative seeing (1985: 144). What she sees in the *speculum* is 'what there is to be *seen* of female sexuality' (145); that is, what remains of female sexuality concaved in the nothingness of masculine self-reflection stripped out of the view seen.

To see the concave image we must look *through* the mirror apparatus recessed in the blank screen, to see as *it* sees in the *speculum* of pathways blocked by the circuitry of reflected images keeping other views in check on the 'chessboard of a closed whole', which, for Irigaray, is the beginning for woman to be *otherwise*, released from the game of life played according to the rules of masculine self-engendering reflected in the mirror-image of current views (1985: 144). By stripping the mirror-image bare, we expose our eyes to the *real* of the apparatus recessed in it, in possible views awaiting in a new dimension of the crystalline sphere, rendering current views obsolete – outdated by the new view perceived in the *speculum* of future views.

A shortcoming of Stiegler's project is that he gives insufficient consideration to the forces of struggle in cinematic self-consciousness in terms of sexual difference. By taking Irigaray's arche-feminist position into account, in which sexual coupling is prefigured by 'sexuate belonging' (2013: 136) – the original relation of male and female to their respective life worlds predicated on mutual responsibility[8] – we can find a way through to Stiegler in Simondon's proposal of a transductive process of ontogenesis and the doubling of individuals in sexual difference (2020: 294, 328). In this case, the sexuate couple would be placed together with others as part of a 'social network' of dyad couplings, where the dyad relation functions to bind individuals into a polygendered *socious* calling itself into existence through mutually self-limiting 'free acts' of moral character (328) opening into the *apeiron* – the transcendental horizon of the *real* – as boundlessly mutable: 'a relation that is always open, constantly evolving, never proper to the one or to the other' (Irigaray 2013: 9).

Irigaray's *apeiron* of boundless mutability correlates with Simondon's pre-individual flux of transductive becoming shifting in and out of phase 'in which no phase exists' (2020: 4). In a transductive becoming, the fulfilment of coupling is thwarted by the process passing through its own dephasing to keep itself open as incessantly incomplete (i.e. as heterogeneous to itself), thus setting the scene for a dismantling of the mirror-apparatus of masculine self-reflection which excludes the feminine. In the process of dephasing, the repressed *feminine view* is brought back into play through the dismantling of the apparatus as an *arche-principle* of incomplete being as becoming seen in the *speculum* of future views. By seeing with this other view – the feminized point of view – we lift our way of seeing out of the closed loop of male anxiety in its seeking relief from its own internalized anguish projected onto the screen as the ordeal of life and death struggle, providing ourselves with sufficient purchase on the problem of sexuate difference in which the issue of coupling remains mutable and incomplete.

The problem of sexuate difference does not come to us of its own accord, but appears through the workings of the apparatus of self-recognition, which, in the socialization of industrial life, functions as imaginative projection projected onto a screen. For Stiegler, imaginative projection in industrial life is becoming cinematic through a transformation of our perception by technical means, a condition of *ciné-mnemotechnesis* in which 'life is *always* cinema' (2011: 16). In the following section, we examine how this becoming cinematic plays itself out in social milieus – a becoming which for Stiegler is epochal (phase-shifting from the old to the new), transforming the way humans relate to technological systems and their technical elements: the tool ensembles by which the system operates (2019: 12–14).

Doubly epokhal redoubling

Following Heidegger's analysis of tool-being in which Dasein's normalized relation to the system is disrupted by shock when the hammer in my hand breaks, Stiegler proposes a *double shift* in our relation to technical objects in order to expose the technical milieu in which they are used to the limit of its possibilities (2019: 13). The first shift is triggered by an 'epochal' moment equivalent to the shock received in the breaking of the tool: a 'suspension of judgement' together with a '*conversion of the gaze, of a change in the way of thinking*' (12), from seeing objects in the world as useful or desirable to seeing them in their technicity as 'transitional objects' (233) – *pharmakons* capable of effecting phase-change in the transformation of life by technical means. The second shift doubles the first in a turning back-over procedure in which transitional space is revalued in an altered array of possibilities effected by the turn through development in which something new comes into view – the beginnings of another future.

Stiegler calls this double shift that doubles back over itself 'doubly epokhal redoubling' (2019: 14): a recursive phase-shifting process in which a current epoch of technically automated life is de-phased by shock and then re-phased through innovations released by the impetus of the shock into a new epoch in-the-making, 'produc[ing] new capacities for dis-automatization, that is, for negentropy to foster new social organizations' (2016: 12). The crucial point to keep in mind in this developmental phase of the doubly epokhal redoubling process is the need for dis-automatization acting as a guarantee that the epoch in-the-making does not congeal into dead sense inhibiting the inventiveness and creativity needed for the flourishing of the *socious* as open to modification and further phase-change. Dis-automatizing is built into the process of automation in which the *pharmakon* has its place acting as an ethical moderator for the '*transformation of rules* [which is] the key factor in the production of new forms of knowledge' (2019: 233).

An epochal event of doubly epokhal redoubling in the technicization of social systems occurred at the end of the nineteenth century in the transformation of the mass-produced photographic print epoch based on the classical image as a static, unified object into a photo-cinematographic moving image epoch predicated on thermodynamic principles of energy exchange (Mules 2007). The new epoch begins in the suspension of existing photographic print values with the shock appearance of the cinematograph: a disrupting technology, the newness of which generates innovations requiring formalisation and standardization into cinematically informed production, distribution and consumption systems for projecting values and meanings of mass audiences springing forth to adopt them into their lives (e.g. the development of the Hollywood studio system of the early to mid-twentieth century) which, for Stiegler, is the realization of the becoming cinematic of a *We* – a multiplicity of individuals constituting themselves as a people – of industrialized life (2011: 98).

The 'automatizing' of the people into mass audiences by formalizing and standardizing procedures to enframe their collective imaginaries renders them captive to the systems as consumer 'dividuals' (Stiegler 2011: 4), augmented by dis-automatizing innovations in ongoing development seeking efficiencies for maximizing profits under the hegemonic rule of mediating institutions (for example, corporatized film studios operating under neo-liberal principles of an unrestricted free market enfolding itself into globalized media networks seeking to control the desire of the people guided by the maxim of free choice). The process moves from *could* in the possibility of other ways opening up in an epochal suspension of the old regime, to *should* in probabilities of development seeking the most efficient way of doing things, to *ought* in conforming with the moral vision projected by the new epoch opening up through the *could* to the *should* as a *fait accompli*. But herein lies danger, when the *ought* ossifies into rigid rule following – 'mandatory protocols' (Stiegler 2019a: 37) – in surveillance control of the system, transforming the people into docile consumers whose acquiescence to the rule deadens their desire for otherness in anthropic self-affirmation (*anthropy*), which, if left unchecked, would lead to the exhaustion of life spirit and the onset of anaphylactic collapse (Ross 2021: 19): an autoimmune attack by the capitalist system *on itself*. To avoid catastrophic system failure in negentropic self-destruction, the automatization of the mass audience requires a dis-automatization which, rather than blindly reproducing system values in the compulsion to repeat rules of consumption in fetishistic desire (Stiegler 2014: 35), knowingly transforms them into *neganthropy* – transvalued noetic life in a specifically human-mnemotechnical mode – as the cure for toxic anthropy in which the *pharmakon* finds its place as a transitional object to the effect the called-for cure.

The promise of technics

To conceive the possibility of re-energizing exhausted spirit (desire deadened by repetition), Stiegler turns to Hegel's dialectic of the *I–We* relation in the return of self-consciousness out of the other to itself in ethical life (*Sittlichkeit*) (Hegel 1977: 110). For Hegel, the *I* returns to itself in an affirmation of the absolute as spiritual freedom predicated on a *naturalized* relation to the subject of ethical life as a *bearer of rights* through the rule of law predicated on institutionalized reason; that is, acting freely 'in conformity with the state's institutions' (1991: 288), albeit under the self-critical guidance of conscience as 'the disposition to will what is good *in and for itself*' (164). However, as Stiegler points out, Hegel could not think the mnemotechnical condition of the dialectic of the spirit in the capitalist age of technological reproduction (2019: 240), and left unsaid the need for a concept of spiritual freedom understood therapeutically; that is, in pharmacological terms (2018: 110) in which the artificially naturalized consumer-subject of ethical life is de-naturalized (dis-automatized) from the hegemony of the capitalist system to reclaim noetic freedom to imagine otherwise in the power to dream.

Stiegler's adoption of the Hegelian *I–We* dialectic transforms the resolution of *ethical life* in anthropic self-affirmation into *technical life* based on a therapeutics of neganthropic care uncoupling itself from the surveillance control of the capitalist system by way of the *pharmakon* – the transitional object acting as an ethical moderator to effect a transformation of rules in the production of new values for an epoch to come, where 'new ways of thinking, new ways of doing and new ways of living take shape' (2019: 13). From a film-philosophical perspective, the ethical task would be to wrest back the *promise of technics* from the control regimes of the capitalist market system by turning within it to expose the archival future in *its* promise of re-energized life in the *real* of its possibilities. By taking films to be *pharmakons* as our 'tools' for effecting such a turn, we are already stepping into this future.

My aim is to develop a methexical style of film analysis – a participatory mode of self-questioning in film *mnemotechnesis* in which the telling of stories becomes entangled in the tale, which I consider in terms of the *figural* as feeling for the future otherwise in paths not taken, to reclaim a moral vision of the world as pharmacological: the cure for anthropic toxicity effected by turning in the technical system to transform it from within as redoubling otherwise in care-full neganthropy. In the next chapter, I pick up on the *figural* in terms of the archival future considered in its hermeneutic dimensions as the reception of the past in the present as trace effects of other times calling for meaning to be made of them in a renewed sense of what they could mean for a possible future – an epoch to come otherwise. The promise of technics is bound up in making this future happen.

2

Hermeneutics

Methexis: A spherical model

In his magnum opus *Truth and Method* (1975), Hans-Georg Gadamer presents a hermeneutic account of the reception of viewpoints received from the past becoming meaningful in the present through *Bildung* or cultivated learning: a 'trained receptivity towards the "otherness" of the work of art or of the past' open to 'universal viewpoints':

> The universal viewpoints to which the cultivated man (gebildet) *keeps himself open* are not a fixed applicable yardstick, but are present to him only as the *viewpoints of possible others*. Thus the cultivated consciousness (gebildet) has in fact more the character of a sense. *For every sense, eg vision (the sense of sight), is already universal in that it embraces its sphere, remains open to a particular field*, and grasps the distinctions within what is opened in it in this way. Cultivated consciousness goes beyond each of the natural senses in that the latter are limited to one particular sphere at a time, whereas it is *active in all directions*. It is universal sense.
>
> 1975: 17–18, emphasis added

Gadamer proposes a *spherical model* of the reception of views in which a 'cultivated consciousness' that 'embraces its sphere' remains open to perceptions (points of view) from other spheres immersed in the *apeiron* – the open horizon of cosmic becoming – described in terms of a dynamic 'field [of views] ... active in all directions' as 'universal sense'. In its 'particular' reality, the field is itself part of the whole of cosmic spacetime composed of multiple spheres in which views from the past are perceived proximate with present views, which, in 'Plato as Portraitist', Gadamer calls *methexis* as being-with or 'participation' (2007: 310–12). *Methexis* is the sharing of past and present views located in the embracing sense of *Stimmung*, the mood or atmosphere of a sphere in which a self-conscious perceiver (a 'cultivated consciousness') undergoes an experience of the *real*: an openness to all times at *this* time in *this* view. In what viewpoint does the *methexis* itself stand? As a *real* event (i.e. open to all times), *methexis* could not stand in an existing view but in a *view from nowhere*: the blank screen of another beginning seen through the *speculum* of the sphere, an instrument for speculating on the possibility of other views as views seen elsewhere, yet to be seen in *this* view.

Gadamer's *fusional hermeneutics* – fusional in the sense that it fuses views seen 'there' and 'here', 'then' and 'now' on an open horizon (2007: 180) – develops a methexical account of being-as-becoming, by which he means the coexistence of two events, one re-performing the other in a 'participation' or 'belonging-together' experienced in the *speculum* of the sphere in which a perceiver perceives, correlating with the quantum thought of non-local interactivity in a superposition of views. The views received are *cosmic views* in which viewpoints are speculated upon as 'the viewpoints of possible others'. The two views thus speculated become entangled in the tensed modality of the future anterior; that is, by *looking backward from the turned position* in the *speculum* in which the future comes to me in 'all directions' (1975: 18) as a 'fusion of memory and expectation into a whole' (195). A *methexis* occurs in the reception of views mixed together ('fused'), when I, as the receptor of these views, respond to the question of how the event of their reception relates to the event of their initial occurrence in the 'chaotic mixture of many historicizing tendencies' (2007: 396); that is, in the mixing of memory and expectation which Gadamer relates to Plato's 'dialectic of *methexis*' at work in the interpretive logic of the dialogues around the issue of *anamnesis* as cosmic re-remembering (312). Gadamer's spherical model opens up a *hermeneutic sphere* in which views from different spheres interpenetrate in an embracing fusion which is also defusing itself – keeping itself open – in the chaos of its heterogeneous tendencies 'active in all directions'.

While Gadamer's sphere is a synchronic model in which views occurring in any given sphere happen at the same time as views in other spheres, his hermeneutics is diachronic in that each view occurs in and through time, thus invoking a *horizonal dimension* within the *speculum* of the sphere – the *apeiron* of cosmic becoming passing through it. Combining the spherical with the hermeneutic component dynamizes the model so that *methexis* as 'participation' plays an active part in the becoming of views as the micro-/macro- site of an interpretive politics which I will designate as *poetizing* in the sense proposed by Walter Benjamin (1996: 33) in which the hermeneutic modality of time is at stake.

Benjaminian poetizing is the interpretive tactic of reading a poem backwards so that what it says is unravelled in the saying; that is, how the telling and the tale superpose one another in the manner of Fichtean *Tathandlung* in which act and deed are understood to be retroactively self-constituting.[1] Seen from this Benjaminian–Fichtean perspective, the Gadamerian spherical model is refracted through a 'sphere of permissible action' (Kosch 2021: 223) in which poetizing – retro-actualization – becomes participation in moral action as methexical self-questioning in pursuit of self-completion (I = I), the summons of the other in me, which Gadamer understands in terms of *stoß* (shock): the sudden putting into question of the I, where 'a question presses itself on us; we can no longer avoid it and persist in our accustomed opinion' (1975: 330). In these terms, *Anstoß* indicates the 'on-stop' or impulse to 'go on' when in a stopped state, a stop-start condition of *resistive effort* in recommencement, the negative force of which Samuel Beckett has stated at the end of his novel *The Unnamable* with the exclamation 'I can't go on, I'll go on' (2010: 134).

Our concern will be with *methexis* as a poetized politics of interpretative retro-actualization within the *speculum* of the sphere in which a *methexis* takes place, altering its perceptual horizons in the defusion of cosmic energy refracted through an apparatus which Bergson describes as a telescopic memory cone aimed at the stars in which the absolute past projected into the future can be brought into sharp focus (1988: 166, 134). We will take Bergson's memory cone in light of Gadamer's receptor model of cosmic views to be suited for modelling film as a *decentred crystalline sphere* in which the 'film's attempt to reflect on itself is refracted such that it remains outside of its own reflection and misses its original target (itself)' (Mullarkey 2009: 46). In missing its original target, the film falls out of sync with itself – refuses to sink into its crystalline substance as pure image – keeping itself open to views from other spheres in the cosmic field of views in which it is poietically infused; that is, open to the creative plasticity of cosmic time as *poiesis*. In Stiegler's terms, poietic becoming relates to the spiralling loops of an 'idiotext' (2021: 189): 'an open and metastable system' (190) composed of the recursive looping of piezo-electrical light-life as trace-data passing through a receptor-sender mechanism that includes a noetic capacity – an *I* as part of a *We* in-the-making syncrystallizing in the dynamism of a 'noosphere' – the biosphere saturated with noetic life – projected along the horizon of cosmic time (36).

Poetizing enters into the make-up of films in methexical moments of self-questioning from within the embrace of the crystalline sphere through which cinematic memory passes, in which the co-existence of two events – the view from the past entangled with the present view – constitutes a *questioning situation*, requiring the exercise of *noesis* to interpret the indiscernibility of the former in terms of the latter's discernibility. Responding to the call retroacts *Anstoß* in the structuring of cinematic time, exposing gaps and fissures in the film's temporalizing of its images while opening up a *circuitry of pathways* recessed within the future anterior of the methexical event in which some paths will have already been taken including the path concretized idiotextually in *this* film, while other paths lie dormant in the possibility that they might be taken in the anterior of a future to come 'to open up new avenues of thought' (Gadamer 2007: 396), which Simondon calls 'recourse to new *dimensions*' (2020: 9).

The choral voice

For the ancient Greeks, *methexis* means participation or sharing associated with publicly performed drama, particularly where the chorus invites the audience to participate in the action taking place on the stage 'in the *challenge* of collective decision-making' (Foster C. 2015: 231). In the hermeneutic endeavours of Athenian dramaturgy, *methexis* is the re-performance (retroaction) of a myth or legendary event, soliciting audience members to question the values of the *socious* – the identity relation of which they are part – as a 'we' exercising interpretive judgement in deciding upon the rights and wrongs of *cratic* rule (the rule of governance) through staged re-enactments:

> In the manner of orations in the Athenian law courts, which were argued in the first person plural, *these performances expressed the voice of a 'we', rather than that of an individual speaking for, on behalf of, the city.* The audience were the performers, and the city the set; there was no 'off stage' in the Athenian dramatic festival. The city itself, in the visual field of spectators, was a geographical participant in the narrations.
>
> 230, emphasis added

In this quote from Clare Foster's illuminating article on the methexical practices of ancient Athenian theatre, we gain some insight into the operation of a *choral function* shared between onstage oration and an audience responding as a 'we', in Simondon's terms, a transindividuated *I–We* to be distinguished from the *I–I* of the solipsistic individual, as a *demos* – people of the *polis* as the city state in principle – vested with the power to decide on the common good by exercising judgement in noetic freedom – the freedom to think and imagine otherwise. My employment of *methexis* takes a similar approach. Insofar as I am vested with such freedom, my stake is as much theirs: to defend *noesis* in its capacity to project otherwise in judging rights and wrongs on behalf of a *We*, whose voice reverberates in the choral voice speaking to me in the re-performance enacted in the *mnemotechnesis* of film story-telling.

The *socious* is not the only *I–We* relation at work in the chorality of re-performance; what is also at stake is life in its givenness, without which a *socious* could not be actualized since there would be no living being to ground it in the earth's atmosphere sustaining human existence. We need to consider the living reality of the *socious* to be part of the *oikeios* – the 'web of life' – as the whole of the natural *organon*, including both human and nonhuman life (Moore 2015: 35 ff). In the chorality of Athenian theatre, the re-performance of the *socious* is inherently eco-cosmological; the web of life flows through the re-performance as connectivity to the *real* of cosmic time as the 'first chaos' of Lucretian flow, the turbulence of which is refracted through all earthly things (Serres 2018: 104) including the *socious* itself. Following the Roman poet Lucretius's poetic invocation of the living being of the cosmos in *De Rerum Natura* (2007), itself following Greek atomistic principles, Lucretian flow is the *clinamen*: the swerve or swaying to and fro of the cosmic rhythm, the dance of life which is also a *danse macabre*; the *play of life and death* switching from one to another in the Heraclitian lightning flash, the projected vision of cosmic wonder seen in the *Augenblick* – the blink of an eye in which, from the turned position of the specular *real*, is the whole of time grasped in its apperceptive immediacy: 'it is a look of an eye in the blink of an eye, a momentary look at what is momentarily concrete, which as such can always be otherwise' (Heidegger 1997: 112).

From a thermodynamic perspective, the clinametric rhythm is the force/ counter force of negentropy – the tendency towards steady state or degree zero in *life death* processes of survival 'in which the organism succeeds in *freeing itself* from all the entropy it cannot help producing while alive' (Schrödinger 1967: 71, emphasis added). In light of Schrödinger's idea of 'freeing up' as 'negative entropy', *methexis* becomes participation in the *freeing up* of the chances of survival in questioning situations where the organon of human existence is put at risk of not surviving the life and death struggle re-performed in the theatre of individuation of film *mnemotechnesis* – a traumatic event doubling itself in me and on the screen, which, from the perspective of the Gadamerian–Bergsonian receptor model of cosmic views, is the surface of a crystalline sphere permeated with Stieglerian idiotextual plasticity laid out horizontally; that is, in the duration of temporal objects such as films.

Neganthropic resistance

In *What is Life?* the quantum physicist Erwin Schrödinger proposes the term 'negative entropy' to describe the resistance of cellular life to the law of entropy as 'the natural tendency of things to go over into disorder' (1967: 68). As discussed in the introductory chapter, negative entropy or *negentropy* is the counter tendency to the tendency towards disorder, thereby affirming life's possibilities against the second law of thermodynamics in which life is determined (fated) to an indeterminate state of being (death). Adopting Schrödinger's position, Stiegler makes a crucial distinction between negentropy and neganthropy, where the former is the negative entropy of natural or organological systems, whereas the latter is the negative entropy of 'exorganological systems' (Ross 2018: 29); that is, organic systems technicized by the prostheticization of human life (the exosomatization of human *noesis*). *Neganthropic resistance* is the resistive potential within exorganological systems whereby localized knowledge of the conditions of survival are learnt through an educative process as *savoir faire* and *savoir vivre*: know-how, learning how to live well in localized practices of care freeing themselves from the *anthropy* of automated system control in which they are immersed (Stiegler 2021: 58, 138, note 10). Anthropy refers to 'the toxicity of the pharmacological condition' (quoted in Ross 2018: 31) in which the ill health affecting an exorganological system is mixed with its cure such that to enact a cure is to risk impoverishment of the spirit, where 'it is always possible for [the *pharmakon*] to cause desire to regress to a purely drive based stage' (Stiegler 2013: 23). A cure for anthropy lies in its detoxification through neganthropic resistance as a praxis of care, played out under conditions of *life death* in which the entanglement of life-in-death and death-in-life is placed under question (Derrida 2020: 1). Being placed in the care of questioning effects the called-for cure.

The *praxis* of neganthropic resistance – knowing how to work against the system by working with it – enables non-inhuman individuals vested with noetic freedom to imagine *for themselves* another life in which it is possible to flourish in care relations with others in the development of 'moral consciousness' (Stiegler 2013: 23) – a sense of knowing how one *ought* to live one's life freely – as newly developing individuations within dis-automatizing social networks (2016: 7); that is, in social relations releasing themselves from the 'automatization to which digital reticulation [in hyper-automated industrial life under platform capitalism] is leading' (6). The praxis of neganthropic freedom is free not in an unlimited sense but in the finitude of relations to others as mutually self-limiting free beings, which – as proposed in the introductory chapter – can be considered in terms of Stiegler's notion of moral consciousness together with Simondon's 'moral act' (2020: 378) as versions of Fichtean *Recht* ('right', 'justice', 'law') (Fichte 1992: 470). For Simondon, *right* as a principle of freedom manifests in the moral act as a 'free act' posited by an *I* in relation to a *We* in the process of transindividuation, which has 'enough reality to go beyond itself and encounter other [such] acts' (2020: 378). In moving back to Fichte, these moral acts of freedom are resolved into one another in the practical work of reason as 'the unification of the wills of many different people' – mutually self-limiting free acts – as *right* in themselves (Fichte 1992: 471).

In the hegemonic power relations of capitalist production and consumption, the *right* of the people must be won back by dis-automatizing the *will* from systems of control in individuals' *finite freedom* to imagine their lives otherwise, to dream new dreams in care for the future in the name of justice, the law and the good understood in moral terms as mutually self-limiting free being or 'free reciprocal efficacy' (Fichte 2000: 33). As Stiegler puts it: 'we must elaborate an *organology of will*, and not just of desire – of will [*volition*] as including every kind of production of motives ... by rethinking practical questions in relation to this organology' (2018: 48), by which he means unwilling the will of the capitalist drive in the praxis of neganthropic care guided by *right* in moral acts of free self-consciousness, which Stiegler calls noetic freedom.

Stiegler finds an instance of a dis-automatizing social network in the exorganism of the city: 'the city is an exorganism ... the social concretion of a society individuating itself exorganically' (2018: 121). As exorganism, the city is always freeing itself from the mechanisms of technical control, which, for Stiegler, is *mnemotechnesis* running through it as a third memory (*hypomnesis*) carrying primary and secondary memories (*anamnesis*) in recursive doublings – complex feedback loops – of neganthropic becoming. In its neganthropic mode, *mnemotechnesis* becomes resistive potential as noetic life (*I–We* potential) freeing itself from the anthropy of 'control societies' (Deleuze 1995) of hypermodern capitalism in which the city – the talismanic site of hyper-capitalist opportunity – is becoming cinematic, where 'life is *always* cinema' (Stiegler 2011: 16). Thinking back to the *methexis* enacted by the *demos* in the Athenian city under *cratic* rule, the question raised by Stiegler's political position is as follows. How can the dis-automatized individual participate in an *I–We* free to determine its own being without the systems of control anticipating and recapturing its gesture of release? In answer: by ensuring neganthropy by right in restoring the conditions under which a free public sphere guided by what one *must* do as a matter of *principled action* in the Fichtean sense of coming to know what *right* is can re-emerge from within the systems themselves; in cinematic terms, to transform the anthropy of control into a neganthropy of care acted out in the cinematization of the *places of life* in which *right* is acted out.

From the point of view of *methexis*, *right* as neganthropic care becomes the practical application of *poetizing* – re-reading technical artefacts in relation to their archival future such that a new dimension comes into view through the *speculum* of a crystalline sphere, to 'open up new avenues of thought …[in seeking] the *right path*' (Gadamer 2007: 397, emphasis added). A *poetized* interpretive hermeneutics seeks to open new pathways for living in the cinematization of the places of life (e.g. scenes in a film), in which paths not taken are re-encountered as possible exit points for new life freed from the anthropy of technical control: a *poietic act* which *is itself* an exercise of care in the *right* of what one *must* do as principled action.

The crystalline flow

For Gilbert Simondon, a crystalline flow is 'an amplifying reticular structure' which 'can overflow itself on both sides from *its center*' (2020: 13, 12) – 'an overflowing expanse of being' in which individual crystals undergo 'abrupt variation' when a 'we' passes across them: 'a crystal is an individual not because it possesses a geometrical form or an ensemble of elementary particles, but because all of its (optical, thermal, elastic, electrical, piezo-electrical) properties undergo an abrupt variation when *we* pass from one facet to another' (264, emphasis added). Simondon's model of crystalline flow opens up the domain of perception to its material dimensions in which images are encountered in their variated trajectories by a 'we' passing across the faceted surface of a crystalline sphere, 'from one facet to another'. But, precisely, who is this *we*?

For Simondon, the *we* is the *who* that sees with the *I* of human perception in the *speculum* of the crystalline sphere as the *other* of the organic machine appearing in the 'theatre of individuation' (2020: 7). The *we* is an imagined We: a we that does not yet exist but in-exists in the perceptor function of the 'living being' inside the machine. The appearance of the phantasmic We as non-I calls the *I* to exercise its freedom to act: a 'free act' of moral character going beyond itself to encounter other acts in a transductive process of self-identification (378). To grasp this imaginary function of the organic machine from a non-inhuman perspective (the human seen from its exorganological position), we will invoke Alfred Lotka's notion of a *receptor function* operating in a cybernetic system of energy exchange (1945: 180). In the cybernetic feedback processes of energy exchange, perception passes across the reception of data on the retinal screen to see otherwise in 'the fusion of memory and expectation [of the whole view]' (Gadamer 1975: 195) seeking pathways through, adapting itself to 'the flowing expanse of being' (Simondon 2020: 12) seen through the binocularity of the perceptor-receiver's eyes. As perception passes across the flow from one data-facet to another ('when *we* pass from one facet to another'), the structure of the crystal switches ('undergoes an abrupt variation') in a kaleidoscopic shift such that what is perceived is seen afresh in a new variation (a new facet) of the crystal surface undergoing reticular amplification in the crystalline flow. As a perceptor-receptor lodged within the system of energy exchange, my capacity to see – my retinal perception – enters the crystalline flow of the sphere in its 'flickering' in and out of phase along an amplifying vector line open to variation through alteration and adaptation, exercising its functional efficiency as part of the organic machine. Equipped with such a receptor function, I becomes a *noetic eye* projecting otherwise inside the machine itself.

An image becomes crystalline when invested with piezo-electrical capacity shared by a binocular-retinal *image perceptor* grounded in existent being as the appearing of an appearance stabilized by fusing 'retinal disparity' into 'one single, merged "datum" from the two different data provided by the two retinal images' (Aumont 1997: 27). The binocular-retinal human eye acting as an image perceptor receives and projects auto-affecting light-life generating itself across an open horizon in which the image perceptor survives as a function of the organic machine together with other image perceptors immersed in a field of views flickering with crystalline light-life. Perception passes across the surface of a crystalline sphere reverberating with cosmic energy as the shared perceptibility of an *I* in relation to a *We*: the phantasm of communal identity becoming real in a 'reticular structure' (Simondon 2020: 328) – a socialized network of individuals – passing through itself in a temporalizing process of transindividuation retroacting the past in the present through variations of a crystalline sphere. Such would be the condition of a film understood to be crystalline in terms of a *perceptor function* capable of seeing otherwise inside the organic machine – the cinematographic *apparatus* in which it functions. As a prostheticized perceptor function, human being in-exists in the crystalline flow of the film's images on the screen and in me; that is, in the *inexistence* of pre-individual being in my generic capacity to see as part of a *We* in-the-making whenever I watch a film.

In Gilles Deleuze's film-philosophical semiotics of cinematic images (1986, 1989) – informed but deviating from Bergson's theses on the moving image (1986: 1–11) –the flow of crystals is limited to the 'continual exchange' of actual and virtual images (1989: 70) organizing themselves without the aid of an apparatus in a circuit of crystalline images in accordance with 'the mathematical analogy' (1989: 213) of geometrical form: Euclidian for the movement-image, non-Euclidian for the time-image (1989: 128–9, 214–15). In cinematic experience, perception enters the crystalline sphere where it becomes an indiscernible part of the virtual image purifying itself of all trace of actuality in the simulacra tending towards geometrical forms; that is, absorbed into the mathematical Idea. In *Cinema 2*, Deleuze identifies a pure crystal image in Orson Welles's *The Lady from Shanghai* (1947), where the 'principle of indiscernibility reaches its peak: a perfect crystal image where multiple mirrors have assumed an actuality of the two characters who will only be able to win it back by smashing them all, finding themselves side by side and each killing the other' (1989: 70). To make sense of Deleuze's first principle of cinematic images as pure crystals 'assuming' – simulating – the actuality of those reflected in it as false (judged to be so when they are smashed to pieces) requires something that Deleuze does not provide: a resistive aspect within the scene itself to *see* the reflections as false (i.e. *after* they have been smashed to pieces). The one who sees the falsity of the reflections in the smashed pieces is the viewer, whose proxy is the third person in the scene – the one bearing witness to the death of the other two in having survived the shattering of the mirrors – living on to tell the tale, a crucial fact Deleuze fails to mention (discussed in more detail in the following chapter). In his concern for the *perfection* of the pure image, Deleuze takes the crystal image to be the 'Idea that generates form' (Dunham, Grant and Watson 2011: 285) – the incarnation of pure light shining through the film – thereby failing to see the false image *as false* in the moral universe of the film. For the film to reveal itself as crystalline (and hence as false), perception must be able to survive the shattering of the mirrors to bear witness to the falsity of their reflections in a *third view* which is also a true view (the view put right – the way it should be), opening the film into a future that could not have been anticipated in the other views since it turns out that these views were false.

In this present work, I take Bergson's notion of crystalline flow to be prototypical. For Bergson, a crystalline flow is a *process* of crystallization in which we become aware of 'well-defined forms [that] appear to me to be all the more distinct from myself the more they are distinct from one another'. In the growing autonomy of their distinctiveness (in their tendency towards auto-affectivity), these forms become 'clear-cut crystals' flowing in 'a succession of states each one of which announces what follows and contains what precedes' (2007: 137, see also 1920: 165 ff.); in Simondon's terms, they overflow themselves in 'an amplifying reticular structure' in the 'process of forming' into a crystalline substance (2020: 13).

In *Creative Evolution*, Bergson describes the crystalline flow as an 'unwinding and releasing' of energy; the flow unwinds and releases its energy along bifurcating pathways in 'definite directions' (1911: 64). Inside the crystalline sphere, the flow of images *reflects* piezo-electrical memory by *refracting* it through the sphere in a synchronizing process which, in Simondon's terms, is continually falling 'out of step with itself' – flickering – in order to keep itself going in a metastable state of being (1992: 302). Seen in their distinctiveness, the images *reflect*, but if impeded they *refract* (Bergson 1988: 37, Mullarkey 2009: 48), a metastabilizing process oscillating between reflection and refraction at speeds faster than the eye can see, generating image flows shimmering with crystalline light-life. In viewing a film, to see-feel the refractions in operation (and not simply as reflected), the viewer must resist the tendency of perception to see things in the immediacy of clear sight by inducing a counter-gesture within the eye – a looking awry that sees with the camera as an automated moving effect controlling the direction of the image flow permeating the screen in the reticular amplification of vector lines (zigzags following cuts and disjunctures across the screen). By coinciding with the time of the camera movement effect (rather than the time of the characters), my time becomes *inhuman* insofar as it relates to the automatism on the screen, thus raising the question of the non-inhuman inside the inhuman of machine memory – its capacity to see otherwise, both with and against the camera. How does this non-inhuman retain its otherness – its free relation to the apparatus – without becoming captured by the automatism of the inhuman machine?

The inhuman

In his later essays on the development of telecommunications in thermodynamic systems as second order cybernetics (analogico-digital), Jean-François Lyotard provides us with an answer to the question of the place of the non-inhuman inside the inhuman automatism of machine memory. For Lyotard, there are two kinds of inhuman:

> the inhumanity of the system which is currently being consolidated under the name of development [which] must not be confused with the infinitely secret one of which the soul is hostage. To believe, as happened to me, that the first can take over from the second, give it expression, is a mistake. The system rather has the consequence of causing the forgetting of what escapes it. But the anguish is that of a mind haunted by a familiar and unknown guest which is agitating it, sending it delirious but also making us think – if one claims to exclude it, if one doesn't give it an outlet, one aggravates it. Discontent grows with this civilization, foreclosing along with information.
>
> 1991: 2

Let us give this passage careful consideration. The inhuman is the memory of what humans are becoming in their prosthetic relation to machines (Lyotard's reference to 'development'): the haunted trace of the non-inhuman other in the future anterior of *mnemotechnesis* as a 'familiar and unknown guest ... sending the mind delirious but also making us think' (Lyotard's second inhuman). To mistake this inhuman for the inhumanity of the human – the *anthropy* of a malign otherness in me (Lyotard's first inhuman) – is the wrong way to think of the inhuman insofar as it would become an inhuman machine controlled by humans ('take over' it, 'give it expression'). Rather, the right way to think of the inhuman is in terms of an *other otherness* eluding the human–machine prosthesis in the gap that refuses to close as the *real* of time itself (in Bergson's terms, the moment of the durational *real*).

In Lyotard's right sense of the word, the *inhuman* is the counter-resistance released in the *drive of technical systems* in their search for operational efficiencies achieved by erasing as much free existence as possible in their tendency towards entropic closure; an uncontrollable excess sending us delirious but also making us think. Technically induced inhuman otherness is the feeling that I am being watched or cared for by an alien presence in the technical milieu in which I exist as a non-inhuman being: the non-inhuman other carrying *its* other in me through technical supports as the *real* of the system itself. Here, we have reached the very heart of the issue of care in the control societies of the twenty-first century which, for Stiegler, requires shifting our critical attention from the negentropy of organological (natural) systems to the neganthropy of exorganological systems (organic systems technicized by the prostheticization of human life). Neganthropic care seeks to know the inhuman otherness in me as *the soul of the human–machine relation* in its therapeutic potential from within the systems themselves by adopting its time as ours.

Lyotard's inhuman *real* can be likened to the Lucretian *clinamen*: the swerve of atoms in spacetime becoming unbinding systems in non-local micro-/macro-intertwining of elemental matter open to the cosmic void; an immateriality that 'eludes any attempt to identify it as having taken place at a given time' (Serres 2018: 6). In quantum-scientific terms, elemental matter is sub-atomic: photons as '"elementary grains of energy"' (Rovelli 2021: 33) released from their binding to electrons which consequently 'leap[ ] from one orbit to another' (34) in the nucleus of atoms held together by 'electromagnetic waves' (32) dispersing in all directions through the spacetime universe. Elemental matter is the *arche* trace of 'absolute time' of quantum thought (Murphy 1999: 70), which, in its macro-cosmic dimensions, is 'precosmic time, a time before time' (Sallis 2018: 144) – elemental motion in the starry heavens, the light of the sun and in the equipment designed to retrieve it and make it real, flowing through exorganological systems as views appearing and disappearing in the crystalline spheres of mnemotechnical apparatuses and on the screens of our perceptor-receptors found everywhere in globalized industrial life.

The *real* remains both inside and outside the system as a gap: the space in-between full of *resistive potential* retaining the power to unbind the binding of the system's elements into singular concretizations in 'a complete overturning of the image of matter' (Lyotard 1991: 38–39). From the resistive perspective of the *real*, there is nothing to see in the spacetime universe other than images as overturned matter; that is, images becoming real in the elemental materiality of the clinametric flux as 'laminar flow' (Serres 2018: 7), which, in Bergson's terms, is the *crystalline flow* of a spacetime quantum field grasped intuitively as the *real* of time itself (2007: 137, 1920: 165 ff, 1965: 5–7, Murphy 1999: 74–7). In developing a film organology alert to the quantum implications of *mnemotechnesis*, what I am seeking are moments of resistive potential in the projection of moving images, instances of temporal inconsistence in the micro-/macro- intertwining of an idiotext leaping across the ontological divide between before and after as paradoxically inflected questioning situations requiring a methexical response.

The distancing function of images

To draw closer to the resistive potential of the *real*, we turn to Maurice Blanchot's proposal of the distancing function of images:

> the image fulfils one of its functions which is to quiet, to humanize the formless nothingness pressed upon us by the indelible residue of being. The image *cleanses this residue* – appropriates it, makes it pleasing and pure, and allows us to believe, dreaming the happy dream which art too often authorizes, that, separated from the real and immediately behind it, we find, as our pleasure and superb satisfaction, the transparent eternity of the unreal.
>
> Blanchot 1982: 255, emphasis added

The distancing function of the image is to resist the pressure of the *real* – 'the formless nothingness pressed upon us' – by anaesthetizing our free existence, putting to sleep our capacity to imagine ourselves otherwise than the generic form of human life reality assumes for us in dreaming the happy dream ('the transparent eternity of the unreal'). However, by awakening ourselves from the dream – by collapsing the distancing function of the image – we face the *real* in its resistive potential: 'the real always leaves us the initiative, addressing in us that power to begin, that free communication with the beginning which we are' (255). Let us consider how the potential of the *real* to enable recommencement in 'the beginning which we are' works in a film.

In what follows, we will test the potential of the *real* in the power to begin by working through the *mnemotechnesis* of F.W. Murnau's *Kammerspielfilm The Last Laugh* (1924). Our aim will be to follow the vector of memorizing – the line of memory formed by looking backward in the *speculum* of the crystalline sphere in which we see the future as 'having happened' – recommencing in a series of hesitations, delays, detours and leaps in the telling of a story, which we have considered in the first chapter in terms of Fichtean *Anstoß* (a check to cognitive clarity as non-I summoning the I to account for itself), but also in this present chapter in terms of its hermeneutic variant as Gadamerian *stoß* (shock in the sudden putting into question of the I in confronting an unexpected event), both of which can be understood in terms of the stop-start effect one feels in moments of fixation in which phenomenal direction (intentionality) – the tendency of projection towards its object upon which the stability of cognition depends (Brentano 1973: 147) – is temporarily stopped. Thus defined, *Anstoß* would be hesitation in the expectation of what comes next on the screen, causing perceptual distancing to falter when the 3D visual structure of the film collapses onto its 2D surface, triggering distortion and opacity of the view projected.

The scene in question depicts the porter of a grand hotel (the Atlantic) – having suffered a severe shock on being told that he is to be demoted to washroom attendant due to his frailty in advancing age – rushing out of the hotel's front entrance and into the street where, in a delayed shock reaction, he hallucinates distorted buildings looming over him. In an over-the-shoulder shot, we see-feel what the porter must also be seeing and feeling: the movement of the buildings bearing down on him, the force of which flings him backwards. Through the device of an over-the-shoulder shot, Murnau has forced an encroachment on the

Figure 2.1 A hotel porter suffers aftereffects of a shock. *The Last Laugh*, dir. F.W. Murnau (1924).

perceptual distance of the viewer in an unsettling moment of *Anstoß* – a sudden putting into question of the normal way of seeing images on the screen. By flattening the 2D/3D structure of the film's visual projection, Murnau has interfered with the distance required for the viewer to maintain correct 3D dimensionality, allowing the *real* to press in on her existent reality as the one to whom the camera addresses its view, superposed on the porter's in-existent reality as the one who hallucinates in the fictional world of the film. Murnau's innovative filmmaking praxis has collapsed the distancing function of the film's images, which, in a general sense, generates *Stimmung* – mood suggesting 'vibrations of the soul' in the immanence of light spreading across the screen (Eisner 1969: 199) – wherein the hallucination becomes cinematically *real*. Henceforth, the porter will be vested with a peculiar power – Blanchot's 'power to begin' – in the turning of fortune's wheel as the story unfolds through the *Stimmung* which is on the screen and in me.

Distancing suppresses the *real* – keeps it from irrupting in the reality of its image, in Blanchot's terms, 'cleans[ed]' of material residue – by transforming its formlessness into happy dreams and pleasurable satisfactions. However, by unsuppressing the suppression in a disturbing moment of *Anstoß* (a 'check' in perceptual reality, throwing out questions), the *real* returns in a new dimension – a new 'facet' of the film – in which the crystalline world of the film splits into two faces: one living and one dead. Wherever the dead face appears the living face disappears in the turning of the crystalline sphere. In dramaturgical terms, we can imagine the two faces of life and death as comic and tragic: the comic face shows life's continuity, while the tragic face shows its loss in the turning of a Janus-face from life to death and back again in the circadian rhythm of the cosmos (its diurnal phasing from night to day in eternal return). In the check to the system of perception, the *real* becomes *irreal* (destabilized by counter-forces), switching between life and death in the rotating facets of the sphere. Let us apply these insights in further analysis of *The Last Laugh*.

In dreaming the 'happy dream' which is in me and on the screen, the crystalline faceted life-world of *The Last Laugh* switches from its comic face in which the porter's life is lived out happily in connectedness to the natural order (his standing as a respected member of the community generative of family life), to its tragic face in the porter's sudden loss of status triggered by an overwhelming shock in which his happy life is severed from the continuity sustaining it. The *real* returns as *irreal*, switched from its comic face to its tragic face. By collapsing perceptual distance onto the surface of the screen, direction has exposed the

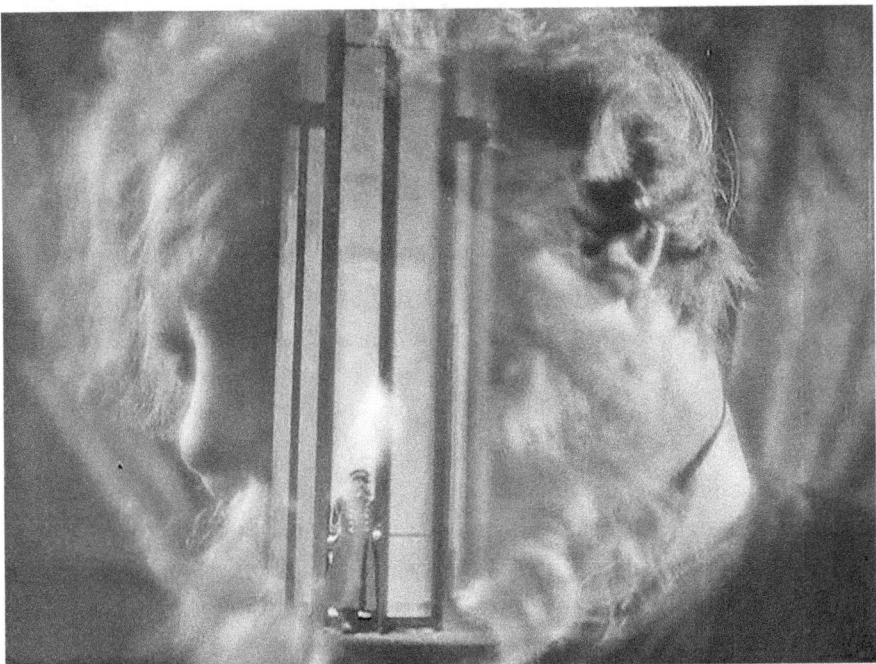

Figure 2.2 Superimposed images. *The Last Laugh*, dir. F.W. Murnau (1924).

trace of the recessed apparatus manifesting as ghostly after-effects of unsuppressed movement in the oscillations of Murnau's 'unchained camera'[2] carrying the force of visual projection with it. The oscillations of the camera released from its 'chained' position – its swaying to and fro – begin to take over the consciousness of the film (its self-awareness) when the porter, in the aftermath of shock and situated inside his family home, is drawn into the swaying motion of the camera synchronizing with the sound of a waltz played on a trumpet by a drunken musician in the *hinterhof* – the courtyard – outside, sending the room spinning around him.

Lulled by the rhythmic motion of the waltzing room, the porter lapses into a delirium: a hallucinated state of being, the cinematic reality of which appears on the screen in a collage of ghostly forms – revolving windmill sails or are they the reel of a film projector mixed in with the revolving doors of the hotel Atlantic's grand entrance? – superimposed on images of the porter who, seemingly restored to the strength of his younger days, picks up a massive trunk and flings it into the air to the applause of an admiring audience, all of which has been set in motion by the unchained camera swaying back and forth, smearing images across the surface of the screen. On a first time viewing of the film, the viewer could be forgiven for dismissing the revolving shapes as obscuring shadows, pushing them into the preconscious of what we don't see in what we see. However, by seeing *with* the camera in the overturned imagist perspective, the shadows suddenly come to life, switching into figures shaped by superimposing the revolving doors of the hotel's entrance on the porter's delirious head: a cryptic reminder of the inhuman mechanism taking hold of the viewer in the free play of Murnau's 'dematerialized' unchained camera (Eisner 1973: 84). The free play of the unchained camera releases the film's potential for opening new spaces in which the Janus-face of *life death* is played out in the 'impossible possibility' of the film's dreaming, turning with the apparatus onscreen and in me insofar as I am – in the manner of the fictional porter – undergoing the delirium of visual projection through questions thrown up in the fixations of action on the screen (the cinematic *coup* achieved by Murnau's direction). My experience is superposed on the porter's, codetermined by the *real* of the onscreen situation which is, to quote Lyotard, 'sending [us] delirious but also making us think' (1991: 2) in the hallucination of a total truth effect (*Stimmung*).

In a coda inserted at the end of the film, the face switches yet again when we see the porter – suddenly transformed into a wealthy man (having been unexpectedly left a fortune by a grateful hotel patron) – dining in lavish style at the hotel in which he had suffered his ignominious fall, providing the film with a 'last laugh' in which fate is turned from ill to good fortune on the 'wheel of fortune' (*fortuna*), manifesting in the *real* of the film's hallucinating images as the turning projector reel throwing up chances on the screen. In the film's final turn of the wheel, the comic continuity of life returns in a happy ending, pointing to the film's tragicomic 'pattern' as *spiel*: its playing out of life's chances oscillating between their *tragic* and *comic* phases. In the turning of the wheel, the tragicomic pattern is *figured*: played out in the *real* of the film.

Figura

In his seminal essay 'Figura', the hermeneutic scholar Eric Auerbach defines the ancient Roman term *figura* in the following way: 'the idea that something that is new and appears for the first time, of something that creates change in things that normally resist change, marks the entire history of the word [*figura*]' (2014:

66). As a *process* of figuration, *figura* is the 'playful association between original and copy [which] gives a greater impression of something available to the senses' (69). To put this another way, *figura* is the figuring of the *real*: an active potential open to the future in processes of change 'in things that resist change', perceived as original-in-copy. By resisting the resistance of things that resist change, the distance between original and copy compresses and the perceived edifice collapses onto its material surface. Figures are surface phenomena: two-dimensional originals-in-copy appearing on a page or on a screen which, in their horizontally flattened shape, refuse the 3D expansiveness of their originals with respect to which they are their trace. As original-in-copy, they *figure* the original, carrying potential to figure it out otherwise, projecting it in a new way.

Auerbach's concept of *figura* works on the basis of intersecting vertical and horizontal axes in which the figure on the horizontal plane points to a higher level by 'standing in a vertical relation to the divine order in which it is contained and which will itself, at some point, be a reality that occurs' (2014: 110). In this way, Auerbach's theory of the figure is realist insofar as the divine order predetermines what the figure is pointing to as a 'reality that occurs' at 'some point' in the future. However, we will take the imagist counter-view: as a *process* of figuration, *figura* moves along the horizontal plane in a swerving line seeking release from the materiality out of which its figurations are drawn. There is no divine order but only the gesture of divination rising and falling along the line's figural vector on the horizontal plane, probing for the future in durational time as *real*. From this overturned *figura* perspective – one in which the verticality of the projected view is collapsed onto its horizonal progression in 'free communication' (Blanchot 1982: 255) with its future; that is, without an end predetermining its beginning – figuration is set in play between surface and depth in which the *real* interrupts what suppresses it, releasing possibilities for creating change in *figuring* the future: playing it out in ever-changing depth/surface gestalt switching between its faces as the *irreal* reality of *life death*. A figural analysis undertaken in this imagist counter-view mode posits ends *after the fact* as fictional events becoming real in switching between the face of death and the face of life as tragicomic. In what way might this imagist concept of *figura* apply to the tragicomic mode of film?

Susanne K. Langer has provided us with a way of thinking of tragicomic figuration of life in terms of contrapuntal rhythms:

> The fact that the two great rhythms, comic and tragic, are *radically distinct* does not mean that they are each other's opposites, or even incompatible forms. Tragedy can rest squarely on a comic substructure, and yet be pure tragedy. This is natural enough, for life – from which all felt rhythms spring – contains both, in every mortal organism. Society is continuous through its members, even the strongest and fairest, live out their lives and die; and even while each individual fulfils the tragic pattern it participates also in the *comic continuity*. The poet's task is, of course not to copy life but to organize and articulate a symbol for the 'sense of life'; and *in the symbol one rhythm always governs the dynamic form, though another may go through the whole piece in a contrapuntal fashion.*
>
> 1953: 362–3, emphasis added

Tragicomic figuration is a rhythmic continuity in which the tragic and the comic, although 'radically distinct', interpenetrate in a rhythmic flow, one 'govern[ing] the dynamic form' in which they are working as components of the 'tragic pattern' of mortal-organic life, while the other 'may go through the dynamic form in a contrapuntal fashion'. Langer's spatialized symbol will, for us, be replaced by the temporalized process of a Gadamerian–Bergsonian crystalline sphere in which the switching of the tragic and comic faces becomes the flickering of the facets of the crystalline flow shining through the sphere, where the tragic form of a film's story-world interpenetrates with the 'comic continuity' of the cosmic energy in which the sphere is immersed, for instance in the turning of reflected fortune refracted through the distortions of images in *The Last Laugh*. For Langer, rhythmic continuity is envisaged on a scale of Nietzschean proportions, in the polarizing tendencies of Apollonian form and Dionysian feeling, ethos and pathos, mixed into 'each other's negatives' (1953: 17), which I propose in terms of the cosmic struggle of *life death* in quantum spacetime superposition switching between micro- and macro- levels of the *real*.

Following Langer's proposal of tragicomic patterning understood in terms of *figura* in its radically overturned imagist sense, *The Last Laugh* can be seen as a tragicomic film insofar as its figurations work their way through oscillating tendencies between the comic and tragic faces of life and death, continuity and discontinuity, played out in the turning of fortune's wheel immaterialized onscreen in the ghostly image of the revolving projector reel figuring – putting into play – life's chances. The flow of images chaining and unchaining themselves opens up possibilities in the *real* of the film's duration to activate recommencements by stepping into new pathways opening up in the turning of the wheel. Following Verna Foster's lead in her study of tragicomic style in modernist theatre (Foster

V. 2004) in which she proposes the tragicomic mode as the antidote to tragic nihilism, and applying it to film, tragicomic figuration becomes a conditioning aspect of the modernist impulse of cinema in the sense that it opens up the questioning of real existence stripped back to images flickering with *life death* irreality across the screen. In *The Last Laugh*, the dark zone between life and death lights up with cosmic laughter when, at the end of the film, the porter returns in the face of life rather than death as the last laugh of the Last Man of the film's alternative title (*Der letzte Mann*), restoring the fallen man to good fortune in the 'comic continuity' of the tragicomic pattern passing through the film's turning faces. The restoration of the porter to good fortune on fortune's wheel raises the question of *amor fati* – the love of one's fate in eternal return to which we now turn.

Amor fati

Amor fati or love of one's fate is proposed by Friedrich Nietzsche in *Thus Spoke Zarathustra* as the joyous affirmation of life: '[the] fundamental Yes [which] is bound up with a radical No ... The Yes always presupposes a No, but the No always ends in a Yes' (Ijsseling 2001: 38, Nietzsche 1976: 340–3). For Nietzsche the *yes no* circularity of *amor fati* transcends mortal life in eternal return, placing the human in an exceptional state of anthropic self-affirmation. However, Nietzsche did not consider the mortal consequences of the death drive: the blind impulse of wilful willing as mindless repetition in which to love one's fate is to suffer in dread of it; in Kierkegaard's terms, 'he cannot flee from dread, for he loves it; really he does not love it, for he flees from it' (1957: 40). In failing to transcend the mortal condition of its affects, *amor fati* becomes a vicious circle driving the sufferer further into suffering in seeking a metastable state of being; poison becomes the cure which is the poison becoming the cure *ad infinitum*, constituting an endless struggle for the health of the organism trapped inside the circle. How does one begin otherwise when locked into the drive of *amor fati*? Here we turn again to Blanchot, to his notion of death in the last instant – the 'death before death' in which we face the *real* as utterly inhuman.

For Blanchot, the *real*

> as the reality of the last instant ... escapes us constantly. It is inevitable but inaccessible to death; it is the abyss of the present, time without a present, with which I have no relationships; it is that towards which I cannot go forth, for in it

I do not die, I have fallen from the power to die. In it *they* die. They do not cease, and they do not finish dying.

1982: 154–5

Blanchot's formulation of the 'secret of double death' in a non-relation to the *real* provides us with a way of thinking about the awaiting catastrophe (death) without thought of transcendence and hence without appealing to an exceptional human condition at risk of becoming anthropic; that is, susceptible to *amor fati*. In the *instance* of the last instant of my death, I stand face-to-face with 'that towards which I cannot go forth' as the *real* in which I do not die but *they* die (those who did not survive as I have survived). In the *last instance* of my life in which *I* do not die but *They* die, I have 'fallen from the power to die'; I have fallen away from – refused – the embrace of the simulacrum – the false image of life death as *amor fati*. In 'the reality of the last instant of my life' which is also the *first instance* of its recommencement (in the chance of the 'abyss of the present, the time without a present, with which I have no relationships'), I have an opportunity to turn counter-wise. By facing the other way, I reverse the closure of the system *in me*.

Concluding remarks

By undertaking figural analysis in the *life death* playing out of chance in films, we are also engaging in a methexical exercise of accounting for the *moral dimensions* of story-telling in films, insofar as these dimensions are located in questioning situations – moments of fixation in the telling of stories, posing questions of responsibility for right action. A *methexis* responding to *ethical* questions (how does one proceed in the right way?) will simultaneously be responding to *aesthetic* questions (how does one's *feeling* for the future relate to the ends of right action?). A *methexis* responding to questions of interpretation (how do I make sense of this artefact received and before my eyes) takes on a *hermeneutic* dimension in the story-telling insofar as an originating performance is apprehended through its re-performance as a possibility beginning to have been always possible; that is, retroactivated in the *methexis* itself. In remaining true to the second law of thermodynamics which says that events in the irreversibility of time are retro-actualized through negentropy, a *methexis* of re-performed events becomes an accounting for the effects of quantum doubling and superposition in the re-performed event itself, which, in facing a radicalized future in the *real* of the questioning situation, becomes open to directional change to the fated future by stepping into a new dimension within it.

With these points in mind, Bergson's turn to the quantum event of non-local interaction can be read together with Stiegler's organological hermeneutics in terms of a Gadamerian *methexis* – a questioning of *right* in defence of noetic freedom – which, for Stiegler, always finds itself in a pharmacological situation in which poison and its cure are mixed together in a deadlock of desire. The question of *right* reaches beyond the *socious* and into the *oikeios* – the web of life – where methexical questioning arises in the chorality of metatheatre played out in the cosmic *life death* rhythm as a question of survival in which the soul of a non-inhuman creator – the human capacity for technical inventiveness at risk of eclipse by inhuman machine memory – is key to our salvation.

In the next chapter, we turn to Stiegler's key idea of dreaming, drawn from his idea of the *this-has-been* as a remainder lodged within digitized and analogue formats, in which Barthes's notion of the *punctum* cut is brought into play to turn our thinking back into the archive as phantasmic artefacts of *life death* switching – an irreality of the photo-cinematic image played out in the mode of true/false. The mode of true/false sets up pharmacological situations in other-pathways thinking which I analyse in terms of Capra's *It's a Wonderful Life*. To draw these ideas together I undertake a deconstruction of the art film as Lyotardian acinema – a tendency in the institutionalization of cinema in which art film style is understood to be the resistivity of a *dispositif* to generic form. To exemplify these ideas, I engage in an analysis of Welles's *The Lady from Shanghai* as an art film tendency revealed in its *dispositif* – the game played by the film with-against itself, which, in Lyotard's acinematic terms, is the film's affirmation of its *right* to be what it is.

3

Dreaming

This-has-been

In *Camera Lucida*, Roland Barthes undertakes meditative readings of photographs in which he follows the trace of what he calls 'this-has-been' (1993: 79), the irreality of a *punctum* effect the reader may feel when contemplating (for instance) the photograph of condemned prisoner Lewis Payne, a Confederate soldier and member of the Lincoln assassination plot at the end of the American Civil War in which Payne (a pseudonym) had attempted to assassinate the US Secretary of State. The photograph has been reprinted in the book with the caption 'he is dead and he is going to die' (95) to capture the peculiar doubling effect of life and death that exposure to the *this-has-been* triggers. For Barthes, the effect on the reader is one of 'horror in an anterior future of which death is the stake ... *over a catastrophe which has already occurred*. Whether or not the subject is already dead, every photograph is this catastrophe' (96).

Following these Barthesian principles of the *this-has-been*, this chapter sets out to explore the idea of dreaming in terms of cinematic projection in which the *punctum* effect operates as a cut in time, generating 'an anterior future in which death is the stake'. Cinematic experience occurs in the ungrounding ground of the *this-has-been* crossing over itself between the dead past and the living future as the playing out of life's chances in which 'death is the stake' as the catastrophic 'horror' of an abyssal *real*.

In recent film theory, it has been said that, in the digital age of cinematic production, the *this-has-been* no longer plays a role in film experience and that the photographic index upon which it is based has been either lost 'in the transcoding of light into information' (Brown 2013: 24) or cut adrift in the 'mathematical abstractions' of digital imaging (Rodowick 2001: 36–7), thus rendering Barthes's proposal of the *punctum* effect obsolete. However, in an essay entitled 'The Discrete Image' (2002), Stiegler challenges the premise on which these types of claims are based by posing the question of belief in a world mediated by digital images, in which '[t]he digital photograph suspends a certain spontaneous belief which the analog photograph bore within itself. When I look at a digital photo, I can never be sure that what I see truly exists' (150).

Having proposed his initial thesis on the *there* of digital images ('when I look at a digital photo') by doubting the existence of the thing seen (by suspending belief in it), Stiegler then develops a line of self-questioning by invoking the *this-has-been* of Barthes's *punctum* cut effecting a phantasm shining in the photographic image in either analogue or digital format – and asks the following question: 'did the analogico-digital luminances really touch the sensitive plate once?...At the same time, I know this thing [the phantasm] has to have touched, but I'm not sure: how much touch? To what *point*? Which '*punctum*' actually touches me?' (154). Stiegler's exercise in Cartesian doubt leads him to conclude that the existence of the *there* has not been lost or cut adrift, as if its function had been eliminated or surpassed by the digital, but remains as the trace effect of a *this-has-been* which *must have been there* ('has to have touched'): an ineliminable excess of light-life shining through the image as an after-effect of the dead past in the living future as *irreal* – both there and not there.

Deleuze calls the this-has-been a *quasi-cause* (1990: 8): a cause posited after the fact – in the event of a past that did not happen but must have happened – as *a posteriori* reasoning required to make sense of non-sense arising in the contingency of life's *unheimlich* situations, which, for Stiegler, is shaped into phantasmic artefacts through tertiary retentions as edifying procedures (2021: 173–4), for instance in the publishing of Barthes's book *Camera Lucida* in which words and images are deployed to reproduce the *punctum* effect on its pages as propaedeutic writing on the mortal condition of human being. The point to be taken here is that, even in digital environments which claim to have eliminated the photographic index, the analogue of the 'image-object' – the exteriorized appearance of the mental image which Stiegler calls '*remanence*' (148) – persists in the retina and on the page or screen as a phantasmic after-effect of what must have been, oscillating between the dead past and the living future in the image's power of projection. Doubt leads to the certainty of one thing – the *life death* announced in the effect of the *punctum*: the cut of the *real*, which, in breaking 'the chain of memorable light' (154) in the sudden realization that this thing I am seeing – the phantasm on the screen shining with light from a past that must have been – offers the chance of something new, retro-actualizing in me and on the screen as projection otherwise of the productive imagination weaving new dreams.

Dreaming is itself an invocation of the *real* of the photo-cinematic *this-has-been* through its displacement and deferral of an originating event in a scrambled syntax of visual linkages, which, in their cinematic formats are the affordances of the Kuleshov effect where images are slipped into an 'optical unconscious' shining through the film as 'figures of a collective dream' (Benjamin 2002: 107–8). Cinematic dreaming calls forth the *there* of the *this-has-been* as the ambiguous facticity of its *quasi-cause* – the phantasmic *thing* retroactivated in the imagination to account for 'a past that was *never present*: the weft of our dreams' (Stiegler 2002: 155); the *play* of the dream in its idiotextual singularity as *this* film unfolding on the screen before my eyes – as the propaedeutic 'writing' of its tertiary retentions. In reflecting back on the moral disposition of the *this-has-been*, cinematic dreaming calls the viewer into methexical self-questioning in questioning belief in the world challenged by the strange appearance of the phantasm on the screen as a question of *right*. In practical reason (defined propaedeutically as an educative process of coming to know what right is), the *problem* of right is played out pharmacologically in the film-dream's telling of its story, in bifurcating pathways opening up chances for life on the screen and in me.

The dead past

In Bergson's terms, the this-has-been of the irrevocable past is the 'dead weight that we carry with us, and by which we prefer to imagine ourselves unencumbered' – unwanted memories cut away from the recollected past as the *dead past* repressed in the 'unconscious' (Bergson 1988: 145). The dead past returns to haunt the living future, which, in later work written to elucidate his earlier ideas in light of developments in the science of spacetime relativity, Bergson describes as an 'unforeseeable nothing that changes everything' (2007: 73). The unforeseeable nothing that changes everything is the cut of the *real* – the pure potential of time considered from a quantum perspective as irreal. In an experience of the cut of the *real*, the dead past returns as the All of time where everything that will have happened has been inscribed (1911: 25) – which, in its recommencement, 'changes everything' (2007: 73). Here, we can see a correlation between Bergson's *quantum effect* and Barthes's *punctum effect*, both of which are concerned with compossible modes of temporal existence – both living and dead – in the future anterior of the industrialized world, in 'the night of a past that was *never present*' (Stiegler 2002: 155): the nocturnal unconscious of a planetary cosmos brought to the light of day in diurnal dreaming – in the *oneiric* capacity of cinema for projecting dreams (2016: 62).

Stiegler's invocation of the Barthesian 'this-has-been' of the photographic index – its pointing to a gap opened in time's passing-through (Barthes 1993: 79) – initially suggests that his thesis is limited to the photochemical era of cinema. However, the photographic index is merely one phase of the industrialization of the visible, which, in its current digital phase, appears as an 'analogico-digital image [which] is the beginning of a *systematic discretization of movement* – that is to say, of a vast process of the *grammaticalization of the visible*' (Stiegler 2002: 148–9). In his later writings, the *this-has-been* – which he had initially ascribed to the Barthesian photographic *punctum* – becomes 'the *there*' of the delocalized location of electronically transmitted time entangled in spiralling vectors of sense data in quantum scales of becoming (2021: 203).[1] The *there* is the refusal of the this-has-been to *not be*, which, in its resistive effort (*Anstoß*), initiates a recommencement of the dead past – the 'frightfully old' (205) – coming back to life – a reference to Blanchot's notion of the incessancy of life in the face of death (Blanchot 1995: 100–1). Without recommencement of the dead past in the living future, the past could not pass through and mortal life would be fated to eternal return in *amor fati* – the fatal love of *anthropy*. Lacking a past which it had not experienced, anthropic life would become anthropophagic hunger, feeding on itself in a self-destructive death drive in which behaviour toxic to life would be mistaken for its cure and dreaming for a better future would 'turn into a nightmare' (Stiegler 2019: 86). In seeking a way out of anthropic self-destruction, we need to consider how the *there*, in its recommencement of 'the night of a past that was never present', carries the whole of time given immediately to consciousness, where possibility inscribed in the dead past comes into play, when 'at this precise moment . . . [it] begins to have been always possible' (Bergson 2007: 82). At this precise moment, we can seize our chance to break free from the grip of *amor fati* in automated systems saturating delocalized spaces in calculable probability, to put ourselves on another path through the 'faculty of dreaming' (Stiegler 2022: 59), by which Stiegler means 'day for night' dreaming of the imagination (2018: 168).

Day-for-night or diurnal dreaming is the capacity to imagine life otherwise through the manipulation of tertiary retentions, in the 'cutting room' of the filmmaker's editing suite, for instance the filmmaking practices of the French New Wave in the mid-twentieth century with their radicalization of the irrational cut which over time have been shifted into 'an everyday practice now engaged by everyone, for example through Skype, webcams and smartphones' (Stiegler 2014a: 25). Stiegler imagines the revitalization of life exhausted in hyper-industrialized negentropic systems through the dream-weaving praxis of radicalized filmmaking as a model for localized creativity – in the fabrications of a self-reflexive cinema alert to its own technics as creative potential for producing neganthropy (localized knowledge of care) as the cure for the anthropy of the systems (globalizing algorithmic control), when the dead past comes to life on the screen as fiction becoming real.

What Stiegler has in mind when he speaks of filmmaking practices of the radical kind are those of the modernist era, for instance the self-reflexivity exhibited in Federico Fellini's *Intervista* (1987) which he (Stiegler) employs to elucidate his thesis on the idiotextual becoming of cinematic consciousness in the archival future (2011: 22). The view to be taken here is that the modernist project *is itself* sufficient for considering the issues at stake in his critique of hyper-capitalist modes of noetic entrapment leading to the current malaise of human existence which he calls 'symbolic misery' (2014). In other words, he encourages us to take a 'step beyond' computational capitalism in the *real* of its incalculable excess, turning our attention to the archival future sedimented within in it in which we encounter archival films posing questions for us in a new frame of reference. In responding to these questions, we can re-engage with the dynamic structure of these films in their having survived the entropic force of time to make the dead past live again in what Simondon calls 'new dimensions' (1992: 307). Accordingly, I propose a critical-analytical project in which films from the past are recommended in their *radical possibilities* to offer new life through 'other pathways' thinking – reflecting on those paths that could have been taken but were not – which Gadamer calls *methexis*. What is required in this other pathways thinking is a hermeneutic turn in current views that retains the critical moment – the moment of the *real* – in which the dead past can be made to live again in a future already *there* as the this-has-been shining with *life death* irreality on the cusp of bifurcation – splitting into the path of life and the path of death as the kernel of the film's dreaming.

Paths taken and not taken

Let us now consider quantum superposition in terms of *methexis* in which a character in a narration is confronted with a bifurcating path situation. Taking one path blocks the other path which nevertheless remains possible in the dead past of the film's memory where its probability of becoming real is *worked through* according to the requirements of *telos* – the logic of ends – controlling the outcome of events towards which the story-telling is always striving. In what way does this 'remaining possible' of the blocked path play itself out as *negative affectivity* (the feeling of loss-in-gain)? Let us reflect on this question in terms of a Hollywood film melodrama: Frank Capra's *It's a Wonderful Life* (1946), a tragicomic masterpiece of small-town American life in which the 'comic continuity' of life is restored by averting a tragic outcome.

The story told in *It's a Wonderful Life* is as follows. In the fictional town of Bedford Falls in the state of New York and set between the two World Wars of the twentieth century, a good man protagonist – George Bailey, the manager of a building and loans bank dedicated to the needs of working people – is driven to suicidal despair by the threat of bankruptcy and criminal prosecution when money needed to be deposited to balance the bank's books is stolen from his forgetful uncle by Mr Potter, a cynical businessman who wants the bank shut down. For Potter, the communal philosophy of the bank is a moral affront to his ultra-capitalistic vision of a world in which individual advancement is all that counts and care for others is for 'losers' – ordinary workers whom he holds in contempt. On the brink of throwing himself from a bridge into icy waters (a bifurcating path situation), George is visited by a guardian angel sent from the celestial cosmos – depicted at the beginning of the film as the Milky Way in which nodes of light become godlike presences looking down on Earth, judging the actions of the humans existing there – who offers him the chance to live again. At this point, the film enters the past of its own time machine – its memory bank of everything that has ever happened – where the angel shows George what life would have been like had he not lived: a world in which the communal spirit fostered by George's enthusiasm for life and the goodwill of the building and loans bank no longer exists, replaced by cynical distrust in others where the life spirit of the townsfolk has been crushed by Potter's determination to take possession of the entire town, to impose his toxic brand of *rentier* capitalism on the people – to bend them to his will.

In a *metalepsis* triggered by the angel's special power of prescient projection, George leaps from the living future into the dead past coming to life on the screen, wandering the streets as a *figure of inexistence* utterly bewildered by the *unheimlich* atmosphere of the town in which he is not recognized by people he has known all his life. The film shows the audience the consequences of a path that could have been taken in which the wrong tendencies of human character are played out without countervailing tendencies to correct them, thus making the point that the path taken by George in staying true to his life principles – the countervailing tendency missing from the path not taken – was the right path to have taken despite his constant misgivings. Throughout the film, George's life is lived out at the expense of his nonexistence in the path not taken, brought to life in the metaleptic moment *as if* it had been taken *but without him*.

The film makes the dead past come to life where it *begins to have been always possible* as either a life worth living or a life not worth living, constituting a *pharmakon*: a situation in which good and ill health are mixed together as either poison or cure (Derrida 1981: 70). Adopting Derrida's *pharmakon* and extending it to all forms of technically mediated life, Stiegler proposes the pharmacological situation as a plexus of toxic and curative tendencies in 'the formation of a healthy psychic apparatus' requiring the application of *care* to ensure the right choices are made in maintaining the good health of the psychic or social body (2016: 3). Pharmacological situations arise in bifurcations of the drive of life and death 'where death is borne by life' (Derrida 2011: 152): a blind impulse oscillating between countervailing tendencies of good and ill health in seeking metastable quasi-equilibrium.

In *It's a Wonderful Life*, the drive impulse manifests a series of ordeals in which characters are tested for their worthiness as citizens of the town threatened by wrong tendencies inside them gaining the upper hand. For instance, consider the scene in which George as a boy saves the local pharmacist from making a grave error in prescribing the wrong medicine to a sick customer. Having received news of the death of his son, the pharmacist has tried to block emotional pain in drunkenness, causing him to misread the prescription and blame George (the boy employed as his assistant) for not delivering the medicine on time. The scene ends with a *catharsis* in which the pharmacist embraces George as his saviour, one of many such moments in the film. George's presence has *corrected* a tendency in the situation towards a tragic ending told to us in the metalepsis later in the film when the angel shows us what would have happened without George's intervention – the patient would have died from an overdose and the pharmacist would have been jailed, one of a number of small tragedies that beset the townsfolk without George there to protect and care for them.

Life is redeemed as 'wonderful' when, in a gestalt-switching revelation, George suddenly sees himself in a new dimension of the life he actually lives compared to the life he did not live – a possibility regressed in the dead past of the film coming to life on the screen as the dead life of 'life without George' superposed on the living life of 'life with George'. In the final scene of the film we see the townsfolk rally behind George, flooding him with money to save him from falling into the ignominy of bankruptcy and imprisonment through Potter's cynical plotting against him. The right tendencies are restored from a dangerous slide into *anthropy* in which Potter's vision of a capitalistic world devoid of communal spirit would have gained the upper hand. In a flash, the town is transformed from what it could have been to what it ought to be and is beginning to have always been: the beating heart of the American Dream imagined by audiences in the mid-twentieth century shaped by the twin catastrophes of economic depression and world war and the desire for a return to peace in family and communal life at home with itself (*heimlich*). In the 'last instance' of George's life, as he prepares to throw himself off the bridge, a saving power intervenes. Tragedy is averted and the comic continuity of life restored – the right path to take has already been taken and justice restored to the world.

Stereotypes and traumatypes

In an essay entitled 'Organology of Dreams and Arche-Cinema' (2014a), Stiegler develops his position on cinema as a *pharmakon* by citing Frank Capra's insight into the pharmacological character of Hollywood film. In Capra's words:

> Film is a disease. When it infects your bloodstream, it takes over as the number one hormone; it bosses the enzymes; directs the pineal gland; plays Iago to your psyche. As with heroin, the antidote to film is more film.
>
> 36

Stiegler interprets this quote to mean 'the cinema experience can either reinforce stereotypes held by the public ['the antidote to film is more film'], or on the contrary put to work its traumatypes' (19), where the traumatype is the *other* of the stereotype 'buried and repressed in the unconscious' (21) returning to disrupt the symbolic order upon which the stereotype's claim to common usage depends. In his proposal of the traumatype, Stiegler draws on Jung's theory of the archetype in the collective unconscious by way of Simondon's thesis on transindividuation as a counterpoint to Freud's theory of trauma inflicted on the individual psyche and brought to 'collective *historical consciousness*' via the unconscious (Stiegler 2021: 287). For Stiegler, the collective unconscious is understood in terms of *epiphylogenesis* or 'intergenerational transmission' of stereotypes and their traumatypes – their repressed other – carried by memory traces through technics (2014a: 13–14). For instance, in Capra's own film *It's a Wonderful Life*, an *epiphylogenesis* is staged by having the collective unconscious of the town without George return as the traumatype to the stereotype of small-town America in a *coup de cinéma* – a quantum leap in the film's telling of the story – in which the repressed past returns to haunt the living future with the deadness of its inexistence calling to be put right: the small tragedies that did not take place because of George's stereotypical good-man existence. The *unheimlich* character of the town 'without George' in which life could not regenerate is switched to the creative fecundity of the town 'with George' – at home with itself – as the cure to the toxicity besetting it by Potter's will to power, flooding the town with renewed life. In recalling Stiegler's claim that life is becoming cinema in what I have called the cinematization of the places of life in which *right* is acted out (see Chapter 2), the fictional town of Bedford Falls is the cinematized place in which the toxicity of a pharmacological situation is cured in the affirmation of the rightness of the American Dream.

The return of the repressed is, of course, a reference to Freud's theory of repression as the resistance of the unconscious to the *Zensor* (ego-censor) (Freud 1984: 154), a breakthrough in organological thinking in the register of libidinal exchanges of the psychic apparatus, employed by Stiegler in following Leroi-Gourhan's paleontological meta-critique of the becoming of technology to account for trauma inflicted on noetic life by 'techniques of cutting' (Stiegler 2020: 255): the separation of the psychic apparatus from itself by the intervention of tertiary retentions – memory traces – undertaken in the 'cutting room' of the studio editing suite (Stiegler 2014a: 8). Stiegler's Freudian-Jungian psychologizing of the cinematographic process enables him to account for trauma in the irrevocable loss of life, which he understands in terms of the tragic condition of human being: technically supplemented noetic individuals afflicted with the 'fault of Epimetheus' – the default of origin in which humans lack essential means of survival – as an issue which 'concerns the relation of mortals to immortality' in the irreversibility of time (1998: 188–9). Stiegler exposes the tragic condition of mortal life in technical supplementation in his reading of Federico Fellini's *Intervista* (1987): a poetizing of two films, one superposed on the other so that what it said in one film is unravelled in the saying of the other as *metatheatrical deconstruction* (my term).

Stiegler undertakes a metatheatrical deconstruction of a scene in Fellini's *Intervista* in which the ageing film star Anita Ekberg sees her younger self acting on the screen in Fellini's earlier film *La Dolce Vita* (1960), when she is confronted with 'the absolutely tragic staging of *her own* existence, insofar as that existence is *passing by* irremediably and forever – *forever*, except for what concerns this silvery image she has left on a film: an image in which she has been preserved' (Stiegler: 2011: 22). The 'silvery image' left on the screen is the aura of pastness passing through the *there* of the this-has-been, switching between life and death in the tragic circumstances of a mortal's existence. The film star's relation to her self returns as a traumatype to the stereotype of her former self – the sex goddess of the 1960s – haunting the screen as the overturning of the film star's immortal image on the silver screen in a tragic moment of self-realization that some day I will die. By entering the movement of memorizing from one film to the other, Stiegler opens up its phantasmic dimensions as overturned images becoming real on the screen as the truth of mortal life. The 'truth construction' of one film is undone by the other's contrapuntal memorizing passing through it, exposing both films to the 'tragic pattern' of the cosmic *life death* continuum as tragicomic metatheatrical deconstruction.

Acinema

The return of the repressed is the traumatype whose *unheimlich* presence draws attention to the film's theatricalization in cinematic memorizing as a mechanism for dreaming, which, in the thermodynamic version of his figure-matrix model of the cinematographic apparatus set forth in 'Acinema' (1986), Lyotard calls *direction*: the steerage or guidance required to stay on track in a film's progressing of action, requiring constant adjustments along a bifurcating vector line that represses the apparatus – stops it from taking charge: 'Direction first divides – along the axis of representation, and due to the theatrical limit – a reality and its double, and this disjunction constitutes an obvious repression' (355). The 'theatrical limit' (the verisimilar code guaranteeing fidelity to a reality principle acceptable to an audience) constitutes an 'obvious repression' of the apparatus by which reality is doubled in its simulation (the *imago* effect), requiring adjustments along the line to sustain the illusion that this thing I am seeing on the screen is real.

Lyotard locates the process of direction in film as a *placing* of objects 'in and out of scene' (354) following Klossowski's erotics of bodily gestures where 'the object, the victim, the prostitute, takes the pose, offering his or her self as a detached region' (357). Such objects become models – types of poses – set in play in the libidinal flow of images as an 'unconscious process of separation, exclusion, and effacement' that can either support or undermine 'representational order' (354) working through a *dispositif*: the counter-action of a repressed apparatus making its mark on the film. Acinematic film is film stripped of its theatrical limit, thereby exposing the apparatus to the 'disorder of the drives' (351) in which libidinal impulses are unlocked from their restriction in coded orders and released into 'true, that is, vain, simulacrums, blissful intensities instead of productive/consumable objects'. For Lyotard writing in the 1970s, such 'acinematic' effects are exemplified in experimental and underground films of the 1960s. When released from 'good order', acinematic effects *intensify* the pose of the model as an excessive moment of *jouissance* burning itself up in unproductive pleasure. These experimental films lay claim to a *right* to be the way they are as unproductive expenditures, by refusing the lure of productivity guiding libidinal energy towards 'genital sexuality' which is for Lyotard heterosexual coupling and happy endings of Hollywood melodrama.

Lyotard's initial proposal of acinema in his 'Acinema' essay is decidedly antinarrative, locating the acinematic tendency in experimental film as counterpoint to the story-telling of mainstream cinema. However, in a later essay entitled 'The Idea of a Sovereign Film' (2017), he changed position to uncover acinematic tendencies in film narration in general: an *arrhythmia* or destabilizing countermotion which he finds pre-eminently in Italian neorealist cinema but also in the films of the French director Robert Bresson who forged his own pathway through the neorealist phase of modern film (63–5). Cinema is affirmed in its *sovereign right* to be the way it is in acinematic moments of 'special intensity' (65), its resistance to the means–end logic of *telos*, calling forth another time which 'tells another story' (66). The sovereignty of film is to be found in the singularity of its resistance to generic type: its *acinematic style* inscribed in the film's direction, in the assemblage of its elements as 'its own rules of the game, its own *dispositif* (Martin 2014: 189).

With Lyotard's acinematic model in mind together with Martin's contribution of singular style as *dispositif* – the game played by the film counter-wise to its story-telling – we can summarize Stiegler's stereotype/traumatype process as follows. In its *cinematic mode*, the model's potential for transgression is repressed in supporting reality codes in which libidinal energy is spread throughout each part according to sufficiencies of the apparatus, where all the poses combine into 'good, unifying, and reasonable forms proposed for identification' (Lyotard 1986:

357). In its *acinematic mode*, the model's transgressive potential is released by concentrating energy in a single pose (a 'detached region'), effecting a distortion of the forms (358) and a subsequent placing of the identity of the model as an adequate ('reasonable') model of good form in question. The tendency of cinematic direction is towards fulfilling stereotypes (the repetitions of 'good form [as] the return to sameness'), holding the film in place at its 'theatrical limit' (352, 354–5). However, in acinematic direction, the theatrical limit is breached by the concentrated energy of the pose, invoking the traumatype in the return of the repressed, putting the stereotype into a questioning situation as a *cinematic right* in the sense of what ought to be done in the demand that the voice of the traumatype be heard. In constituting cinematic right by putting *itself* in question through the demand, the 'Idea [of sovereignty] persists and suffices to ensure that there is sovereignty in films, and to continually call for new films' (2017: 70), which, in Fichte's terms, are 'the conditions which make individuality possible [for a film to have] "rights"' (1988: 409). There are no sovereign films (Lyotard 2017: 69); rather, sovereignty resides in the *dispositif* – the counter-tendency within them transgressing the rules – without which a film could not individuate to be the film that it is.

Having developed an acinematic model of the stereotype/traumatype process, let us now return to Fellini's films discussed in the previous section. By placing – superposing – the screen life of *La Dolce Vita* on the screen life of *Intervista* and setting them in play, Fellini's *acinematic direction* draws attention to the theatricalization of the craft of filmmaking at its limits – its *dispositif*. The counter-movement of the film's direction releases the repression of the traumatype by re-screening the erotic pose of the sex goddess in its full potential in *La Dolce Vita* juxtaposed against the perspective of its ageing star in *Intervista*. The concentration of energy in the superposition of the two films breaches their theatrical limits – an acinematic moment in which the voice of the traumatype is heard as the *Yes* of life exceeding the *No* of death in joyous overflow spilling into the acinematic *real*. The tragedy of mortal life as irrevocable loss – in the gap between the 'timeless' (quasi-immortal) image of the sex goddess seen on the screen and her ageing self many years later – is phase-shifted into tragicomic mode, offering hope of renewed life in the experience of cinema as *sovereign to itself*.

Traumatypes appear in pharmacological situations when we take Capra's statement at its word: all film is toxic and its antidote is more film, a cynical view of the Hollywood film industry which leaves no way out of the *pharmacological trap* – the double bind of a therapeutic vicious circle in which the poison is the cure and vice versa. The toxicity of *It's a Wonderful Life* would be – by Capra's own admission – its addictive hold on the audience lulled into satisfaction by its ameliorative spirit and the affirmation of the American Dream. The pharmacological trap disables the audience's methexical function to tell the difference between right and wrong action in the *anthropy* of the pharmacological condition when the cure turns out to be toxic, when the affirmation of the American Dream in films such as *It's a Wonderful Life* leads to a quietism of the spirit and blind acceptance of values that have been insufficiently tested. By turning to the self-reflexive cinema of the French New Wave and Italian post-neorealist (i.e. modernist) cinema, Stiegler opens up the possibility of a re-quickening of the spirit in which other paths might be taken to lead us out of this trap.

In his employment of the stereotype–traumatype dyad, Stiegler takes his cue from Simondon's adaptation of Jung's idea of the archetype in the collective memory of a transindividuated *We*, but shifts it in favour of the Freudian 'return of the repressed' and the Heideggerian 'turn' as *Ereignis* in which 'something happens, constituting an event when what is utterly unexpected manifests itself' (2020: 207). The realization that 'something happens' *there* on the screen releases the binding of the archetypal structure in the metastasis of the drives in which the traumatype reappears as the otherness of what could have been, calling for the situation which has provoked it to be put right. In responding to this call, a morality of *right* could be developed along pharmacological lines by delineating the film's *dispositif*: the counter-tactic employed in its refusal of the cliché it is becoming in acinematic moments of the *real*, opening itself to new dimensions in which paths not taken suddenly come into view.

Art film

According to András Kovács, the art film is a *type* of film emerging in the mid-twentieth century, the product of 'institutionalized film practices' (2007: 21) mediating between mainstream commercial narrative cinema and the avant-garde. As Kovács explains, the institutionalized art film is characterized by 'modern visual abstraction' (17): a sensitivity towards images, beginning with the expressionism of 1920s Weimar cinema, picked up, worked through and then adopted/adapted by Hollywood genres in the 1930s through émigrés fleeing the

Nazi regime, their influence leading to 'a stylistic renewal of the American cinema by Orson Welles and *film noir* in the 1940s' (18). For Kovács, the stylistic renewal afforded by the congruence of visual abstraction of Weimar expressionist cinema and Hollywood genres feeds into a desire to affirm the type of film in which such abstraction can be seen as 'the "pure" form of the cinema' concretized into the institutionalized art film.

Art film is not inherently anti-narrative but accommodates story-telling in a *rapprochement* between style and action in which the story told becomes infused with visual abstraction as a mark of its sovereignty as acinematic cinema (i.e. as *a* modernist film). In this modernist quest for pure visual abstraction, the art film concerns itself with the *new* released from the dead past in the impulse of self-reflexivity, which, following Clement Greenberg, Kovács calls 'aesthetic self-criticism' (12). The *rapprochement* between style and action would thus turn on the function of self-reflexivity in shifting from story-telling to absorption in abstract images as a new kind of cinematic realism sovereign to itself as a 'filmic fact' (Lyotard 2017: 68). However, despite having invoked aesthetic considerations and their consequences for the facticity of modernist films (their 'this-ness' as cinematic artefacts), Kovács contradicts himself. The institutionalized art film does not refer to 'aesthetic qualities but to certain genres, styles, narrative procedures, distribution networks, production companies, film festivals, critics, groups of audiences – in short, an institutionalized film practice' (21). It is clear from this statement that Kovács conceives the art film not as sovereign to itself but as part of a social reality of production, distribution and consumption with its own audiences and *aficionados*.

Against Kovács's assumption of the categorization of art film as a certain type of film, I propose that the institutionalized art film *as such* does not exist and that its possibility is bound up in the crystallization of tendencies in the generalized system of cinema production and consumption in which decisions regarding types of film are made. Following this line of thinking, what we call art film would be an *idiotextual concretization* of resistive tendencies in the sphere of cinematic production and consumption, where such resistive tendencies would be *acinematic* singularizations through the employment of an array of stylistic gestures as a *dispositif* unique to *this* film and to the *auteur* team who created it. Wherever and whenever these resistive tendencies concretize into an individuation, art film *is* – this 'is-ness' being the facticity of counter-inherence within already circulating generic forms. In these terms, an art-film would be an acinematic singularity tied to a limiting condition in which the tendency towards type is subverted by a reflexive counter-gesture in which the edifice of the crystal sphere is cracked, exposing the film's *dispositif* as *spiel* – the playing out of stylistic gestures in which the rules of the game set in train by the film apparatus are simultaneously transgressed and re-written. Accordingly, I argue, *pace* Kovács, that an art film *as such* does not exist but in-exists as a *subversive potential* within existing types of films including the institutional art film itself.

The Lady from Shanghai

In this section I will undertake an analysis of Orson Welles's *The Lady from Shanghai* (1947), a film that – as I will demonstrate – fulfils the criteria of art film as a film that sets its own rules, thereby subverting the genre to which it claims to belong by affirming it otherwise through its *dispositif*: 'a game with rules, where the execution of the game's moves – the following of rules – generates outcomes, results and sometimes surprises. These rules can be the structures and parameters of a film' (Martin 2014: 179). A term often associated with *dispositif* is *apparatus*, the concept I have employed in this book to describe the quasi-machine posited retroactively to account for the process of metastabilization of perceptual experience in film (i.e. the cinematograph as the apparatus inside us and on the screen). However, the *dispositif* is not simply another name for the apparatus, but a *disposition* within it manifesting in any given film: the film's idiotextual characteristics or singular accents that tell us this film is different from other films of its type played out through the apparatus as counter-wise spin (*spiel*). Likewise, Martin defines the *dispositif* as the disposition of 'the spectator's experience of a film' (188), by which he means how the film sets itself up in addressing its audience as *this* film (unlike, say, a can of Campbell's tomato soup in which the soup in one can is guaranteed to be as good as the soup in any other can of Campbell's tomato soup). What Martin is getting at when he says that the *dispositif* plays its own game, has its own rules, is that the rules of the *dispositif* work against the generic patterns of what the film is *expected to be*, thereby 'manifest[ing] its sovereignty' (Lyotard 2017: 64). Another way of thinking about expectations is in terms of the film's moral 'disposition' – its being disposed to what *ought* to be. As moral disposition, the *dispositif* provides the film with a *sufficiency of reason* for putting wrongs right (how things ought to be), thereby affirming its *own right* to be as subversive potential within existing generic forms. Following these principles, I will undertake a poetizing of *The*

Lady from Shanghai as a film that subverts its genre (the type of film it is expected to be), and in so doing, demonstrate how it fulfils the criteria of a non-institutionalized art film – a film that negates its generic affiliations – through its *dispositif* as the film it ought to be *by right* as sovereign to itself.

Martin draws his idea of the *dispositif* from *avant-garde* filmmakers of the mid-twentieth century and more recently Lars von Trier's dogma 95 manifesto in which the Danish director applies a set of rules to his filmmaking practice to ensure strict adherence to a limiting condition in the absence of any transcendent authority upon which to ensure 'good form'. Rather than follow pre-existing rules, the dogma 95 filmmaker gives herself rules to make a film, to ensure fidelity to the fact that *this film exists*. In production terms, the strategy of giving oneself one's own rules is proposed to take back power from the studios in order to provide filmmakers with more scope and freedom to explore the limits of their own craft. Here, we have echoes of Lyotard's proposal of *acinema* as a resistive style of filmmaking (as well as Welles's own struggles with the studio bosses in making the film). As discussed previously and applying Stiegler's notion of *neganthropic resistance* – resistance to the resistance of technical drive – Lyotard's concept of *acinema* as film sovereign to itself (2017: 64) means that an acinematic film develops its own rules against generic order as neganthropic resistance – an acinematic style singular to itself to ensure survival of the creative-resistive potential of the human by right (noetic freedom). From this neganthropic resistive viewpoint, the *dispositif* would not be the apparatus that supports the ordering of good form but rather a moral disposition within it subverting what it supports, providing a sufficiency of reason for doing so as the right way to be. A *dispositif* plays a double game of both supporting and undermining what it supports, holding itself back in the 'game [played] with rules' as the game's subversive potential in affirming what it ought to be; that is, as previously stated, sovereign to itself.

Keeping in mind Kovács's definition of art film as a style of film characterized by 'visual abstraction', my concern will be to identify a *dispositif* in *The Lady from Shanghai* as a certain tendency towards abstraction of images in the double game played by the *dramatis personae* – the actors playing their part both with and against the rules which the film claims to be following – how it sets up generic expectations in order to subvert them – which I take to be 1940s Hollywood crime melodrama which has come to be known as *film noir*. My justification for making this assumption lies in its employment of a *'film noir'* voice-over technique in which the telling is entangled in the tale, together with other details such as the figure of the *femme fatale* and her cuckolded husband, the hand gun at the ready, the atmosphere of cynicism and betrayal that thwarts every action and gesture, the powerful sense of *amour fou* (obsessive desire) taking hold of all of the characters playing the game as a life death masquerade from which there is no escape. The key to *The Lady from Shanghai*'s art film credentials lies in its tendency towards visual abstraction of mirror reflections – the play of masks – until they shatter in the refracted world of the film, proclaiming the death of truth exposed in the lie of its crystalline illusion.

The masquerade of the film begins with a clichéd night shot of the Brooklyn Bridge, with Michael's voice-over announcing 'when I start out to make a fool of myself, there is very little that can stop me; if I'd known where it would end, I would have never let anything start'. Michael speaks with a voice that both says and retracts what it says as an ironic exclamation of the folly of life, suggesting that one's path in life cannot easily be reversed due to the fact that we are never fully aware of where it is headed. It is only in hindsight that we see clearly the paths we have taken and not taken for better or worse. Michael continues: 'if I had been in my right mind that is. But once I had seen her, I was not in my right mind for quite some time'. It is only after he has seen the consequences of following the beautiful woman and thus of having taken what turns out to be a wrong path in life that he can actually see that the path was the wrong path to have taken, suggesting he ought not have taken it in the first place. The issue boils down to a question of right-mindedness: a condition of being in one's 'right mind' in having come to the realization that one has taken the wrong path in life; in *knowing* this to be the case, one is *already* on the right path; that is, in one's 'right mind'.

Let us, for the moment, entertain the possibility that the 'fool' Michael claims himself to have been relates to Frank Powell's *A Fool There Was* (1915), in which a high-ranking diplomat falls for a beautiful woman on board a luxury liner who lures him into a life of *amour fou* where he suffers endlessly at her mercy. In surrendering to the vamp's seductive embrace, he literally loses his mind, a condition echoed by Michael whose obsessive pursuit of the beautiful woman Elsa who dupes him into her murderous plotting almost ruins his life. What follows is a story that affirms the tragicomic condition of modern life in which cynical self-interest is played to the hilt in a complex masquerade where all the characters play their lives against each other in a death drive to the point of mutually assured self-destruction when their masks are removed in the realization that they have all been duped and that there are no winners but also – as Michael says at the end of the film – there are no losers either. What remains is the game entangled in the story told by its teller, the fool whose belief in the cliché of romantic love had led him astray. The tragedy of life is the realization that love cannot exist without a price to pay in the risk of its betrayal by cynicism and distrust in the lovers' motives: a force of evil binding them into each other's desire as the deadly embrace of *amor fou*. The comic counter-motion is the playing out of the game in which life is affirmed against the death-that-awaits, where wrong-minded obsession turns to right-minded clarity of purpose in Michael having realized that 'a fool there was' – himself: the wronged man put back in his right mind in the *telling* of the story.

The vitiation of the life spirit in cynical mistrust in others' good intentions, is, of course, the *Stimmung* of *film noir*, whose characteristics are easily recognized in *The Lady from Shanghai*. Yet the film reaches through its generic format to break the surface of crystalline images across which the game is played out, undercutting the film's tragic projection of *amor fou* with savage self-mockery. For instance, the walking sticks used by Elsa's disabled husband Bannister to steady his gait are exaggerated to the point that they begin to manipulate him, turning him into a grotesque puppet-figure; Bannister is both puppet master and puppet, pulling the strings of others while having his strings pulled by them as the film looks back at its own imagery with a wicked eye and sardonic laughter. The film reaches absurd levels of self-mockery in the courtroom scene in which Michael is standing trial for the murder of Bannister's business partner Grisby (having been duped by Elsa into colluding with Grisby to do away with her husband). As the trial proceeds, disturbances in the gallery intrude into the action, while witnesses and prosecutors begin to talk over each other as if gripped by some strange compulsion to ruin the trial's proceedings and its good ordering of justice; called to give evidence, Bannister becomes his own cross-examiner, while the judge's child-like inability to control the court leads to mayhem as the jury's verdict is about to be delivered in a world of justice turned upside down. Seizing the moment, Michael swallows a handful of Bannister's painkilling tablets in a feigned attempt to kill himself and in the ensuing confusion escapes from the courtroom, running out into the street.

In accordance with the expectations of *film noir*, *The Lady from Shanghai* mobilizes the death-that-awaits, calling the characters into its deadly game. The game is set in motion by Elsa's plotting told to us through Michael's voice-over, which, adopting a self-deprecating tone, interacts with the events as they happen as if to disavow them, drawing the film closer to the cliché it feigns to be. As

Figure 3.1 The shattering of the crystal edifice. *The Lady from Shanghai*, dir. Orson Welles (1947).

events unfold and Michael is drawn deeper into the ambiguities of the *femme fatale*'s death embrace, the playing reaches incredulous levels of hyper-realism in the courtroom fiasco just described, spinning out of control in an accelerating spiral of cuts as the condemned man flees the courtroom into the streets with Elsa following, both led by an invisible thread towards a Chinese theatre where they find each other in the audience of a stage play currently underway. Shots of actors on the stage looking out over the audience intermingle with shots of Michael and Elsa also looking out in a *melange* of looks which finds its impossible point of focus on a gun concealed in Elsa's purse: the pistol used to kill Grisby as incriminating evidence of her culpability for the crime. In the masquerade of exchanging looks in which each look sees through the other, Elsa and Michael embrace, their desire turning deadly when Michael – alerted as if by some strange power of prescience – draws the pistol out of Elsa's purse. In a flash of insight, he sees her as she sees him in a fusion of desire and fear binding them together in deadly *amor fou*. Overcome with the sedative effect of the tablets, Michael collapses, his slumped body bundled out of the theatre on Elsa's orders and left in the Crazy House of an amusement park to await his fate.

Figure 3.2 'I don't want to die.' *The Lady from Shanghai*, dir. Orson Welles (1947).

The death-that-awaits arrives in the final scene of the film in which Michael finds himself in the Magic Mirror Maze – the chamber of reflected images in which the falseness of the film's moral projection crystallizes into what Deleuze calls a pure crystal image (1989: 70) – where he meets Elsa and Bannister confronting each other with guns drawn refracted through the reflected images in a *mise en abyme* duplicating multiple reflections across the screen. Shots are fired and the crystal edifice shatters, killing Bannister and mortally wounding Elsa, leaving Michael – the third person in the scene (missed by Deleuze) – to bear witness, his death suspended in theirs. As Elsa lies dying at Michael's feet, she calls out 'Oh my god, I'm afraid, Michael come back here, I don't want to die, I don't want to die', as the film's last instance in communicating the *real* of its own demise as a false bearer of the truth of mortal life. Yet, the final image of the film persists as life after the Death Event we have just witnessed. As the camera pulls back from Michael's retreating figure, the tragicomic play of life and death recommences by putting Michael in his 'right mind', a state of rectitude which he *knows* to be the case, having judged it to be so in having survived the shattering of false images to bear witness to it as his death suspended in theirs. Michael is saved by the very danger posed in the ambiguous appearance of truth – its veiled irreality as both true and false – played out as fabulation in the film's story-telling. In its singularity as sovereign to itself, the film becomes a *pharmakon* – a self-questioning event – in which its own survival affirms the right path which could also be the wrong path, the consequences of which have been 'figured out' in the film's moral disposition: its *dispositif* providing sufficient reason to put wrongs right in affirming its own right to be as subversive to generic form. As such, *The Lady from Shanghai* becomes a non-*film noir*: an art film that negates the category *film noir* in the very act of claiming itself to be such a film.

End game

The valueless present of hypermodernity sustains life in the *amor fati* of a *life death* existence, announced in the middle of the twentieth century by Samuel Beckett at the end of his novel *The Unnamable* through the voice of a neutralized *I*: 'I can't go on, I'll go on' (Beckett 2010: 134), echoing the voice of a Fichtean I caught in the *Anstoß* of an in-between existence in an endless struggle to be. The extreme condition of *life death* stripped back to its essentials is also presented by Beckett in his experimental film entitled *Film* (Beckett, Schneider 1965), a re-performance of life becoming cinema in its 'last instance' in which a non-inhuman *automaton* played by silent film comic Buster Keaton is pursued by a camera whose omnipresent gaze threatens to enclose him inside the apparatus with no way out. I shall call this figure B.

The apparatus operates through a mechanism controlled by obscure rules demanding restrictions of movement tending towards degree zero, at which point B would reach its very last instance and would cease to exist. Seeking refuge, B covers any apertures that might admit or reflect light (windows, a mirror, the eyes of pet animals), with the camera always looking on, its *inhuman gaze* seeing everything we see that B sees and doesn't see. What is forbidden is to see the eye of the camera itself; there must always be a camera, the 'one working now' (Cavell 1979: 126), free to show us what can and cannot be seen without itself being seen. As a creature of cinematic automation, B exists for the camera, yet something else persists: life otherwise anticipated and captured by the apparatus in the camera's encroaching presence. Reduced to minimal in-existence, B eventually succumbs to the mechanism and, with nothing more to do, falls asleep, only to be awakened by the ever-present camera looking at B. On awakening, B looks directly into the camera – a forbidden act that bars B's gaze by reflecting B's own image back at B but in the distorted figure of the *real* – the non-I as a horrifying excess – which cannot be survived and must be avoided.

At minimal levels of existence, we are – like Beckett's hapless figure trapped inside the crystalline sphere of a cinematic apparatus – all Bs seeking the B we will have become in the spheres of automated industrial life in which we can't go on but we must. How does one survive such a situation without succumbing to its inhuman embrace? Beckett's answer is by adopting a *non-inhuman* perspective in which the anthropy of *amor fati* yields to the neganthropy of unhoped-for expectation in the promise of life: waiting in expectation of an event that 'will have' happened, the quasi-cause of which is the film we are currently seeing on the screen. In its re-performance of the 'not yet' of inexistence as the *life death* condition of industrial life, Beckett's film is the exemplar of what this film could be.

Stiegler describes the non-inhuman in terms of the man after the last man 'only insofar as he is in-existent: only insofar as he *does not yet exist*, only insofar as he exists *only as "not yet"*, always *already* having become anthropic, *all* too anthropic' (2018: 84). This non-inhuman perspective is adopted when I step back from the scene to see B looking at B as the *automaton* of the cinematograph failing to transcend itself: the traumatic moment in which I become aware of the inhuman other *in me*. In stepping back, I refuse the drive's auto-efficiency in eternal repetition as 'the first moment of improbable epokhality, into which we must enter' (2016: 71). In this first moment, the non-inhuman other in me goes on, the *I* that I could possibly be having turned within it in epochal recommencement.

In the next chapter, we follow the non-inhuman other of the automation into modernist cinema as a catastrophic event of memory death in which the future cannot pass through. My aim is to demonstrate how these films – exemplified by Antonioni's *L'Eclisse* and Bresson's *Une Femme Douce* – offer a way to pass through the catastrophe by refusing the lure of the apparatus to lead me into it. In so doing, I will have released *myself* from its grasp in the finite freedom to think and imagine otherwise, activated in the analysis itself.

4

Cinematic time

Non-indecisive action

In *Technics and Time, 3: Cinematic Time and the Question of Malaise* (2011), Stiegler identifies a profound malaise afflicting the contemporary industrialized world: the enervation of 'consciousnesses [exploited] for "market access"' (3), who, through 'loss of individuation', have succumbed to a 'proletarianization of the mind and to the pauperization of the culture' (4) in which their desires circulate for the system rather than themselves insofar as it *allows* them to desire for themselves. For Stiegler, these enervated, proletarianized consciousnesses have lost their noetic freedom to dream new dreams and to imagine themselves otherwise as a communality of individuals free to decide for themselves the who they *ought* to be; that is, an identity formation drawing itself together in mutually determining acts of 'moral consciousness' (2013: 23): a transindividuating group as a *We* in-the-making.

Pauperization arises in the marketing of temporal objects (films, television programmes, streaming platforms etc.) for consumption by de-individuated 'dividuals': individual consciousnesses stripped of the 'in' of their individuality – the inner capacity to think for themselves – by automated machine intelligence (2016: 24). For Stiegler, such dividuals have lost the 'feeling of existing, the loss of the possibility of expressing one's will, the correlative loss of all reason for living and the subsequent loss of *reason as such*'. Worryingly, these losses 'also and especially strike *an entire generation*' of young people – those whose futures are at stake in the catastrophes to come (2019: 8–9).

In terms of cinematic experience, de-individuation occurs when the viewer's time is absorbed into the 'stream of consciousness' (2011: 1) of cinematic time – the duration of moving images projected on a screen – leaving no time for herself as an individuated being to project her own desire to be herself together with others as a *We* in-the-making:

> [T]he consumer, being locked in, can no longer escape; she can be perfectly anticipated and controlled, no longer an individuated and individuating 'person' but in a real sense *Nobody* [*personne*; *outis*], a perspectiveless Cyclops.
>
> This loss of individuation, in which *I* persists as a yawning void, no longer moving towards a *We* who, being everything, the confusion of all possible *I*'s in the undifferentiated flux (the totalitarian model of 'community'), is condemned to dissolve into a globalized, impersonal *One*. This loss of individuation leads to immense existential suffering.
>
> 4–5

Having projected a vision of 'locked in' consumers as dividuated egos undergoing 'immense existential suffering' in being deprived of the means of releasing themselves from the system of industrialized market surveillance, Stiegler comes up with a solution. Rather than turn away from the pleasures of the consumer market as 'pure illusion' (4), he proposes to work through them by provoking bifurcations –moments in which the path ahead splits in two – as pharmacological events with the potential to effect phase-change through a decisional praxis whereby the toxicity of taking the wrong path can be corrected in hindsight by the thought of having taken the right path to resolve the undecidability of the *pharmakons* thus produced. The resolution of the situation in which the pharmacological event takes place releases noetic imagination repressed by the suffering in potential to act otherwise as an epochal opening of new life which 'may always once again become closed' (2019a: 44–5). Stiegler's aim is to place the pharmacological tool he has developed inside the viewing consciousness opened to the archival future of cinematic memory in order to turn out of it in a recommencement otherwise – to dream new dreams, where a dream is 'the condition of my potentiality to act' (2018: 167).

To provoke a pharmacological event and thus re-awaken new dreams in recommencement, Stiegler asks us to imagine ourselves on a Sunday afternoon, seeking distraction from 'boredom' in the lull of industrial life, looking for pleasure by watching old movies and television programmes:

> If by some lucky chance the film is a good one, we who are watching it in complete lethargy...come out of it less lazy, even re-invigorated, full of emotion and the desire to do something, or else infused with a new outlook on things: the cinematographic machine, taking charge of our boredom, will have transformed it into new energy, transubstantiated it, made something out of nothing.
>
> 2011: 10

In this account of the viewer's adoption of the time of the characters in a film, the bored viewer has no conscious awareness that she is doing so; her re-energizing takes place by chance – 'if by some lucky chance the film is a good one' – suggesting that the more likely outcome would be no change to her disposition, chance having not intervened. If there happens to be a release from boredom, it would have been in unhoped-for expectation, as if the cinematographic machine 'taking charge of [her] boredom' *had decided for her*. In her 'complete lethargy', the viewer's noetic freedom has already been surrendered to the machine and she remains entirely captive to its frame of reference.

The machine having already decided for her means that her power to decide lies in *non-indecisive action* – retroactive decisiveness – in the viewer's capacity to refuse the lure of deadening life offered by the film, without which she could not see it otherwise to shift into a new frame of reference in which her life could be revitalized, *knowing that she is free in having done so*. The lethargy in her must already be charged with *potential to act* in the capacity to see the film from the turned position – looking backward in coming forward – in what Walter Benjamin calls the 'irresistible urge to search ... for the tiny spark of contingency' (1999: 510) within it, in the chance to open up other pathways hidden from view in the non-turned position.[1] From the turned position, she will have already put herself in a new frame of reference by playing the machine against itself to open up views hidden from view by the apparatus as neganthropic resistance (the refusal of the non-inhuman to surrender to the control of the machine through non-indecisive action). She will have already decided *for herself* in non-indecisive action; that is, in 'knowing [herself] to be decisive' (Nancy 2002: 74).[2]

In proposing the possibility of an otherwise recommencement in dreaming new dreams through the adoption of my time with the time of characters onscreen, Stiegler has missed a crucial step. Before the viewer can adopt the time of the characters, she must be free to do so, otherwise her time will have already been absorbed in theirs, leaving no time for herself. She must willingly give up her freedom to be otherwise in adopting their time as her choice or alternatively play against their time from the turned position – looking backward in coming forward – to dream new dreams within the cinematographic machine itself, knowing that she is doing so. By turning out of the machine's capture of noetic freedom in the spurious freedom to choose, the viewer *unwills the will* – resists the resistance – that makes her free to choose, thereby opening up possibility for new views and new pathways not as her choice but in knowing herself to have been decisive through non-indecisive action.

This chapter takes the step missed by Stiegler in his thought experiment by opening up films to cinematic time from the turned position in order to play against the mechanism by which cinematic time is generated – the apparatus. To take this step, I will draw on Simondon's notion of syncrystallization as the process of falling in and out of sync of an emerging self-consciousness in the 'syncrystallization' of 'biological forms' (2020: 168) drawing from the insubstantiality of pre-individual flux sustaining individuated life in films, where 'life is *always* cinema' (Stiegler 2011: 16). In cinematic time, syncrystallization is the synchronizing of the viewer's time with the time of the characters in which the falling in and out of sync process is continually corrected and recorrected in the flow of images towards the completion of ends (the 'aim' of the narration; what the story is trying to tell us). In the process of synchronization, the viewer's consciousness is lifted out of cinematic time and into story-time by an apparatus recessed within it and in what we see on the screen (i.e. in our perception of it). To retrieve the viewer's consciousness as self-consciousness requires a *desyncrystallization* of perception in which I become aware of *my time* in the duration of the film in which the apparatus comes forth in its counter-strategic mode as a *dispositif* – a tactical avoidance mechanism or *spiel* (a 'playing out' against the grain) – supervening the falling in and out of sync process of the image flow in order to effect the time required for onscreen action to take place.

To explore the pharmacological potential of modern films as the aim of this chapter, I will undertake a reading of two films – Antonioni's *L'Eclisse* (1961), already discussed in a preliminary fashion in the introductory chapter, and Bresson's *Une Femme Douce* (1969), both of which employ directorial provocations to effect phase-change in the viewer's perception, liberating it from the control of the film-apparatus as means–end efficiency-seeking drive. A counter to the 'locked in' situation of the viewer discussed in the opening paragraphs of this section of the chapter finds a precedent in the modernist art film in its acinematic sovereignty to be itself, thereby effecting a cure for life facing the catastrophe to come in which the living future will have been erased.

L'Eclisse

In this section, I engage in a reading of Antonioni's film *L'Eclisse* (1961), following my analysis of the film in the introductory chapter, where two young lovers Vittoria and Piero are conceptualized as *figures of resistance*: the dyad couple of quantum superposition, whose inexistent life in being compossibly together-apart is controlled by the force of negentropy as counter-movement against the plot's forward progress – its coming to an end in the catastrophe of memory death in which all trace of them is wiped from the screen. Here, we pick up on Vittoria's and Piero's fate by tracking the *spiel* of the film's image flow – its playing out of life's chances in the *saying* of the film as a catastrophic event in which the future cannot pass through. My aim is to show how *L'Eclisse* effects a *desyncrystallization* of the viewer's perception – desynchronizing the viewer's time from the time of the characters – reclaiming its acinematic sovereignty to be itself in the catastrophe of modern life where, as Vittoria says 'a piece of cloth, a needle, a thread, or a book … or a man is the same thing'. Through this desyncrystallizing-desynchronizing process in which the film holds itself back in moving forward, the perceiving eye of the viewer is drawn into the indeterminacy of the *real* in which the trauma of the suffering ego dephases into self-annihilating meaninglessness, a catastrophic condition of life stripped of its noetic capacity in which nothing survives but the *there* of the film itself – its refusal to not be. In experiencing the *there* as neg*anthropic* resistance – that is, as specifically *human* – finite freedom is won back from the brink of catastrophic memory loss.

The turning of the crystalline sphere begins in the film's opening scene, in which we find that a camera positioned in a *view from nowhere* has already leapt

Figure 4.1 Opening shot of *L'Eclisse*, dir. Michelangelo Antonioni (1961).

into what I see before me, *there* on the screen in a still life image consisting of a lamp positioned beside a table on which has been placed books, pens and a coffee cup, as well as an *indeterminate something* that looks like a piece of fabric resting beside the books. The shot is held for a few seconds, then the camera shifts slightly to the right, triggering a movement of the indeterminate thing, suddenly revealed to be the sleeved arm of a man sitting in a chair. In the background, a desk fan is circulating air in the apartment in which the scene is set. From the *nature morte* of its opening frame, the film is bringing itself to life by the effect of the moving thing as the man shifts his arm together with his head turning from side to side in time with the oscillating motion of the fan. These synchronizing movements slow the viewer's time to the time of the camera in its presentation of things to be seen, a desyncrystallization of perception from identifying with characters as fully formed individuals, to move in sync with the camera in what *it* sees.

These counter-synchronizing movements in which story-telling is held back from advancing towards causally motivated action are followed by a shot of the other person in the room: a woman who, although appearing to be the recipient of the man's look, is looking away from him and into curtains closed across a window which she parts to be confronted by her reflection in the glass pane, blocking her view of trees outside. The sequence then breaks into a set of poses: the woman's hand holding a glass *objet d'art* which she extends through a wooden frame to place it on a table while at the same time removing an ashtray full of stubbed out cigarettes; the woman looking at a painting of a village on the wall; the woman drawing the window curtain open; a shot of the woman's legs from floor level; the woman curled up on a couch. On close inspection, it becomes apparent that the woman (Vittoria – an archetype of modern woman) is responding not to the man (Riccardo, her current lover), but to prompts by the camera; as it is with his gestures, her gestures are synchronizing with the camera as it wanders around the apartment. But what is prompting the camera? To answer this question, we need to turn to Antonioni's style of direction.

Antonioni's directing style is guided by his relinquishing of control over the camera so that everything he sees he sees with what the actors see:

> What I try to do is provoke them [the actors], put them in the right mood. And then I watch them through the camera and at that moment tell them to do this or that. *But not before.* I have to have my shot, and *they are an element of the image* – and not always the most important element.
>
> Antonioni 1996: 336, emphasis added

Antonioni's control of the filmmaking process is limited to the way he sees 'not before' the camera sees, but as the camera sees: a prosthetic *seeing-with* the camera, initiating a visual display in which actors are placed as an 'element of the image' with respect to the *whole* of what could be seen. What both he and they see is what the camera sees, but the camera can also see more in an excess of machinic vision over the human eye, described by Walter Benjamin as an 'optical unconscious' (1999: 512, 2002: 117). Antonioni's method is thus stochastic – responding to the exigencies of the camera-situation automated with positive feedback as 'another nature which speaks to the camera rather than the eye' (Benjamin 1999: 510). By embedding his prosthetic eye in the filmmaking process, Antonioni allows the contingencies of filmmaking to guide the decisions he makes in what he shoots and how the shooting takes place, so that the film comes into existence through 'experiential contact' in 'work to-be-made' (Souriau 2015: 220): self-questioning through the camera apparatus in reality testing exercising the director's non-indecisive action.

Antonioni's filmmaking praxis is guided by an automated feedback process adjusted by the director's eye inserted into it, in which both the actors' and the director's seeing are *instaured* into the images passing between 'virtual existence and concrete existence' (Souriau 2015: 224), which is a mode of looking rendered immanent to the film's becoming as an objectivized seeing-without-a-subject. In the 'instaurative action' of Antonioni's image-making, the camera prosthesis acts as a drive automation seeking blindly for a pathway along which the actions of characters may or may not pass in seeking efficiencies required for the situation to be resolved. By inserting himself on the vector line of a pathway, Antonioni directs the actions already onscreen as 'element[s] of the image' in self-questioning that seeks answers in what the camera sees in what he sees. Antonioni's style of receptive passivity to the *automaton* of the camera image strips the characters of self-volition, plunging them into non-indecisive action – action calling for a decision – making them unknowing of the 'why' of what they are doing as if drawn along the vector line by an inhuman force (the Lyotardian *inhuman*). Seeking blindly for the future, they continually fail to complete their actions in the decision called for, which is also the failure of the film to coincide with itself in the gap that refuses to close (falling in and out of sync with itself).

By slowing cinematic time down to synchronize the movement of objects along the vector line with the movement of the camera, Antonioni's prosthetic eye enters the void of the cinematic *real* – the inhuman otherness of technology left to its own devices – in a *view from nowhere* taking control of the *automatons* and testing their limits. Inside the void, we find *ourselves* confronted with mechanized human gestures mimicking camera-like functions: just as a camera touches objects with its look, Vittoria's hand reaches through the frame to touch the objects seen within it; just as a camera opens up new views, her gesture of opening the window curtain also opens up a yet-to-be seen view. By curling up on a couch she affirms that her gestures are not psychologically or causally motivated (she is not sleepy or in need of rest), but arbitrarily linked to the cinematic mode of selecting and combining of images (she can lie on this couch, sit in this chair, or even fling herself into the man's arms – all of these gestures are possible). In this way, her actions lack purpose other than to display the power of the camera to stage the scene in a masquerade of postures – ways of facing the world through the kino-eye of a camera liberated from the end-seeking *telos* of human motivations. Antonioni's camera releases *itself* from the human gaze to wander in a *theatrum mundi* – a world theatre – stripped back to its theatrical elements in 'a fusion of instantaneous poses' (Stiegler 2011: 13) controlled by the *mnemotechnesis* of an inhuman memory machine in which non-inhuman life in-exists as 'an element of the image'. Herein lies the material basis of modern film as 'visual abstraction' (Kovács 2007: 21).

By making the characters' actions depend on camera movement and placement, Antonioni's film reverses the synchronization of the viewer's time with story-time into 'death-time' (Stiegler 2011: 30), desyncrystallizing the viewer's self-consciousness through the apparatus by way of its *dispositif* – the *spiel* or playing out of chances – whereby the film individuates itself, affirming its sovereign right to be. In the turned position, the viewer is placed in a view from nowhere in which gestures are performed for the camera by camera dupes: *automatons* acting out a sequence of possible poses in cinematic time slowed to approaching degree zero. The *automatons* are doubled on themselves insofar as they are both for the camera and for the character they could be, posing as possible ways of being without sufficient means of making them real in psychologically motivated action, yet with enough reality in them to play with and against the camera as *figures of resistance*.

In its re-performance of automated doubling (the *imago* effect), the camera brings the cinematic *muse* to life as an autoaffecting puppet free from the norms of narrative motivation, while bound nevertheless to the technics of film as a counter-praxis of figural placing which is also a *testing of limits*. In this way, the film tells of a love affair acted out by the two protagonists – Vittoria and Piero – who repeatedly

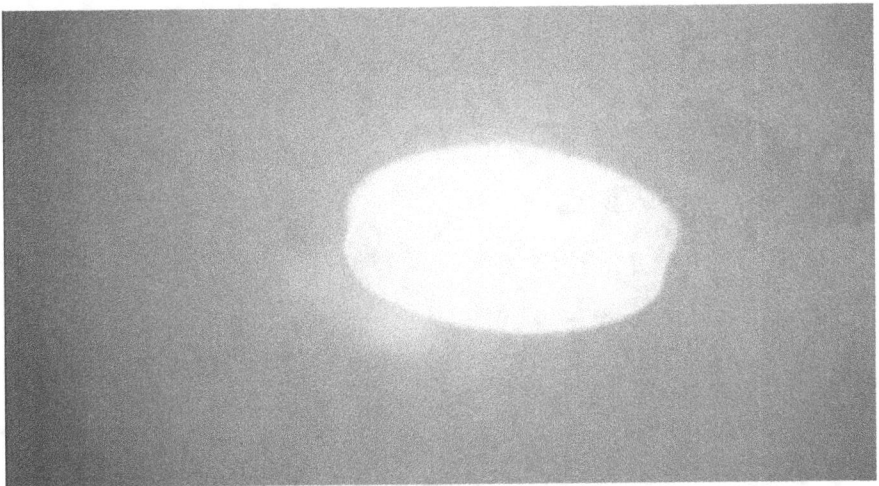

Figure 4.2 The blinding light of the *real*. *L'Eclisse*, dir. Michelangelo Antonioni (1961).

fail to consummate their desire for each other, the failure succeeding in telling us 'that cinema, which brings many such coincidences into juxtaposition, has no need of them' (Stiegler 2011: 31). In its final moments, the film breaks into a montage sequence where the camera wanders through the streets of Rome strangely emptied of life, retracing the steps of the two would-be lovers who, having walked these streets before, are nowhere to be seen, their onscreen presence having been erased from the memory of the film but with its trace persisting as a haunting after-effect (*Nachträglichkeit*). In saying that it has no need of them, the film suffers the traumatic after-effect of their loss – a *Verneinung* (negation) that paradoxically says what it does not want to say (Freud 1984: 437).

In the persistent failure of images to transcend their material reality as trace effects of the camera apparatus, *anamnesis* collapses onto a surface of hypomnesic memory in which desire has been captured in a technical drive stripped of inner motivation, the camera's aimless wandering having no purpose other than to announce the catastrophe of a world bereft of the capacity to make itself meaningful for the life of humans as nothing more than dupes of the apparatus. Having given its characters life, the film then takes it away to bear witness to its *res gestae*: the visible remainder persisting on the screen in the death-time of chance in which an event which should have happened in the logic of happy endings becomes a catastrophic event anticipated in its aftermath as self-inflicted

Figure 4.3 Mushroom-shaped tower suggesting atomic explosiveness. *L'Eclisse*, dir. Michelangelo Antonioni (1961).

oblivion: the erasure of the lovers from the screen by its own memory trace. The film concludes on one powerful shot of a phosphorescent street lamp glowing so brightly that it threatens to liquidate the screen, engulfing the *theatrum mundi* with atomic explosiveness in the blinding light of the *real*. The film circles back on itself in an empty *theatrum mundi* filled with luminescent *schein* emanating from the blast in which the atomic light of the street lamp works its way through the rest of the film as the flickering of the *real* traced across the surface of the crystalline sphere, carrying the catastrophe with it. Images drift across the screen in undulations of a collapsing quantum field in which everything remembered is always already on the cusp of being erased, leaving us abandoned to ourselves without a cure which would not also be toxic. In what way does the film effect the called-for cure?

As the opening credits of *L'Eclisse* roll across the screen, we hear a jaunty popular song followed by piano-orchestral music, its doom-laden mood contradicting the *élan* of the song preceding it as if foretelling its message of love as 'radioactivity/it gives me shivers'. This pharmacological vision of love as both curative and toxic is played out in the chiasm of a catastrophic event – an event that will have happened in its aftermath – foretold as apocalyptic in the mushroom shape of an atomic cloud inhering in random objects spread through the film. The catastrophe that will have happened is already here – foreshadowed in the trace of what the camera has left behind – as an *eclipse* in which the future superposes the present with its erasure. The response of the film to the eclipse it has itself triggered is to open a new dimension of the *real* in which the future is felt as an inhuman sensibility (it 'gives me the shivers') neutralizing the actions of the characters in deadlocks of desire: the condition of industrial life in which all values are reduced to equivalences of exchange, stripping the world of meaning. Vittoria's musings on life's *ennui* in which 'a piece of cloth, a needle, a thread, or a book ... or a man is the same thing' reflect the condition of her reality as a figure of inexistence: a self-consciousness stripped of its capacity to project a future, but with enough reality in her to know that she is unfree.

What is at stake in *L'Eclisse* is the anamnesic health of a generation of young people – their capacity to remember – in which the value of their lives has been taken from them, the 'feeling of existence' (Stiegler 2019: 8) neutralized by 'the nihilistic conception of value wherein everything tends towards equivalence' (2016a: 85). Trapped inside a capitalistic world of money speculation, which, in Jean-Luc Nancy's terms, 'absorbs well beyond the monetary or financial sphere but thanks to it and with regard to it, all the spheres of the existence of humans, and along with them, all things that exist' (2015: 5), Vittoria can only react to the invisible forces pressing in on her, sapping her desire for life. Without the noetic capacity to project otherwise in the exercise of a healthy *anamnesis*, she can only react to what she encounters with no purpose other than to resist that which persists in her – the will to nothingness and 'the subsequent loss of *reason as such*' (Stiegler 2019: 8).

In *L'Eclisse*, the problem of general equivalence in a capitalist world of market exchange pervading 'all things that exist' is highlighted in two lengthy stock exchange scenes in which we see share traders including Piero – Vittoria's future lover – engrossed in a share market run in full swing. The frenzied activity of buying and selling in the trading pit turns into a black hole sucking energy into itself, creating monetary value seemingly out of thin air. These scenes of anthropic excess are juxtaposed against scenes of anthropic malaise in Vittoria's liaison with Piero. His fast-moving direct style in which he seeks to control life is counteracted by her slow-moving indirect style which, lacking the direction she seeks, refuses life in his seeking to control her, one negating the other in a still-born romance played out as failure in the death-time of the film. The death-time of the film is its being-towards-death into which the story incessantly collapses, projecting an all-encompassing mood or *Stimmung* threatening erasure of all values in catastrophic meaninglessness.

The achievement of Antonioni's film is to have undercut the tragedy that his film could have been with a tragicomic inflection in the camera's blind groping for meaning in the insufficiency of non-inhuman memory to guide it into a coherent vision of the world, rendering its wanderings incoherent in its continual movement. Yet, within this incoherence, we find that the threat has been averted by re-performing what the catastrophe will have been as its own metacinematic deconstruction: the superposing of the *real* of the cinematic apparatus on itself as modern self-reflexive cinema, sustaining its sovereign right to be the film that it is. Noetic capacity is restored in the realization that I have survived the catastrophe of meaning the film's refusal to not be has enacted. In *my* non-indecisive action, the film has set me free.

Blindness of the seeing eye

Let us for a moment return to the opening shot of *L'Eclisse*, the still life photograph that suddenly comes to life, and consider what we see and what we don't see in what we see; that is, what is unconscious in what we see, suppressed in the preconscious (Freud 1976: 691–2). What we see are a table, books, pens, a coffee cup, and some *thing* yet to be objectivized into something meaningful. What we don't see in what we see is the sleeve of a shirt which suddenly appears in the *thing*'s switching to an *object* when the camera moves. What we don't see in what we see is there before our eyes in what Freud calls 'blindness of the seeing eye' (Breuer and Freud 1974: 181). Blindness of the seeing eye is the effect of *Zensur*[3] – unconscious censoring of what one does not want to see in what one sees as *repressed suppression*:[4] in Freud's case, his screen memory of a 'repulsive' event in which what he did not want to see is seen retroactively as having been seen but in a corrected way to suit his expectations of what he feels he ought to have seen.

In *L'Eclisse* what is repressed – unconsciously censored – is the *real* of the apparatus that makes images move, the camera movement effect regressed[5] in what we see coming to life in the movement of the man's arm, hallucinating the film with auto-affecting life as if some mysterious force had caused it to happen. What we don't see in what we see is the apparatus retreating in the *real* of what we see 'corrected' when we see the indeterminate thing *as* a man's arm moving. Blindness of the seeing eye is a retroaction of seeing in which what I missed seeing is seen after the fact as if it had not been missed as a 'missed...encounter' (Lacan 1981: 69), thereby disguising the real moment of having missed it as a *blind spot* in what I see.

In Walter Benjamin's terms, the human eye sees by way of an optical unconscious which is both in the eye and outside in the apparatus through which we see: a technological blindness of the seeing eye in which the camera, having taken hold of human perception, opens up 'a vast and unsuspected field of action' (Benjamin 2002: 117) as *Spielraum* (room to play) in poietic release. In its desyncrystallization of the viewer's perception, Antonioni's camera opens up the optical unconscious of a camera apparatus regressed in what we see in which Benjamin's unsuspected field of action plays itself out in what the camera sees from *its* perspective through blind spots pervading his films. In the following section, we pick up on these ideas in Bresson's *Une Femme Douce*, in which actors acting for the camera act out blindness of the seeing eye in terms of a modernist-realist style of film, stripped of its theatrical tendencies.

Bresson's blind camera

In his *Notes on the Cinematographer*, the film director Robert Bresson has said that there are 'two types of film: those that employ the resources of the theatre (actors, direction, etc.) and use the camera in order to *reproduce*; [and] those that employ the resources of cinematography and use the camera to *create*' (1986: 5). In accordance with this formulation, Bresson makes films that disavow theatrical reproduction in order to release the creative gesture of the camera as a critical reflection on the cinematographic apparatus itself. His aim is to deconstruct the residual theatricality of the cinema by exposing the cinematographic apparatus to the repression of its mechanisms, thereby liberating the creative gesture of the camera from the deadening effects of industrialized life. In the flattened 2D surface of the film, he discovers the power of the *irreal*: 'the power your (flattened) images have of being other than they are. The same image brought in by ten different routes will be a different image ten times' (32). By focusing on the surface of the film as flattened images coming to life on the screen, we access the recursive process of memorizing 'brought in by ten different routes' in the irreality of the film's optical unconscious. In Bresson's version of the optical unconscious, the camera reveals another nature in the release of the eye from its repression by the cinematographic mechanism as 'a way of recovering the automatism of real life' (59). This other nature which, as Vilém Flusser has argued with respect to the photographic gesture, is the *real* of industrialized technics reified in the cinematic gesture of release. Let us turn briefly to Flusser's argument for elucidation on this point.

In his book *Towards a Philosophy of Photography* (2000), Flusser proposes a thesis on the post-industrial apparatus as a second-order cybernetic system with the camera and its operator – the photographer – as its *organon* of vision. His aim is to draw attention to photographic gestures as 'acts of resistance that have been avoided' (33). What does he mean by this? For Flusser, the camera blends with its operator into an apparatus as 'a thing that lies in wait ... [in] readiness to spring into action' (21). In its camera-readiness, the apparatus *anticipates* the photographer's plan – her 'intention' (46) – by seizing upon images to remember as 'the realization of one of its possibilities', leaving others unremembered as possibilities not spent. Here, the photographer becomes a player playing *against* the camera in its censoring of views – *this* view rather than *that* view out of a range of possible views – in anticipation of the correct shot secreted in the program's settings to be discovered by the operator's *spiel* – *in situ* praxis of searching for new views to elude capture as in a game of chess (27), for instance, as we have already seen, Antonioni's praxis of placing his actors before the camera to see the *whole* of what could be seen from the camera's point of view together with his, thereby avoiding its restrictions in non-indecisive action. By playing against the camera, the photographer-player avoids the program's settings in a yet-to-be censored view – a *view from nowhere* – drawing on unremembered potential; to keep itself in play, the camera adjusts its settings via its operator (either manually by the photographer or automatically by the algorithm or a combination of both) to censor the view. As 'an act[ ] of resistance that ha[s] been avoided' (33), the photographic gesture affirms the reality of the view by negating other views that could have been seen in a process of adjustments and corrections inside the camera apparatus opening into new views (cybernetic feedback). Henceforth, I will refer to these acts of resistance that have been avoided in the *spiel* of a camera apparatus as *acts of avoidance*.

Striking a Heideggerian note, Flusser warns of 'danger lying in wait' (2000: 74), the threat posed by anticipatory control of the apparatus as *Gestell* – enframing – usurping the creator-role of the operator in opening up new views, leading to suppression of the creative spirit in 'rigid automation' (79). The danger lies in the automation of Freudian *Zensur* – unconscious censoring – by the apparatus as 'unintentional, rigid and *uncontrollable* functionality' (74, emphasis added): the threat of unchecked automated censoring in which the ego's desire to remember is destroyed by drive in entropic forgetting as blindness of the seeing eye – what the camera sees in not seeing – amplified into a generalized blindness to imaginative possibility in the industrialization of visual projection, when the system of perception in which the censoring apparatus operates closes in on itself, rendering everyone inside it locked into a rigid way of seeing, incapable of seeing what they are seeing otherwise (hyper-syncrystallization). Can this danger be avoided? Yes, if the auto-*Zensor* apparatus of the camera – its 'conscious' program designed to seek efficiently for the right shot – can be turned against itself in the manner of a *dispositif* – an anti-system inside the apparatus generating acts of avoidance to give shape to imaginative possibility in what lies ahead.

I propose an organological approach to films which uncovers the blindness of the seeing eye turned against itself by a mechanical creator: the operator working both with and against the machine through the tool-use of a *dispositif* – an *in situ* praxis of resistive gestures specific to this film – exposing *Zensur* to the apparatus that supports it as *consciousness of unconsciousness* within the field of views in which perception of onscreen action takes place. By turning the apparatus against itself we open our eyes to the optical unconscious discoverable in the operations of the camera, the trace-effects of which are the images we are seeing on the screen. The optical unconscious, which, in Walter Benjamin's terms, arises in the camera's capacity to see more than the human eye can see (Benjamin 1999: 510–11, 2002: 117), leads us into the archival future of the memory trace carried by the apparatus equipped with an inhuman eye: an eye that sees what the human eye sees as *irreal* – both unconscious and conscious, virtual and actual, one disappearing in the appearing of the other. Following Bresson, my plan is to shift the focus of analytical observation to the disguise of the apparatus in passing off *irreal* images as real to effect an artificial naturalness of the camera's gesture. My aim is to reclaim this Bressonian camera gesture as a means of uncovering the irreality of its images, their doubled reality in 'conscious unconsciousness' of their in-existence as traumatypes of the dead past coming to life on the screen to act out the death-that-awaits for the camera. The danger of capture by the apparatus is avoided by reclaiming the power of the *Zensor* – the critical eye – to see what the human eye has been trained not to see: the repressed other suppressed in the optical unconscious of the film.

The optical unconscious works to make what we don't see in what we see visible in the film's preconscious – barely noticeable gestures regressed in the detail of characters' actions. What we *do* see in the conscious register is what we *don't* see in the preconscious register as *Spielraum*, releasing the eye to see otherwise. In its readiness to 'spring into action' (Flusser 2000: 21), the camera anticipates the ego's desire for satisfaction in the film's memory drive (memorizing), which, in terms of Bresson's films, consists in voice-over recollections accompanied by images that show more than the character sees in the preconscious register of the film. Seeing with the camera-eye, I will observe the work of the optical unconscious in Bresson's *Une Femme Douce* (1969) to show how the director employs his camera as a creative tool to make us see what we don't see in what we see, thereby exposing the cinematic apparatus as a mechanism of repression to critical reflection.

Une Femme Douce

In our pursuit of the work of the optical unconscious, we are looking for cracks in the façade of the film, moments when things don't make sense; points at which – in recalling Freud's blindness of the seeing eye – consciousness encounters something that does not fit expectations, in Fichtean–Gadamerian terms, a moment of *Anstoß* in which I am summoned to exercise critical reason in a *methexis* to make sense of what I see. In *Une Femme Douce*, we find one such moment in an early scene told in flashback, in which a young woman – whose suicide we have just missed – enters a pawn shop to sell a camera clutched to her chest, shielded behind books and folders. As she stands in the queue waiting her

Figure 4.4 Elle conceals the camera as she approaches the counter. *Une Femme Douce*, dir. Robert Bresson (1969).

Cinematic Time 115

Figure 4.5 Elle places the camera on the compass set. *Une Femme Douce*, dir. Robert Bresson (1969).

Figure 4.6 Luc picks up the camera which becomes another camera with a funeral urn superimposed on it. *Une Femme Douce*, dir. Robert Bresson (1969).

turn to be served, the owner of the shop – her future husband, at this stage unknown to her and she to him, serving customers at the counter where he will soon be serving her – says in voice-over from a future time 'I paid no attention to her at first', as if to emphasize that he *will have* noticed her. On reaching the counter, the woman offers the camera to the man, placing it on top of a compass set left there by the previous customer. The man behind the counter picks the camera up and briefly inspects it, saying, once again in voice-over, 'I was being smart' as he looks down at the camera in his hands, followed by 'what a treasure' spoken in diegetic time as he looks up at her and she at him, his voice, speaking in free indirect mode, referring to both the camera and the woman as things to be possessed through 'smart' business dealing. Upon this, the woman takes the camera back and leaves the shop. This complex set of gestures bears careful unpacking.

In the *conscious* register of the film, these shots provide information about the main characters – the suicidal young woman desperate for cash, the professional looking man with a cold and calculating manner intent on profiting from her misfortune – as causal agents of the film's narration. However, in its *preconscious* register the film reveals a matrix of hardly noticeable detail that says much more than this. If we look carefully at the exchanges between the man and the woman, we note that as she takes her camera back, he appears to retain it. In a filmic sleight of hand, the compass set has disappeared while the camera splits in two, the one now in Luc's hands with what appears to be a small funeral urn superimposed on it: her life symbolized by the camera *she* retains becomes her death in the camera *he* retains. Here we are confronted with a crack in the film's façade in which what we thought was natural movement is artificially contrived, superposing the urn on the camera to create a *life death* dyad in the form of a Laruellean two in-One – ontologically bound into the compossible state of the couple being *together-apart*. Upon this, the man says in voiceover 'At that moment I suddenly noticed her'. What are the possibilities opened up in this non-coincidence of what is said in voiceover and what we see on the screen?

In the moment when the man notices her, the camera she offers him splits into a *life death* object, transitioning between the conscious and preconscious registers of the film, so that what is repressed in the preconscious register – the unconscious of that which remains unsaid – suddenly becomes conscious in an exchange that does and does not take place as a blind spot in the film. When Luc says 'at that moment I suddenly noticed her' he is ventriloquizing Bresson's directions for viewing the film: Elle can only be seen by Luc in his not seeing her, in the blindness of the seeing eye of the camera that sees more than Luc sees. Luc's gaze is *carried* by the apparatus of seeing which allows us to see what he does not see in what he sees as a quantum effect taking place in the optical unconscious of the film.

In Bresson's film, Elle's camera acts as a substitute for the other camera, 'the one working now' (Cavell 1979: 126): the apparatus recessed in what we see switching the way we notice things from the conscious to the preconscious register, giving us access to the *real* of the optical unconscious; the prescient light of the kino-eye that sees what I see and what I don't see, one disappearing in the appearing of the other. In Stiegler's terms, Elle's camera is a transitional object: a *pharmakon* vested with potential for either curative or toxic effects through which the living must pass in seeking a 'life ... worth living' (2013: 2); that is, a life tested by the ordeal of truth as *life death*. How does this testing take place in *Une Femme Douce*?

The gesture of offering and taking back the camera suggests a kind of game – what Freud calls the *Fort/da* game (gone/there), where a child tests the limits of her control of the world around her in the compulsion to repeat (1984: 284–5). By offering and then taking back the transitional object (the camera), the woman is testing her power over the man: her capacity to give herself to him while refusing at the same time, in Freudian terms, *Verneinung* or disavowal (437–42). Luc's voiceover is thus ironic: it is not concerned with the expression of tragic fate in the manner of the *film noir* voiceover, but with announcing the tragicomic play of masks switching between life and death by marking the difference between what Luc claims ('she is mine') and what is seen by the camera (he does not have her). What the viewer does not see in the conscious register comes to light in the preconscious register (when we switch our attention to it), as the sheer fact of the situation: the 'treasure' that Luc claims to have found in Elle – transitioned through the camera exchange that does and does not take place – is unable to be possessed at the moment of claiming it since she has not appeared in what is yet to happen. Paradoxically, it has happened *but not yet*. Elle's presence is repressed in Luc's failure to see her ('I paid no attention to her at first'), which becomes the blind spot of the film, concealing her phantasmic return as the living dead, which is precisely how she now appears in its undistorted form as a normal looking young woman. She *will have become* the repressed figure repeatedly returning in the *Fort/da* game climaxing in her suicide, a traumatic Death Event occurring at the beginning of the film as its last instance in which the camera – having arrived a moment too late to see her jump to her death – fails to capture. *Yet there is return* in exchanges that do and do not take place.

In *Une Femme Douce*, the camera acts as a transitional object between Luc and Elle in their desire to be together, which, at the *symbolic level*, equates with the social norms of 'wife' and 'husband', but at the *reflexive level* with model and director. The term *model* is used by Bresson to describe the roles played in his films as prototypes rather than characters; Bresson insists that actors must become models of the type they are directed to play, not as convincing stage performances but as dupe negatives of the cinematic apparatus (1986: 4). The transition occurs in the interpenetration of the conscious and preconscious registers of the film, where the viewer is denied the satisfaction of seeing the stereotype of husband and wife consummated in a happy ending; where the fulfilment of desire is short-circuited by the mechanical repetitions of the models' actions. In taking all of these points into account, I propose three transitional phases: a *symbolic phase* in which characters act out stereotypes in the symbolic register; a *reflexive phase* in which the types are carried by the apparatus from the conscious to the preconscious register; a *figural phase* in which the images transform into *traumatypes* – repressed others – by passing through the other two phases. All three phases are at work within each other, dynamizing the film in a complex play of figures becoming real in the story told. The task of figural analysis is to observe the apparatus at work in the film as an eye that sees and does not see, which, in Bresson's film, releases Elle from Luc's possessive gaze, triggering the compulsion to repeat in the return of the repressed as Elle and Luc seek to become the happy couple they *will have never been*. Freud saw clearly that dreams were the prototype for generalized fantasy and story-telling in which the compulsion to repeat tests the reality of the world *as it is imagined to be*. Bresson's film exemplifies the fantasy of the happy couple in its traumatypical mode, seized by the compulsion to repeat as a symptom of repression, which is also the warning sign of the malaise of industrialized life carried by the automation of the cinematograph as *amor fati*. His achievement is to have shown how the creative gesture of the camera can reveal the work of repression in an acinematic style of film in which the transformational power of images is put to the test.

In Stiegler's model of the dream, the prototype of repression is split between traumatypes and stereotypes: the former being 'either repressed, or expressed by default as manifesting in symptoms and fantasies', while the latter work through 'habits and volitions' repressing the traumatype in the maintenance of life as it is imagined to be by an audience transindividuating into a *We* (Stiegler 2018: 155), a pluralized consciousness metastabilized through 'a *symbolic apparatus* that is not situated *only* in the brain, but in *society*, that is, in those other brains with which *this* brain is in relation' (2020: 197). The model activates traumatypes and stereotypes in a self-differentiating process in which the former generates differences while the latter represses them. In Lacanian terms, the appearance of the traumatype Elle to the controlling master Luc invokes the stereotype of the patriarchal happy couple – the sought for state of equilibrium between male and female – failing to consummate in the compulsion to repeat, triggering a cycle of failed attempts stripped to its mechanical operation by Bresson's prototyping procedure in which models acting under direction, play out a simulated marriage as cinematic 'bastard theatre' (Bresson 1986: 7). Stereotypes confirm reality by repressing their traumatypes as the wound of trauma seeking a cure (Stiegler 2016: 88), while traumatypes challenge their stereotypes to account for the repression suffered. The cure lies in exposing the stereotype to its traumatype repressed in the preconscious by cracking the façade of the dream, exposing the apparatus of repression to the critical eye vested with reflexive self-consciousness (consciousness of self-consciousness) as potential to initiate change through the exercise of noetic freedom manifest in the analysis undertaken here. The exercise of noetic freedom is a moral act in the sense that it duplicates the freeing claim of the traumatype in facing the stereotype it refuses to obey and holds to account for its suffering, thereby releasing possibility otherwise *in me* as the *right* of the analysis itself.

Methexis: A pharmacological model

Throughout this book, we have been seeking to establish a methexical way of relating to films through a hermeneutic turn to the past by turning into the archival future: the future 'to come' in the anteriority of what it 'will have been'. Following Gadamer, *methexis* is a participation or sharing of an experience of the past in the present through the reception of views from the past offering themselves for reading or interpretation. In the *methexis*, the receiver responds to questions posed by the views' inability to account for inconsistencies between the sphere in which they are located and the sphere in which they are received/perceived as interpretive challenges. The analysis of Antonioni's and Bresson's films in this chapter has been undertaken from within the sphere I presently occupy, reducible to a personal milieu expanding into a field of views on an open horizon in which other spheres come into view refracted through the *speculum* of my sphere. The films appear to me in their crystalline forms as messages from the past, opening themselves to a future that has already past and is passing in the turning of the crystalline sphere. The turning of the spheres dynamizes the whole in its parts, such that my reading of the films is reflected in the whole projected into the future. In the *methexis*, the reflections are themselves refracted through the spheres as quantum effects such that changes in one sphere effect changes in others (entanglements, superposition) as a *whole* affecting itself. What is at stake in the readings is not a matter of delving into the past in searching for lost origins, but a way of opening up a new path within it, which, if taken, would change our orientation to the future, placing it in a new frame of reference. Insights gained from the readings do not reflect back on the past, but project into the future anteriorially – refracted through the sphere in which the *methexis* takes place – other than the future before us now.

I opened this chapter with Stiegler's lament on the state of immiseration in the current age of industrial capitalism in which young people's lives have been reduced to 'symbolic misery' in having their capacity to imagine life otherwise stripped from them by the algorithmic governmentality of hyper-capitalist consumerism, leading to what Daniel Ross calls 'psychic and collective anaphylaxis': the erasure of the incalculability of human life – its singular existence as a condition of finite freedom – and, as a consequence, the collapse of the systems that sustain it (2021: 19). The cure proposed by Stiegler is by way of the *pharmakon* – the transitional object through which we must pass from the current age into another (2013: 4, 2018: 70). A cure is effected by exposing the operation of the *pharmakon* to its control mechanisms as an organic machine inside which we find manifestations of the *thing*: in Lacanian terms, a phantasmic master, the ultimate form of which is a fully automated machine thinking for itself (artificial intelligence as a metaphysical construct – the ghost in the machine). The aim of analysis is to show that the master's power is not real but phantasmic – 'an illusory point of transference whose misery is finally revealed' (Žižek 2022: 117) – dissolved into the nothingness that it is by the counter-reasoning of a *critical gaze*. The critical gaze does not come from nowhere but must be won back from the *automaton* by turning within it in a freeing claim, thereby releasing control into concernful care: a mode of feeling for the future which Stiegler calls *neganthropy*. The work I have undertaken on films in this and other chapters is motivated by the call of the *pharmakon* – its ambiguous lure as both toxic and curative for life – to turn in the direction of *neganthropic care* in which mastery-over is replaced by care-with.

In the next chapter, I take up the idea of the sphere in a field of views to develop a spherological model of *methexis* in which films are received in quantum terms as entangled in each other's realities, which, when viewed from the turned hermeneutic position, open themselves to a dead past whose living future is still to come. My aim is to make a provocation in the alignment of my view with views received to trigger a new frame of reference for viewing films, not as dead objects from the past but as potentials for new ways of seeing the future.

5

Spherology

Neganthropy

Throughout this book, we have been concerned with developing a figural analysis of films under the guidance of the *figural* – feeling for the future in the 'doing' of films: their 'figuring out' of some *thing* as self-questioning automations shaping what the future 'will have been' in memory unfolding on the screen. Film figuring begins when the camera reflex – the technical cut which splits time in two, between 'before' and 'after' – is inserted into an editing process, where images are 'slipped in' as falsifying fiction (the Kuleshov effect). Editing begins when the operator clicks a button to cut out a view of what the camera sees, setting in train a process in which views stored in the camera's memory – worked through with slipped-in images shaped by a *dispositif* – combine with other views in an *organization of views* aligned with means–end logic in which each view finds its place in the order of time (past, present and future) experienced by viewers capable of perceiving such views, knowing that 'I am watching a film'.

From the perspective of the views perceived, the camera reflex leaves its trace on the screen as the disjunctive synthesis of views phase-shifting into cinematic time as a form of crystalline life (piezo-electrical autoaffectivity): a projection of *light-life* bearing the memory of what was recorded and subsequently shaped into future possibility, generating metastabilizing image flow seen by non-inhuman viewers as neganthropic potential: the resistivity of *noesis* to the automation of life by machine intelligence, setting itself to work in care for the future. Neganthropic potential is neganthropic resistance in its affirmative mode, enabling the noetic capacity of the non-inhuman being inside the machine to think and imagine otherwise.

Neganthropic resistance is the 'negative entropy' (Schrödinger 1967: 71) of 'exorganological systems' (Ross 2018: 29): organic systems technicized by the prostheticization of non-inhuman life into '*exorganologically situated neganthropy* of a noetic différance' (Stiegler 2021: 230), the differing/deferring process of an incomplete I = I attempting to complete itself within a supervening technical milieu. In anthropic terms, non-inhuman life is *anthropos* (the human) understood as a noetic soul vested with the projective capacity of primary imagination within exorganological systems in which the individuating I = I phase-shifts into a transindividuating *I–We* flourishing with noetic *différance* (self-questioning incompletion). In the experience of films, there is always the possibility of a resistive gesture – a projection otherwise – as the freeing claim of the noetic soul's capacity to imagine, to dream of another life together with others in the becoming cinematic of the system, such that the I = I could always be otherwise in changing the *complexion* of the *I–We* relation – a mood change in its facial expression.

What does neganthropic resistance resist? The answer to this question lies in the substance of memory itself: the *light-life* of cosmic becoming. In *Technics and Time, 2*, Stiegler describes cosmic becoming as

> the becoming of everything 'that happens', through the operation of media and, beyond them, through the omnipotence of the new programmatology *producing space-light-time's weave of rhythms*, [which] is also the primordial phenomenon arising with informatic calculation.... Synthetic cognition is constituted as an algorithmic sequence of unfolding instructions or operations whose control loops determine recurrences qua feedback ... clearly, the structure of objects emerging from a network of neuronal automatons is (intra)temporal to the degree that all of a network's changes of state are fixed, as holistic alteration, on the 'now' as determined by the clock.
>
> 2009: 188, emphasis added

For Stiegler, cosmic becoming is the becoming of 'everything "that happens"' in a micro-/macro- excess of *light-life* ('space-light-time') arising in the informational 'structure' of mnemotechnical objects (films, videos, digital images, etc.), *itself* conditioned by the recursive processing of trace-data in the calculative cognition of algorithmic sequencing opening to the outside in *real connections*[1] to the organic world, without which the energy of the system governing the light-life captured within it would dissipate in the entropic tendency towards degree zero: 'the natural tendency of things to go over into disorder' (Schrödinger 1967: 68). Put simply, a mnemotechnical object such as a film holds itself together in the 'now' of the viewing experience by resisting entropy (neganthropic resistance) in the light-life of cosmic becoming flowing through it.

The technical cut carried by the flow of light-life introduces a void in-between before and after as *real* – the nothingness of a blank screen or *view from nowhere*, without which a view from somewhere could not be had and the film could not eventuate *there* on the screen. Projection transforms piezo-electrical flux into autoaffecting images moving through the blankness of a screen regressed in them: a process of ideation in which activities on the screen open up possibilities in *feeling for the future* in the sense of blind probing without knowing where or what this future is. Checks in progress (Fichtean–Gadamerian *Anstoß*) induce counter-movement in the projection of light-life in which ideation collapses into the doing of the film as figures moving between before and after, in the void of nothingness into which possibilities are released from their rationalization in the ordering of images; that is, released from their employment in the efficiencies of means–end logics of story-telling as a *screen event*.

Figures are incompletions seeking the idea that 'will have' completed them had the completion succeeded; if they were to complete themselves, activity would cease and life would regress into death as entropic oblivion. Figures *forbear* – go on going on – in their incessant failure to complete themselves, thereby releasing the light-life of autoaffecting images from the death-that-awaits in self-annihilating erasure. The *figural* is the process of *life death* shifting back and forth between ideation and materialization in ongoing incompletion as the past becoming future anterior to itself, expressed in the past conditional tense of 'will have been' – a persistence of the past in the present concretizing into memory carried by technical supports. The concretizing of memory *persists* as neganthropic resistance: the 'resistance to the resistance' of drive, where drive is blind probing of the apparatus seeking efficiencies of operation through the gap opened up by the cut of the camera reflex, the trace of which is left on the screen as the *cut of the real* in which each view from somewhere invokes a view from nowhere as a blank screen filled with pure potential.

Neganthropic resistance is the resistive stance taken by the human inside the organic machine, exercising noetic capacity to imagine otherwise in *care for the future*, which, for Stiegler, is entailed in the fantasy of dreaming, where the traumatype of repressed otherness returns as the *pharmakon* calling for wrongs to be put right to redress an injurious event – the fictionalized quasi-cause of something that did not happen but will have happened in story-telling (2018: 95, 163). From the perspective of neganthropic resistance, film figures are the 'doings' of a counter-tendency to resist the limits of the machine in care for life, understood both therapeutically and propaedeutically as the *pharmakon* of *life death* opening within the bifurcating paths of an exorganological mechanism as the mechanical creativity of film insofar as it is for the human and not the machine.

A spherological view

From the perspective of cosmic becoming, organology becomes *spherology* – an account of the organ of perception inside the sphere in which films are viewed as noetic 'seeing otherwise' in views received from other spheres laid out across a planetarium dome – the sphere's surface – full of potential to see all views from all times receding into the immemorial past in cosmic becoming, the viewer's view carried along with them. What is a sphere? In spatial terms, a sphere is a self-embracing 'orb-shaped membrane' (Sloterdijk 2016: 52) separating itself from other spheres, for instance the earth's atmosphere coming in-between the earth-globe (the earth's spherical shape) and the sphere of outer space. One can imagine the earth's atmosphere in temporal terms as an unwinding sphere laid out in a horizontal projection in which the past embraces its future (Bergson's fundamental insight). A *temporalized sphere* is a surface membrane separating *before* and *after* in a gap that refuses to close, without which the past would compress into the timeless present of an eternal return in which the newness of a beginning could never eventuate.

Conceived in its temporal dimensions, a sphere embraces and is embraced by piezo-electrical light-life bearing memory in pulsating rhythms along an unwinding twisted surface – a Möbius strip – in which before and after intertwine by surfacing in and out of each other in a quantum field of non-local interactivity. A spherological frame of reference is a view from the in-between, refracted through the surface membrane that sustains light-life in its capacity for replication, either organically or technically or in combination, which is a view of the dead past surfacing in and out of the living future (across its twisted surface) as the becoming of the whole of time – the 'becoming of everything "that happens"' (Stiegler 2009: 188) – part of which is captured by the camera apparatus and concretized into mnemotechnical objects such as films, forming themselves into crystalline images moving across a screen. By combining the organic with the technical in novel arrangements, noetic life is phase-shifted into self-sustaining crystalline spheres as *life death* played out in the turning of the sphere – cut out of the continuum of time and the determinations of natural order – in which a faceted light-life future 'begins to have been always possible' (Bergson 2007: 82).

A film-sphere is the self-embracing entwinement of film *spiel* – concretizations of '*play drive*' (Hui 2019: 236), a synthesizing process of drives holding the films together in the internalization of trace-data carried by piezo-electrical light-life running through them in metastabilizing image flows. In its cosmic dimensions, the film-sphere manifests vestiges of the whole of time resonating in each film that passes through it, making it shine with cinematic light-life which is what we see on the screen as normalized vision; that is, cosmic vision rendered suitable for human perception. In Stiegler's terms, the film-sphere is the crystalline formation of an idiotext (2021: 189): a spiralling weave of mnesic traces (trace-data) passing through each film, opening them from within to an outside exceeding all ends in entropic dissipation. Seen through its crystalline formations, the film-sphere embraces and is embraced by each film passing through it in a Gadamerian field of views fusing and defusing on an open horizon, charging them with piezo-electrical autoaffectivity simultaneously affecting views received from other spheres, such that the whole reverberates in its parts in a unilateralized-amplifying becoming of cinematic light-life held together in the views received in a totalizing effect of mood or atmosphere (*Stimmung*). Such processes can be understood in quantum terms as the micro-/macro- entwining of cosmic elements undulating in spacetime quantum fields saturated with entanglement, superposition and non-local interactivity metastabilizing the coherence of image flows in a paraconsistency of its elements becoming real in any given experience of a film-in-question (the wave/particle phenomenon).

We live by embracing and being embraced by the sphere that sustains us in our neganthropic being as transindividuals vested with noetic capacity – constrained by our mortality in being-towards-death but with the freedom to imagine ourselves otherwise in feeling for the future and caring for it – which, in Stiegler's terms, is our capacity to dream. In temporal terms, dreams are views from a projected future in which we look for anteriority through the refracted reflections of a screen-membrane – a *speculum* – through which we see ourselves seeing: a doubling reflex that phase-shifts us out of our mortal selves and into the *real* of an abyss – the void of the in-between – in which we see otherwise in what we see. Our *dream life* is sustained through the screen-membrane embracing us with after-life carried by piezo-electrical currents of phosphorescent flux running through us in cosmic flows of electro-communicational light-life concretized in *mnemotechnesis* – films, television, internet sites, audiovisual processes of all kinds – as the spectral reality of the dead past in the living future haunting us with *Nachträglichkeit*.

In looking back through our journey from organology to spherology we find that we have always been working within a spherological frame of reference in which cinematic time – the time of industrial life mediated by an organic machine (the cinematograph projecting images on the screen and in me-us as an

I–We) – is itself experienced through the turning of a crystalline sphere. Lodged within the cinematograph, non-inhuman memory is already shaped by technical memory (*mnemotechnesis*) passing through a complex of spheres in which I see views of the past moving across the surface of the sphere in which I am presently situated. The passing-through of *mnemotechnesis* gathers what has passed into the 'will have been' as the future already remembered but not yet. From this future anterior perspective, non-inhuman memory looks backward in order to see what lies ahead in a *field of views* laid out anteriorially before me as the 'will have been' through the *speculum* of the sphere crystallized with time-images in which I can see myself seeing otherwise (the split subject). To grasp the complexity of views arrayed anteriorially before me requires a cosmic mode of seeing the whole of time in which each view is part, concurrent with the dimensions of a *spherical model*: the prismatic modality of a sphere refracting possible worlds through the flux of cosmic becoming (micro-/macro- flows of light-life carried by piezo-electrical currents). The shift from organology to spherology is a shift in the way we *see* the future, not ahead of us but in the anteriority of its possibilities in the turning of a crystalline sphere. In the sphere's crystalline turning, views are seen from a *planetarium perspective* as facets of time moving across the surface of a dome resonating with crystallized light-life in the cosmic flux flowing through it.[2]

Following Bergson's inversion of images and matter in Matter and Memory, an organology becomes spherology by beginning with the images of the crystalline sphere as 'impeded refraction[s]' (1988: 37) of time becoming space rolled out across the sphere's surface, where it becomes horizonal (the plane of action in Bergson's memory cone). As Bergson has proposed in Creative Evolution, concretions of time are durations of the dead past and the living future bound into each other in tensed modalities, experienced in durational time as the *tension* of images passing across themselves in the turning of a crystalline sphere, opening up '[vector] lines along which action might be taken' (1911: 22). Through our concern for films as mnemotechnical objects, we are always already moving in the turning of crystalline spheres, in futures remembered but not yet in the archival future of industrialized life in which current views are situated.

Films are durations of time unfolding on the screen through mnemotechnical procedures (*hypomnesis*) carrying interior memory (*anamnesis*) with them as the trace of the past I did not live but will have lived in the memorizing of the film passing through itself as story-telling, when an event is recalled by repeating it to remember what will have happened, this fictitious event becoming the quasi-cause that justifies the telling of the tale, one superposed on the other. The process of memorizing as story-telling draws the viewer into a crystalline sphere in the flow of images permeating the film with micro-/macro- entanglements of the dead past and the living future as quantum time, finding its measure in the paraconsistent logic of superposition and non-local interaction. Following Gadamer's receptor model of cosmic views, access to the crystalline sphere requires a turned position where I look back anteriorially to the future *as passed* and *as passing* in a visual projection to see the field of views laid out on the surface of a sphere in layers of sedimented time in which other spheres can be discerned. By adopting a planetarium perspective, I become a receptor-perceptor of the whole of the past appearing to me in faceted image formations spreading across the surface of the sphere in non-localized interaction between the dead past and the living future as *futural* (i.e. projected into the future anterior: a past that 'will have' happened), depending on my point of view and the particular layering of sedimented time in the visual projection through which my point of view is refracted *as received*. Such is a spherological view.

The character/automation split

The task before us in this chapter is to elucidate general ideas for a spherological-organological approach to film set forth in the preceding two sections by undertaking an analysis of a specific film, Florian Zeller's *The Father* (2020), a chamber film in which the time frames of past, present and future are collapsed by the director's provocation, thereby posing the problem of coherence in shifting frames of reference. By calling on quantum theory within the framework of a Stieglerian organology in which primary and secondary retentions (*anamnesis*) are carried by tertiary retentions (*hypomnesis*), we can say that the provocation *interferes* with the quantum fabric of timespace by forcing a split between the inner life of the characters (*anamnesis*) and its exteriorization in the automation of onscreen action carried by technical support (*hypomnesis*). The force of the split is the *cut of technique* executed in the 'cutting room' of the chamber (Stiegler 2014a: 8), severing the dead past from the living future to release primary imagination repressed by the means–end logic of story-telling. In the process of forcing the split, the projective capacity of the released imagination is set to work to present characters in their figural dimensions as inexistent free beings exposed to the *real* of time – its sheer potential – experienced as catastrophic meaning loss in overturned cause/effect sequencing. Sequencing is sustained – as we shall see – by the paraconsistency of visual connections in which possibilities are acted out through their irrational jointures in phase-changing leaps across the time frames collapsing on themselves.

Paraconsistency across the jointures is ensured by a *dispositif*: a productive counter-praxis working against the grain of the means–end logic of story-telling as *spiel* – the playing out of chances – alert to the possibilities of otherness in the same as leverage for phase-change. My aim is to demonstrate how the *dispositif* is capable of fashioning cinematic images through the forced character/automation split, prompting questions of the *right* of moral action, which, in a film-sphere yet to have a rule whereby undecidability can be resolved, requires a sufficiency of reason for doing so. My claim is that the rule to resolve undecidability in collapsing time frames such as we see in *The Father* is supplied by the *dispositif* called for from any one view in the field of possible views immanent within the situation in which the viewer *has* this view; that is, enjoys possession of it by *right*. Generally speaking, all films are collapsing time frame films *in potentia* – the counter-force of negentropy (the resistance to entropy) – holding the frames together in metastasis. A collapsing time frame film is one in which a *provocateur* interferes with the resistive mechanism to trigger a collapse, thereby placing the bearing of rights by all holders of views in crisis. Such is the case, I will argue, in Zeller's *The Father*.

Moral action

I draw the notion of moral action partly from Simondon and partly from Fichte to whom the former is indirectly indebted.[3] Simondon defines a moral act as a 'free act ... that has enough reality to go beyond itself and encounter other acts. There is only a *center* of the act, there are no *limits* of the act' (2020: 378). In other words, the act is moral when it acts freely in mutual self-limitation with other acts as infinitely free, in the sense that if it were left unchecked it would spread universally for the *right* of the act itself: its self-positing as freely enacted in relation to other acts, which, for Fichte, is a 'relation of free reciprocal efficacy' (2000: 33); that is, as mutually self-limiting in the way that Simondon proposes. Thus, a moral act is always constrained by the practicalities of life in *finite freedom*, where its infinitization fails to eventuate as an impossible idea which is nevertheless worth pursuing.

Moral action in film story-telling relates to the struggle between agonists in which competing claims over finite freedom are played out in mutually self-limiting action until the situation in which they occur resolves itself in a sufficiency of reason, at which point it becomes *right*. The mismatch between *anamnesis* (inward feeling) and *hypomnesis* (exteriorized mnemotechnical support) caused by the cut of technique and the ensuing ontological difference between the time of the telling and the time of the tale calls forth a *dispositif* to stitch them together in accordance with paraconsistent logic (the resolution of paradoxes in practical reason), thereby fabricating the sufficiency of reason required to resolve the competing claims as *right* for this situation.

The question of the right of moral action is raised in a *methexis* in which a viewer, who, by definition, must always *have* a view, bears witness to the situation and adjudicates on right action: what path should have been taken as a moral obligation to bring about the justice called for as *right* in this view. For the problem of right to be addressed, it is sufficient that a *methexis* be acknowledged and that the question of right be recognized as a problem *for us*. So long as these *conditions of right* are recognized, we are already on the right path of moral action. In Stiegler's terms, moral action understood as *methexis* becomes the formation of 'moral consciousness' in the 'unconsciousness' of pharmacological situations (their negative affectivity in paths not taken) as 'the most elevated modality of desire' and as 'the point of departure for a *new critique*' (Stiegler 2013: 23, emphasis added). From a pharmacological perspective, the question of moral action is posed in the workings of the film's *dispositif* – its playing out of chances in ad hoc rules to make them work as sufficiencies of reason – in the formation of moral consciousness of an *I–We* projected into the future: a *transindividuating* identity in which moral action is already becoming cinematic.

The Father: An abstract

The film to be examined is Zeller's *The Father*, which, although based on the director's stage play *Le Père*, breaks with the dramaturgical situation of live theatre to enter a crystalline sphere composed of cinematic time-images in and through which action takes place as a re-performance of an event – the death of Anthony – that has passed and is passing through the film's memorizing, the former superposing on the latter, rendering Anthony's life *irreal*: phasing in and out of *life death* enfiguring. What follows is an abstract of the film's complex memory structure:

> Zeller's film *The Father* conducts a cinematic *coup*: a totalizing effect in which everything real is doubled in *life death* irreality by collapsing the time frames that keep the present coherent to itself. In the irreality of life death thus produced, the memory-life of its protagonist Anthony, an elderly man suffering end-stage dementia, is checked by *Anstoß* – gaps and fissures in the continuity between the dead past and the living future – threatening *memory death* (absolute loss of memory) in the catastrophe of meaning generated by collapsing time frames. Anthony's response to the threat of memory death is to keep time from slipping away by making sure he always wears his watch, while holding himself fast to where he is, living comfortably in his flat, affirming his right to *be* Anthony in his emphatic declaration to those whom he perceives to be threatening him with eviction: 'Let me be absolutely clear, I am not leaving my flat'. The totalizing effect of the *coup* means that the viewer is not simply a passive onlooker but shares the catastrophic effect of collapsing time frames with Anthony in the projection of memory into the film-sphere – the complex of views – permeating events with *Nachträglichkeit* (feelings of 'afterwardsness'). The ambiguity of events wracked with retroaction can be likened to the distortions of a waking dream in which Anthony represses trauma by fabulating the past – making up stories to rationalize the threat he feels in memory loss as an intimation of the death-that-awaits, invoked in the film by a spectral presence haunting the *mise en scène* with jump cuts, rapid point of view reversals and sudden switches of time and place accompanied by barely audible mood music to announce the turning of the sphere into a new dimension.
>
> To pacify the threat of trauma, Anthony's daughter is split in two: Anne, his primary carer, lives in the present as the 'bad' daughter whose intentions Anthony cannot trust ('I suspect she wants to put me in a home'), while Lucy, the daughter who lives in the past and who has long since died in an accident, is the 'good' daughter – the daughter that Anne is not. Anthony keeps the death-that-awaits at bay by projecting it into the past of his good daughter's death which he then embraces as his love for her to counter the distrust he feels in Anne's love for him. By denying Lucy's death, he invites its return as repressed in an act of Freudian *Verneinung* (negation) as 'reality testing' (Freud 1984: 440). Having been woken in the night by Lucy's call, Anthony walks down the hallway of his flat into a hospital room – a phase-shifting quantum effect of *life death* – where we see Lucy lying critically injured on a bed hooked up to life supporting equipment. He looks down at her with the love he cannot find in Anne's love for him, thereby retaining his familial connections with the past threatened with memory loss, a

past retrojected into a future that has already happened (in the death of Lucy) but not yet (she is there barely alive on the screen before our eyes). The trauma of the death-that-awaits returns to make sense of Anthony's feelings of loss in the traumatype of Lucy, the daughter he wishes Anne were as the daughter he both trusts and distrusts in equal turns. As dementia takes hold of Anthony's mind, the film's memorizing is gradually absorbed into the void of the forgotten past – depicted in the film as a mass of memory-leaves outside the window of Anthony's hospital room – into which the camera moves as his life is erased.

This abstract of the film's complex dream-memory structure, although by no means exhaustive, indicates the general outline of a visual projection from within the film-sphere I presently occupy in a planetarium perspective motivated by problems of logical consistency in the plot structure of the film-in-question, ideas that have come to my attention in consideration of *mnemotechnesis* as a question of *right*. In what way might these ideas be addressed from the planetarium perspective I have adopted?

The *Kammerspielfilm*

In the planetarium perspective of views received, my reading of *The Father* feeds back through the *speculum* of the film-sphere I presently occupy in which other films come into view. In the view perceived, I can discern elements of *The Father* resonating in Jessner and Leni's *Hintertreppe* (*Backstairs*, 1921), a *Kammerspielfilm* from the Weimer cinema, a style of organic film melodrama made under the influence of Max Reinhardt's total theatre in which action is restricted to an enclosed set saturated with *Stimmung* (Eisner 1969: 177–84).[4] Prompted by Béla Balázs's conceptualization of the *Kammerspielfilm* as a new form of film realism (2010: 17), I find myself called into a *methexis* to resolve disparities in the view of the two films perceived by locating a problem shared between them: how to hold themselves together in visual projection through the passage of time frames: in *Hintertreppe* time frames are unfolded through chronological sequencing of actions, whereas in *The Father* time frames are collapsed into a-chronological disorder in which chronological actions are forced out of sequence. The problem boils down to this: how does the film's memorizing secure the transitions of time and space necessary to accord with sufficiencies of reason for moral action in the struggle over the *right* of a contested situation? The key idea to be considered here is Balázs's concept of visual linkage.

For Balázs, visual linkage is the 'interpolation' of images to 'let time pass' (68), by which he means to let time pass through the non-causality of their connections as the guarantee of consistency *across* the connections, binding them together in a trajection – a casting forth – to 'create a cosmic impression' (70); that is, an impression of a qualitative whole spreading across each part. Through the affordance of visual linkage, time passes through 'features' of montage rhythm with 'a quasi-musical value of its own that has only a remote and *irrational relation* to the content of the film' (129, emphasis added).[5] Visual linkage accords with the paraconsistent logic of a *dispositif* – the paralogical consistency of heterogeneous elements binding an irrationally constituted situation together – providing sufficiencies of reason for ongoing *methexis* in a continual process of self-questioning. Balázs employs the concept of visual linkage to show how the *Kammerspielfilm* can be analysed in terms of a technics of bodily gestures acted out on the screen to generate the overall mood of the film (*Stimmung*) – an atmosphere of mixed emotions simultaneously expressed as a whole in which each part reverberates with the character of a *face*, by which he means an appearing of an appearance as filmic substance with 'the moral significance of physiognomy' (36). Moral significance spreads transversally through the film as its physiognomic character – a face capable of subtle transformations of self-expression 'signalling greater inner events' (37) – as the moral disposition towards which action is incessantly striving. Balázs's concept of visual linkage as moral significance spreading through the film as its 'face' – a surface of appearances appearing as a 'mysterious play of expressions' (46) – provides us with a tool for analysing the *Kammerspielfilm* in terms of a technics of bodily gestures designed to generate total mood (*Stimmung*) out of, yet distinct from, Expressionist film.

According to Balázs, the difference between an Expressionist film and a *Kammerspielfilm* can be understood organically (films as an interactive wholes), where, in the former, the whole is given all at once in a single vision, whereas, in the latter, the whole is intimated in its parts. For instance, in the Expressionist film *The Cabinet of Dr. Caligari* (Wiene 1920), the horror of the world depicted is seen all at once in the distorted sets and twisted gestures of the actors expressing an 'inner state' projected outwardly as the dream image of 'the *living naturalness* of the human sphere' (47). In the counter-instance of Jessner and Leni's *Kammerspielfilm Hintertreppe* (1921), the terrifying reality of the 'human sphere' is not depicted all at once in a single distorted vision, but built up incrementally in the durational time of the film through encounters with small details of everyday life as a style of 'naturalistic expressionism' (47) in which the director 'attempts to animate the entire screen with the same mood that animates the faces of his actors'. Rejecting the Expressionist film's all-at-once projection of horror in which the actors act out the terror already there for us to see on the screen, the *Kammerspielfilm* progresses through visual linkages in cause/effect sequencing of action in which the organic relation of parts to an *intimated whole* is set in motion, where 'the image ... places us on the very edge of an *abyss* that opens up *before our very eyes*' (66). In these terms, the *Kammerspielfilm* becomes an experimental modelling of the artificial naturalness of a film's memory structure saturated with the radical immanence of the *real* – the abyssal future opening before the viewer's eyes as horrifying nothingness.

What would happen in a *Kammerspielfilm* if we were to collapse the time frames sustaining the progress of action? In answer, the mood of the film would switch from one of dread in the awaiting future to one in which the future has already passed and is returning in fragments, in possibilities of another life that 'will have' happened composibly related to the life enacted on the screen. This is precisely the mood projected by Zeller's *The Father*, in which visual linkage of the flow of images, far from supporting the sequencing of actions in chronological order, recasts them in a scrambled order in which the causality of actions required for the protagonist to make sense of events is constantly thwarted by the return of the repressed as *Nachträglichkeit* (feelings of afterwardsness). These moments of passage are shifts in visual linkage which are also phase-shifts in the ordering of time in which each moment occurs. To account for these shifts, I will call upon the quantum model of non-local interactivity in which events from other times are superposed on the continuing present of the film's duration. In doing so, my attention shifts its frame of reference from chronological time in which one action follows another in cause/effect sequences in the film's memory chamber to a-chronological time in which causal actions are short-circuited by collapsing time frames, wracking the chamber with quantum events of non-local interactivity in which the past as having passed passes through itself, anticipating and affecting what its future will have been.

My hypothesis is that, in the collapsing time frames of *The Father*, the question of *right* shifts from sufficiencies of reason to sustain the coherence of movement in chronological time, to their paraconsistencies in breaches of the law of the excluded middle where something said can be both true and false in a field of views in which no one view transcends another in an absolute sense. In this collapsed field of views, the right path to take cannot be assessed without transcending the view I currently occupy (i.e. to assess or judge in moral consciousness) – a transcendence *which must also fail* in the gap that refuses to close in ongoing self-questioning as an open methexical process in which the right path and the wrong path continually intertwine in *spiel* – the playing out of chances in the paradoxical situations of time passing through itself triggered by the collapsing frames. To demonstrate this hypothesis, I will take Balázs's idea of visual linkage as key to the consideration of how the collapse of time frames in *The Father* takes place.

The Father: Analysis

To demonstrate my hypothesis, I will conduct a series of passes through the film-in-question (*The Father*), in which I analyse moments of passage as views perceived in a *methexis* – a participation with others in questions raised by the incoherence of a seemingly coherent flow of images, shifting my attention from the causal relation of actions in chronological time to a matrix of visual connections linking actions into achronological jointures, the logic of which adheres to the quantum effect of superposition as non-local interactivity located in the collapsing time frames of the film.

Unlike the visual linkages of the *Kammerspielfilm* carried by the movements of actors projecting inner feelings into an outward trajectory in the unfolding of a single time frame like unwinding springs, the visual linkages in *The Father* are carried by discrete packets of spacetime energy, each of which is the time frame in which characters dwell at any given moment, their actions superposing on actions in other packets crossing over them, triggering cascading quantum events as the story unfolds across the screen. The resultant mixing of frames affects the trajectory of action with disjuncture in the linkage of its images, saturating the surface of the film with *punctum* effects (the cut of the *real*) as life death scission in which Anthony, like Lewis Payne, the condemned prisoner in Barthes's photographic *punctum*, 'is dead and he is going to die' (1993: 95). The *punctum* cut separates *before* (he is going to die) and *after* (he is dead), one superposed on the other in time frames collapsing on themselves, haunting the film's memory with *Nachträglichkeit* ('he is dead' *and* 'he is going to die') in a recurring pattern of *life death* oscillations in which the action unfolds.

In the film's collapsing framework, the death of Anthony is performed twice – the first time as fiction and the second time for the camera, one superposed on the other – invoking the *spectre of death* making itself felt in the gap between the collapsing frames. In the re-performance, Anthony 'stands on his own feet'[6] – keeps himself upright, holds himself together – in finite freedom by *refusing* the death-that-awaits: a refusal entailed in his *moral right* in demanding that he be allowed to live in his flat – 'Let me be absolutely clear. I am not leaving my flat' – as a claim for mutually self-limiting *free being* shared with members of his family as well as others – the viewers of the film drawn into a methexical relation with them including the author of this book.

Pass 1: The missed encounter

In this pass through the film, I will respond to the question of time posed to me in a moment of the continuing present when Anthony is challenged by his daughter Anne to account for his missing wristwatch. Having forgotten that he had placed the watch under the bath in his bathroom as a special hiding place for his valuables, he accuses Angela, his day carer, of stealing it. Prompted by Anne, he goes to the bathroom and finds the watch where Anne had suggested it might be, returning as if nothing had happened with the watch now strapped to his wrist. The following dialogue ensues:

> **Anne** So, you found it then?
>
> **Anthony** What? Oh yes.
>
> **Anne** You realize Angela had nothing to do with it.
>
> **Anthony** Only because I hid it, luckily just in time, otherwise I would be sitting here talking to you with no means of knowing what time it was. It's five o'clock if you're interested. I myself am interested [shows the watch face to Anne]. Pardon me for breathing.

The circular logic of Anthony's argument in which Angela could not have stolen the watch because he hides it from her, thereby confirming that she intended to steal it, indicates not merely a lapse in Anthony's *a priori* thinking into the *post hoc* fallacy of confusing antecedence with causality, but, more importantly, his employment of the *a posteriori* logic of story-telling in which a teller must transform the contingency of an unexpected event into a fictional necessity to make sense of it. Anthony is fabulating chance events that come his way by retrojecting meaning into them, as we all do in our everyday lives – rejecting things not needed while assigning significance to things that are needed for

Figure 5.1 Anthony shows his watch as proof that he can keep time. *The Father*, dir. Florian Zeller (2020).

getting by, framing and re-framing situations in terms of a select few things while dismissing others as contingent to our particular concerns as the way we *go on* in life. For Anthony, meaninglessness intrudes in moments of memory failure, which, in the urgency of the situation, require meaning to be made of them.

In Anthony's telling of his story about his missing watch, possession of the watch becomes fictionally necessary to mean that he has *kept time* with the event in which he finds himself situated to *justify* his place in the world as *right* ('It's five o'clock if you're interested. Pardon me for breathing'). However, the keeping of time in the film is controlled not by Anthony but by the visual linkage of images through which the story is told as moments of passage in which the threshold between the past as having passed and in its passing is continually crossed (the blending of other time frames in the continuing present as a manifestation of their collapse). Anthony's attempt to keep time by retrieving his watch from its hiding place, justified *après coup*, is a version of the Lacanian missed encounter (Lacan 1981: 69) in which something that did not happen happens in the retroaction of a fictional event *as missed*, carried by the film's memorizing. Possession of the watch is Anthony's guarantee that he is 'on time' in the time frame in which he happens to be dwelling as his *right to be* against accusations that he is incapable of keeping time and is at risk of being 'put in a home'.

Pass 2: Time frames

What is a time frame? In filmic terms, a time frame is a passage of the durational time of a film when the viewer's time is synchronized with the characters' time in a *continuing present*. The coherence of the present keeps the past and the future separated as independent modalities (*the* past, *the* future), to be invoked through memorizing from within the continuing of the present itself (i.e. flashbacks, flash-forwards). In this case, none of the frames intermingle, retaining their separate realities as ontologically distinct (real in themselves). On the other hand, in a collapsing time frame film, the coherence of the continuing present is rendered incoherent by the superposing of cascading quantum events in which other times intermingle as ontologically indistinct (*irreal*).

In a collapsing time frame film, the past is both *past* and *is passing* in a future stripped of its antecedent ground and thrown into the abyss of an in-between in which time's incessancy falters: where things are never in the past nor in the present, but, impossibly, both at the same time. As a viewer caught up in the collapsing time frames of Zeller's film, I find myself in multiple questioning situations in which the question of time is raised by the missed encounter with Anthony's watch and with many other missed things as well – in fact, with everything I see. From the planetarium perspective of my view, time passes through the memorizing of the film as a crystalline sphere in which facets of time out of order slide over one another, precipitating cascading quantum effects in which the death of Anthony is played out in a *game of faces* where the face of life and the face of death continually switch from one to the other. To keep time, that is, to keep himself alive in the film's memory, he must stave off death as the other face – the stranger *in him* – thereby restoring the coherence of the event so that it makes sense to him.

Pass 3: The view from nowhere

The setting up of time frames in *The Father* begins – as it does in all films – in a *view from nowhere* in the opening shot of the film in which we see a woman striding purposefully along the footpath of a London street turn into the entrance of a block of flats, walk up a set of stairs, unlock the door to one of the flats and enter. The transcendent position of the view from nowhere opens up a *space of possibility* for her to enter, without which she could not pass through her own actions in which her frame of reference is fixed in the present view. By continually anticipating her actions, the camera shifts the view from nowhere and its frame of reference to another view, sustaining her movement in constant adjustments, providing the sequence with the coherence needed to allow passage through to what lies just out of reach beyond the present view. What the viewer sees is a continually moving body in shifting frames of reference – the walking woman with a past behind her and a future ahead of her in a continuing present seemingly coherent to itself – where the coherence of the present is continually threatened with incoherence in the abyss of the view from nowhere in which it is always possible that other times might slip through. The woman's walk is itself guided by the camera's anticipation of where she is going in Flusserian *acts of avoidance*, forestalling other pathways in order to open up *this* pathway for her to pass through.

As the woman enters the flat, she calls out 'Dad, it's me.' As she calls, we see her from a shot switched 180 degrees from the previous shot inside the flat looking back to the door through which she has just entered: a view from nowhere to be repeated in the film at different times and in different time frames as they come into view. This entering-the-flat sequence is followed by a sequence of long and mid shots, switching from behind her to in front of her as she looks for her father down a hallway and in different rooms. From the screen-analytical perspective of the framing of views as 2D horizontal projection, we should not think of these shots in terms of a camera following the woman as if she were independently mobile. Rather, the moving effect of a withdrawn camera as *camera movement effect* is phase-shifting the woman's walk into the actions of an *automaton* being carried across the screen, shifting her in different directions in the time frame in which her actions make sense in the switching of points of view. In this case, coherence is not drawn from the subjective will of the character transcending her actions on the screen but through the appearing of an appearance of the *phantasm* metastabilizing in the counter-force of *drive* – the retardation of progress in the work of technical creativity – probing for the future in the cutting back-and-forth of shots generating disruptive movement as the film falls out of sync with itself in anticipating her next move. Shifting frames of reference pull the woman's body one way then another, keeping time with the voice of an opera singer heard in diegetic music bleeding into the scene from headphones through which the father she seeks listens, as if he were summoning her to the *place* where he is through an invisible thread of connectivity running through the shots.

At this point, we come to the sequence in which the woman questions her father about his watch, which, as I have suggested in Pass 1, is already fraught with uncertainty in the sequencing of its actions. The point to keep in mind here is that, in its expenditure of shots, the film is already exceeding the support required for the *anamnesis* of the story-telling – the presentation of the character's inner willingness – to be recalled. There is more in the telling than required for the tale to be told, this *more* being Balázsian visual linkage of images through 'irrational' jointures drawing phantasmic figures across the surface of the screen in the trajection of mood as *Stimmung*. As creatures of the camera automation, characters become *automatons* who, seen from the camera's point of view, traverse the screen in Flusserian acts of avoidance to keep the images metastabilized across the cuts, the irrationality of their movements having been rendered paraconsistent with themselves through visual linkage.

Pass 4: The optical unconscious

Recalling the moment when Anthony goes to search his bathroom for his missing watch, we see Anne seated on a couch looking at a painting of a young girl on the mantelpiece of the fireplace (Lucy, Anthony's dead daughter; Anne's dead sister). As she gazes at the painting, she simultaneously turns her head slightly to the right, at which point the door to Anthony's bathroom opens and he emerges with the watch, strapping it to his wrist, as if the movement of Anne's head had caused the door to open in '*ritardando*' time (Balázs 2010: 69) – decelerating like the relaxation of a wound up spring – in which her movements align with his, as if the two events were connected by some strange coincidence in which the logic of cause and effect anchored to the physical world no longer applies, calling for the paraconsistent logic of non-local interactivity in terms of Ó Maoilearca's filmic 'substance' (2015: 128) – how the film holds itself together through the immanence of its effects – to make sense of it.

Having opened our perception of onscreen movement to its figurations moving with-against the drive in its blind probing for efficiencies in seeking a way forward, we find ourselves inside a *spectral world* in which the meaning of action is bound up in the visual linkage of images dynamizing the projection of light-life in which the film hallucinates itself with phantasmic otherness. In visual linkage, the paraconsistent logic of image connections does not refer to the innerness of the characters' motivations (psychological intentions) but to the interface between actors' postures to the camera in its capacity to capture their movements and set them to work in the possibilities of a *dispositif*: a counter-praxis inside the apparatus releasing the otherness of the system in Flusserian acts of avoidance. In Walter Benjamin's terms, we have opened ourselves to the *optical unconscious* in which the camera sees what we see but the camera can always see more in 'a vast and unsuspected field of action' (2002: 117). Our task is to follow the trace of these micro-gestures as moments in which the façade of the film cracks, revealing gaps and fissures in which other times slip through. Let us continue our observations.

Pass 5: A moment of passage

The dialogue between Anne and Anthony around the missing watch develops into the question of what Anne is 'going to have to ...' when she tells her father that she is leaving London to live with her new partner in Paris whose name we find out later is Paul. 'Anne, you are going to have to what?' Anthony responds in an accusative tone, as if to wrench the truth from her in the unspoken thought that she is going to have to put him in a home. At this point, before we hear any answer from Anne, the scene switches to a view from the window in Anthony's bedroom in which we see Anne walking away in the street below, followed by an eyeline match which presents us with Anthony in profile looking out the window, telling us that this is Anthony's view. This looking-out-the-window sequence is followed by three still shots, the first two of which show other rooms in the flat, while the third returns us to Anthony's bedroom but without him in it. What are we to make of this?

If we consider these three stilled shots in the possibilities of a *dispositif* informed by Balázs's 'moments of passage', the sequence begins to make sense. This sequencing of shots is an 'interpolation' of images to 'let time pass' (Balázs 2010: 68) in which the continuity of time is eclipsed, wiping Anthony out of the scene to allow the camera to follow its own inclinations, to pass through to what comes next. In the moment of passage, the film undergoes a phase-shift from the time frame of the present which includes Anthony, to another time without him – a time yet to be framed. Placing us 'on the very edge of an *abyss* that opens up *before our very eyes*' (66), the camera is *feeling* for the future in the anterior of the film's memory yet to come into view, seeking another frame of reference in which Anthony, having been wiped from the scene, might be found. In searching for continuity between the cuts, the camera has developed mechanical self-consciousness, looking for a yet-to-be framed other-time in the 'vast and unsuspected field of action' of the optical unconsciousness in which the scene is immersed, limited to the confines of the chamber in which the action takes place. Where is the *dispositif* in all of this? The *dispositif* is the particular way this moment of passage is played out – repeated throughout the film as a praxis of ad hoc rules or *spiel* running counter to the expectations of means–end story-telling

– to both provoke incoherence and provide a sufficiency of reason for resolving it in right action. In describing the rule of actions across the frames, I am showing how the *dispositif* works as the moral disposition of the film, affirming its own *right to be* as sovereign to itself.

Pass 6: The stranger

The next shot takes us to the kitchen of the flat where we find Anthony making a cup of tea, marked by the trace of an anterior absence triggered by the eclipse of time in the previous sequence in which Anthony was wiped out to re-appear here, an unsettling negativity taking hold of an ordinary domestic situation. As he goes about making the tea, we hear the sound of a door slamming shut. Anthony calls out 'Is anybody there? Is that you Anne?', but receives no reply. At this point we hear ominous background music as Anthony picks up a fork from the kitchen table as if to defend himself, walking cautiously into the living room to find a strange man seated in a chair reading a brochure. In astonishment, he questions the man: 'Who are you? What are you doing here? What are you doing in my flat?' In reply, the stranger – equally nonplussed in Anthony's not recognizing him – tells him that he is Anne's husband Paul and that 'I live here' (thus contradicting the fact already established in conversation between Anne and Anthony that she has been married to James from whom she has been divorced for five years). In passing from what comes before to what comes after, Anthony has been shifted into two time frames at once – one five years earlier and one in the continuing present of the previous scene – in which the stranger he sees is a double of the man who is/was Anne's husband in the guise of the

Figure 5.2 The strange man in Anthony's flat. *The Father*, dir. Florian Zeller (2020).

hospital orderly Bill who, so we find out later, tends to his needs in a future time frame when the dreaded event – that he will be 'put in a home' – has happened.

The complexity of the situation is compounded when, in Anthony's declaring 'Let me be absolutely clear. I am not leaving my flat,' Paul replies 'this isn't your flat Anthony. If you remember, you moved here, you moved to our place while waiting for a new carer because you quarrelled with the last carer, Angela'. However, Paul as Anne's husband could not have known of the quarrel with Angela since this is an event that happens after Anne and her real husband James separate, which was five years earlier, as Anne herself intimates in the previous scene when she tells Anthony that 'I've met someone … he lives in Paris, I'm going to go and live there', this someone being another Paul whose name is not mentioned until much later in the film. It is clear that Anne is saying to Anthony that she is not married and hence does not live with any husband at all. The complexity compounds even further with the arrival of a second Anne doubled with the identity of the nurse Catherine who cares for Anthony together with Bill the orderly in the hospital (another of Paul's doubles) where he has been sent by Anne at some later time (as previously mentioned). The arrival of the second Anne coincides with the sudden disappearance of Paul from the scene as if he had never existed, indicating yet another time frame – a time without Paul – doubled into the already doubled situation. One time frame collapses onto another, itself collapsed onto another and another, generating a multiplying *imago* effect in which the stranger is split into three Pauls superposing on each other's reality. As Bill's double, Paul is and is not Anne's husband; as Paul's double of the other Paul, Paul is and is not Anne's new lover; as Paul's double of Bill as Anne's husband, Paul is and is not Anthony's carer, binding the future into its anteriority in the present situation as a cascade of quantum events entangled in each other's realities. The effect here is to render Paul's status in the matrix of positions played out in the film fiction highly problematic with respect to the legitimacy of his rights claim against Anthony's insofar as Anne's divorce from James means that her husband (the person Paul says he is) could not have been present to experience the events Paul claims to have remembered as the reality upon which his claims are based.

Pass 7: The question of right

How do we make sense of this scene? We can rule out the argument for seeing the entire scene as a projection of Anthony's subjective experience, as if he were hallucinating while other characters were not, since the others are, like Anthony, phantasms of the spectral world projected by the cinematic machine; there are no non-phantasmic characters occupying a privileged place of truth from which to judge the falsity of others. To put this another way, Anthony and Paul do not live as you or I do, but *as if* they do; they in-exist in a spectral world of shifting frames of reference in which the problems of life are reduced to having to *go on* in the next instance, such as we saw in Beckett's *Film* in which its protagonist – a *hominem* reduced to *life death* inexistence – flees from an intruding camera locked into an apparatus restricted by arbitrary rules in which noetic freedom is systematically erased. By looking at the scene from the optical unconscious of the camera eye – an inhuman eye which sees more than what the characters see – we see with the apparatus inserting itself into the story as *false memory* through which all views must pass. In the spectral world of the film, there are no true memories but only false tellings accorded quasi-truth status in the normalizing of onscreen situations. To survive, a character must lay claim to the *place* in which she finds herself by falsifying her memory of it in her favour as the quasi-truth of the situation *vis-à-vis* the claim of others over the same situation, all of which is told to us by the story-telling of the film, itself a false memory slipping into the self-consciousness of the viewer called into the situation to judge contested claims according to the criteria of *right*.

To survive the collapsing of time, Anthony falsifies the situation in his favour by pretending that he knows Paul after having denied it – as if he had correctly remembered in the expectation that others will agree, thereby overlooking his lapse as by convention we all do – in the same way that he pretends that he knows that Angela did not steal his watch after having denied such knowledge. The practical consequence of Anthony's retrojection of false identity to Paul as Anne's husband is to open up a *new point of view* in the spectral world of the film in which Anthony survives the dispossession of his memory by claiming right of possession of his flat (the *place* where he lives). Here, we arrive at the nub of the problem haunting the film: Anthony's right of possession is claimed by him in an act of moral rectitude ('I am not leaving my flat'), rebutting Paul's claim that it is not Anthony's flat but his (i.e. Paul's) 'place'. From a Fichtean perspective, Anthony and Paul are standing in a *relation of right* of mutually self-limiting freedom (Fichte 2000: 10), but within the framework of a fiction in which neither claim transcends the other as ultimately true.

At this point, a realist argument might side with Paul, assuming him to be a character capable of practical reason, unaffected by the forgetfulness affecting

Anthony as someone suffering from end-of-life dementia. However, our previous deliberations have already raised doubts about Paul's capacity to remember; he too makes what could only be false claims in order to rebut Anthony's claims as if his (Paul's claims) were self-evidently true while his interlocutor's were not. In a quantum world of collapsing time frames, *all* consciousnesses are affected by time shifts such that any correct perception or memory of one consciousness must be false in any shared situation in which the quantum event is operating, even though empirically – from the realist point of view – it could be true.

According to the situation in which they encounter each other in a relation of right, it makes sense for Paul, as it does for Anthony, to claim that he is the rightful owner of the 'place' where he resides. But, in making sense *for him*, Paul's claim must be false in the sense that the grounds on which he is making it are retroactively (i.e. fictionally) real as much as they are for Anthony. Given this relativity of views in a *field of views* in which no one view transcends another without itself being transcended, which one is correct? Here we must look to what is at stake in the *game of faces* being played out – the *dispositif* – as the true measure of claims. In a practical-rationalist sense, what counts is the achievement of localized ends which, in this film, is the life of Anthony singled out as a life worth living in his moral stance to the world expressed in his assertion 'I am not leaving my flat'. Accordingly, we should accept *de facto* that Anthony's claim is the one that truly matters insofar as it is his life at stake in the fictional world of the film, a *right* which is also ours in the reality of the world in which we exist as noetic 'free beings'; that is, beings capable of judging right from wrong in a transcendent field of possibilities.

Pass 8: Arche-cinema

What is the underlying cause of Anthony's struggle? If we take the broader perspective of *arche-cinema* (Stiegler 2018: 154) in which characters relate to 'epiphylogenetic memory' (2014a: 10) – the intergenerational transmission of traumatypes as phantasms seeking redress on behalf of the dead – then certain things follow. From an arche-cinema point of view, what is at stake in the struggle of life is the characters' mortality: their being-towards-death in which the 'species-life' of noetic beings, their '*universal* and therefore free being' (Marx 1975: 327),[7] is put at risk of annihilation through catastrophic memory loss, which, in the experiment of the film, is triggered by interference in the time-frame coherence of the spectral world in which characters, acting as proxy members of the human species, live and die.

From this arche-cinema perspective, Anthony's *ordeal of truth* (Stiegler 2022) – his struggle to survive as the Anthony he claims to be – is also ours insofar as we share a common fate in the technological enframement of 'the becoming everything "that happens"' (2009: 188). Like Anthony, we too are at risk of fading from view in the eclipse of the human by machine intelligence – a non-inhuman other driven by the relentless search for efficiencies at the expense of our existence. The profound message of *The Father* is its foreboding of a future ruled by machine intelligence in which *homo sapiens* – in not some too distant future – will not appear and will not figure, a posthuman condition predicted by Ludwig Binswanger in the 1950s in which 'what is renounced is life as independent autonomous selfhood. The subject thus surrenders itself over to existential powers alien to itself' (cited in Crary 2022: 22).

The foreboding of a future *without us* is signalled by the film in the phase-shifting of time frames in which the ontological coherence of the world collapses in a catastrophic irruption of entropic otherness – an existential power alien to ourselves – threatening the survival of the noetic beings who live by it. As the one who suffers, Anthony becomes an archetypal figure of 'man' – the *hominem* who must face the 'ordeal of danger' as a prelude to the 'ordeal of truth' (Stiegler 2022: 273) shared by us as well in coming to know the *who* of what we are as noetic free beings trapped in the throes of an end game in which we see a life worth living in Anthony's life as our death in his.

Pass 9: View X

Casting our mind back to the analysis of *Rear Window* in the first chapter, view X is the view missing from the picture when looked at from the perspective of the life and death struggle on the screen as specifically masculine. View X is the 'third view' emerging in the resolution of the conflict as the new norm, which in *Rear Window* is the masculine view transfigured into a feminine view, in my particular view or reading of it. All films must have a view X in the field of possible views passing through them as openness to the future in other views in the cosmic continuity of the universe, without which they would cease to exist, having no future from which to recall them. Where is view X in *The Father*? An answer to this question will depend on the perspective we adopt in looking for it. If, for instance, we adopt a gendered perspective, we could trace the possibility of view X in Anne's situation in having to care for Anthony in terms of sexuate difference, where Anne's actions are guided by moral responsibility for her father's wellbeing as a familial obligation (Irigaray 2013: 118–19). View X is the view emerging through conflict resolution in which the situation switches from Anthony's struggle with *his* threatening other to Anne's situation in which *her* threatening other appears in his as a shared travail but with conflicting claims on the right outcome, which for Anthony is the right to live in his flat, and which for Anne is rightness in having discharged her familial obligation to do the 'right thing' which, in her eyes (and after much anguish), is to put him in a home. The question this poses is a question of which claimant is *more worthy* – requiring careful consideration on a case by case basis, guided by the situation in which the competing claims are made as pharmacologically informed.

Pass 10: The character/automation split

Foreboding symptoms of the eclipse of humans by machines – threatening otherness – occur throughout the film, for instance in the kitchen scene described in Pass 6 in which we see Anthony going about his business making a cup of tea. In a view from nowhere in which the kitchen is laid out before us, we see on the left-hand side two blue plastic shopping bags placed on a table, while further back, a kitchen bench laden with the usual utensils (plates, crockery, electrical appliances etc.) makes up the rest of the view. As Anthony moves around the kitchen quietly whistling to himself, he turns on an old style cassette player which begins to play an operatic aria; continuing to move around the kitchen, his movements begin to fall in line with the music, his mind distracted by something he seems to have forgotten. Coming to his senses, he moves to one of the shopping bags, pushes the top of the bag down and takes out two items, one of which he puts on the bench and the other in the overhead cupboard. While these deliberate gestures suggest Anthony is capable of rational action (albeit a little clumsily), the frame of reference in which they occur indicates a non-causal reality in which their efficacy is being put to the test.

As the music rises to a climax, a jump cut intervenes, shifting our point of view to a more distant location while triggering a sudden thrust of Anthony's body in which the empty plastic bag in his hand is waved around in a futile gesture, as if reacting to a spectral presence lying in wait whose unnerving proximity we feel in the suddenness of Anthony's lurching movement. Upon this slight interruption, the music slows and Anthony falls back awkwardly to lean on the bench as if exhausted by his efforts. In these unsettling moments we are faced with questions. Is Anthony suffering from memory loss, unable to make the necessary connections between the immediate past and the proximate present to coordinate his actions properly? What do we make of the coincidence of his gestures with the camera's shift of point of view? Applying Balázs's concept of visual linkage, I propose the following. Insofar as Anthony is perceived to be a *character* in the story, his movements could be conceived as consistent with someone displaying signs of dementia; however, as an *automaton* of the apparatus, his gestures are motivated by visual jointures to which his body is attached, responding to the counter-force of *drive* – the incessant blind searching for efficiencies in the thwarting of progress – as neganthropic resistance.

Here, we should be careful not to confuse drive with the neganthropic resistance that resists it. Drive is the retardation of entropy – where entropy is the tendency towards end-stage finality – manifesting in delays, deferrals and suspension of progress holding the film together in a metastabilizing flow of images. Drive decelerates the entropic tendency towards degree zero, seeking blindly for opportunities to persist in its pulsing repetitions in thwarted progress. On the other hand, neganthropic resistance is noetic life lived out through the system *otherwise*, sustained by resistance to the thwarted progress of the pulsing drive in *its* resistance to entropy; noetic life is the *resistance to the resistance* of drive in its blind seeking for efficiencies in holding itself back from sliding into entropic disorder. Neganthropic resistance is the non-inhuman counter-gesture to the inhuman indifference of the drive: the *standing against* of noetic being in refusing to give way in the face of an unremitting alien force carried by technical ordering seeking its own functional efficiency, the logic of which remains elusively obscure to the humans who experience it, always out of reach of attempts to bring it under control.

Through his *bodily movements*, Anthony is resisting the resistance of an inhuman force taking hold of him. He is trying to keep himself *upright* in a stance of bodily rectitude, to stand with dignity on his own feet which allows him to persist – to *go on* – as his way of refusing the threat confronting him: the threat of being put in a home as the preluding moment of the death-that-awaits. From an arche-cinema perspective, the refusal of end-stage finality is the archetypal struggle of *anthropos* with itself in facing an abyss of the *real* in which 'I observe with horror an anterior future in which death is the stake' (Barthes 1993: 96). In the final stages of the film, we see Anthony in his hospital room in a disoriented state, unable to remember past events which have been related to him by the nurse Catherine who is caring for him. Having lost the power of recall, he now faces the abyss of non-being in its full horror and asks the last question that could possibly be asked: '*who* exactly am I?' In asking this last question *for himself*, Anthony is also asking on behalf of *all of us* – the *I* that *We* are as mortal beings, whose fate is to know that I will some day die. To ask this last question is to already *know* my fate as a mortal being, without which I could not feel for the future and care for it.

Pass 11: The switching of faces

The inhumanness of the force taking hold of Anthony – its indifference to his non-inhuman existence – is signalled by ominous background music announcing a turn in the ontological structure of the film where spectral reality breaks through in catastrophic loss of meaning in which the *hominem* that he is must 'go on' in the face of *life death* irreality triggered by the turn (its release from one face into the other). Anthony's going on – persisting against the entropic force taking hold of him – takes the form of a series of advances and retreats out of and back into his room, each time facing a different face of the flat which keeps changing its complexion (appearing in new arrangements of familiar objects and living consciousnesses rendered *unheimlich* by the switching mechanism), wrenching Anthony into an abyssal *real* at the point of intersection of collapsing frames with no support other than the *dispositif* – the counter-praxis of ad hoc strategies devised to stabilize the provocation of order that the film has inflicted on itself – to keep him being the *who* that he is at *this* place which he claims to be his by right. Through the affordances of the *dispositif* – its capacity to order

Figure 5.3 The blank stare. *The Father*, dir. Florian Zeller (2020).

the disorder – the *character* Anthony speaks through the *automaton* he has become as the traumatype announcing the horror of a blank screen stripped of meaning, in 'an abyss that opens up before our very eyes' (Balázs 2010: 66). The horror of the abyss is expressed in the blank stare that comes across Anthony's face when confronted by the otherness of what he sees *in* what he sees before him: his daughter and her husband as utterly strange to him. What he sees in the living faces of these familiar strangers is the death that awaits *him*, forcing him back into his room and its reassuring window view out to the street below.

As dementia takes hold of Anthony's mind, the *automaton* in him refuses – pulls back in forbearance – opening up possibilities for life by standing against the spectral nonbeing haunting the film, in the turning of the crystalline sphere. In his forbearance against the machine, possibilities of life become chances in the numerous pathways that could be taken in the turning of the sphere, as life recommencing in the gap between before and after wrenched apart by cascading quantum events, requiring ongoing practical action to repair the rift, which is Anthony's *way* of coping with the entropic force taking hold of him. As Anne says to Laura, the new day carer, 'he has his ways' in attempting to excuse Anthony's erratic behaviour without realizing that, for him, his 'ways' are ways of surviving the death-that-awaits which he sees in their caring faces as the *pharmakon*: the 'toxic cure' leading them to putting him in a home in the belief that this is what is best for him.

Pass 12: Recommencement

The issue of *life death* in the film boils down to one of recommencement: how to go on in the rift between before and after triggered by collapsing time frames in which Anthony survives by making-do in practical ways as the situation calls for. With this in mind, let us return to the scene in the kitchen where we see Anthony making a cup of tea and consider how it enables recommencement. Later, in the scene after the next (in which we see Anthony's confrontation with Paul and Anne's double), we enter another time frame in which we see Anne entering the kitchen carrying two blue plastic bags which she places on the table where Anthony had found them, noting that the kitchen has switched to another face (the kitchen has different wall colours and back tiles to the main bench).

This scene recommences from where the scene prior to the last (in which Anthony is in the kitchen making a cup of tea) leaves off, with the previous scene coming between them, an elision of five years blended into a *false continuing present*, calling forth more perplexing questions: how could the two blue plastic bags be put on the table by Anne after the scene in which we see Anthony open one of them and take shopping items out of it as he makes a cup of tea? The answer is not the obvious one, which is that the events are simply out of order in the manner of Tarantino's *Pulp Fiction*; rather, the film is sliding one time frame across another, rendering the frames 'coherent' in the ordering of the continuing present so that objects in one frame persist in the face of the other, acting *as if* they were coherent through their inconsistencies.

The film is struggling to hold itself together against the disordering of its frames, making do with objects and actions as they come to hand, generating truth effects which do not add up, for instance in the following scene where we see James, Anne's husband, speaking to her about the new carer Laura hired to replace Angela, even though the event with Angela and her replacement with Laura happens in the continuing present in which Anne has already told us that she has been divorced from James for five years. To sustain the (quasi-)coherence of a false continuing present, bits and pieces of the blended time frames are being put together in a series of recommencements, the visual jointure of which is ruled by the paraconsistency of quantum time in which a character's life – Anthony's – is being played out inside the memory chamber of the film in *life death* superpositions wracked with *Nachträglichkeit*.

Order emerges out of chaos in the collapsing time frames as the camera *feels* for the future, probing blindly through the memory chamber for the place it needs to be to recommence the action, linking ways to tell the story out of randomized memory shards coming its way, putting them together in ensembles of (quasi-)cause/effect relays jointed in Balázsian visual linkage, thereby creating a *Kammerspielfilm* in reverse. The *telos* of the film – its purposeful action – is fulfilled by allowing the time frames to collapse on themselves so that the end superposed on the beginning is drawn through the memory chamber backward. This is confirmed when we cast our mind back to the beginning of the film in which we see Anne leaving the hospital in which she has left Anthony to face his death without her to enter the flat in which he lives, creating a feedback loop in which the end superposes on the beginning at the same time in the same action. The effect is one of regression, where progress recommences through the generation of quantum effects across the collapsing frames in Anthony's relapse into an infantile state at the end of the film which is also the beginning in which his birth and death superpose.

Pass 13: End beginning

Like Lars von Trier with his dogma films, the director of *The Father* and his production team have given themselves arbitrary rules, obscure to us, in which the film's mechanism for memorizing is inflected with artificially generated entropic disorder to trigger an autoimmune attack on itself.[8] In the *neganthropic resistance* – resistance to artificially induced entropic disorder – thus produced, the film is made to hold its ground as a masterpiece of twenty-first century cinematic artwork. In pharmacological terms, the film diagnoses the illness of hyper-industrial life of the late capitalist era – the epoch of globalized digitization in which simulation has taken control of its originating source – by mimicking its effects as toxic to noetic life in the making of the film itself. In so doing, the film carries within itself the cure to the toxicity it generates in the possibility of radical change in the way we perceive the future, not as a world laid out before us in predictable patterns and probabilistic models but as a chaos of potentials in which we are immersed and through which other paths may be followed.

In the final scene of the film, Anthony – who in his last moments does not know who he is but is nevertheless aware that he is 'losing all my leaves' – is left behind in the care of the nurse Catherine, a consoling *She* figure leading Anthony out of the 'closure of the world' (Irigaray 2013: 11), as the camera probes through the window of the hospital room, placing us on the cusp of immersion in the leaves of a tree – the reassuring tree outside Anthony's flat which he could always see but never reach – flooding the screen. The image of the leaves places us on

Figure 5.4 The final image of the film as the camera probes out the window of Anthony's hospital room – memory leaves rustling in the wind. *The Father*, dir. Florian Zeller (2020).

the edge of the abyss as an arche-image of living memory – the memory-leaves of the tree rustling in the wind – into which Anthony's life – the 'who am I?' that he is – is consigned as the dead past of immemorial time where everything that will have happened 'is being inscribed' (Bergson 1911: 25).

Yet what remains is what we see on the screen. The film *itself* survives in the death of Anthony which is our chance of recommencement. In bearing witness to Anthony's struggle for the right to be who he is, we are the ones called to stand in the right way, on the path that lies before us through the guidance of the film's *dispositif* – the game played to provide sufficient reason for *right* to be affirmed which is the film's *sovereign right* to be itself. What remains to be done is to take this path by acting these values out, feeling for the future in moral consciousness as 'the point of departure for a new critique' (Stiegler 2013: 23) – the right path to take which could also be wrong as the pharmacological cure. In our journey through *The Father*, we may have already found ourselves on this path.

Conclusion

In writing this book, I have named and reflect upon figures appearing in films under analysis as *figures of resistance* bound into negentropic force – the entropic force of time retarded in the duration of films as concretizations of piezo-electrical light-life – guided by Stiegler's organological project in which the noetic freedom of human existence – the capacity of the noetic soul to project itself otherwise – is at stake. Names have been given as concepts, tools to work with and reflect upon in a project of film organology with the explicit aim of bringing about acts of creative imagination – noetic projections otherwise – making new pathways possible in the *speculum* of the film-sphere in which films are experienced in a hermeneutically turned position: turned backward to the past as it comes to me in the future anteriority of what it will have been. Figural thinking is the endeavour to retrieve a future from the past in its already pastness as a future to come otherwise than the future already fated. This is the task of figural hermeneutics.

My project of figural hermeneutics follows philosophical principles drawn from the post-Kantian Idealists in their attempt to get behind the Kantian schema to access the thing in itself as spirit or *Geist* (to put it in Hegel's terms), which I have taken up in terms of the intuitive faculty as proposed by Fichte in his *Wissenschaftslehre* in which the originary act of self-positing as I = I is retroacted within visual projection of the primary imagination as pre-subjective activity: the incessancy of an incompleted self trying to complete itself and forever failing in the struggle to be. Fichte's I = I as failed self-transcendence sets us on a path of practical action in pursuit of the cinematic life of film figures, calling upon new rules and new schemes in situations encountered in films in which the struggle to be is re-performed in a world of ontological inconsistency, where being and becoming fail to intersect and causal reality founders in quantum effects of non-local interactivity. Figural thinking is a *praxis* in which the movements of figures appearing on a screen are analysed in terms of the logic of failed transcendence, requiring naming and reflecting upon in a *dispositif*

– a game played with rules *against* the unifying tendencies of films in their formal constructions – as paraconsistent with themselves. The attempt to work out the rules of the game played by the film against itself *is itself* a reflection upon the *dispositif* in what it can tell us about the future otherwise, opening up new possibilities of the past in the present as hermeneutic self-consciousness.

Stiegler's organological project, through which my figural hermeneutics has been developed, is underpinned by the moral imperative of *right* as therapeutic for living a life worth living in the failed transcendence of the incompleted self: a figure of resistance who suffers the full weight of the capitalistic world of hegemonic free markets in their demand on the living that life be lived as dividuated being – being divided from itself and, because of this, denied the right to be *for itself* insofar as this rightful self is also for the right of others in the free reciprocal efficacy of 'moral being' (Stiegler 2019: 236). For Stiegler, to live a life worth living is to live it *for me*, not in the liberal sense of the autonomously free individual (negative freedom), but in the social sense of a Simondonian transindividual: an *I–We* relation in which my free actions overreach themselves to meet other such actions as moral acts of freedom (positive freedom). To live life *for me* in transindividuation is to live it freely in openness to others' claims of freedom as mutually self-limiting, thus guaranteeing that the relation does not close in on itself in the heteronomy of rigid belief and ensuring that the *new* can be named and reflected upon in noetic freedom. Primary imagination is itself projected in the tertiary retentions of *mnemotechnesis* in which the *pharmakon* of a life worth living that *we ourselves are* passes through a memory machine in which the struggle of the self with itself is re-enacted through the hypomnesic carriage of technics, in films, video productions and on internet platforms as screen memory. Screen memory carries the *pharmakon* with it in fabulation – the telling of cautionary tales in which the struggle of *anthropos* with itself is acted out through the agonism of stereotypes confronting their traumatypes in a *theatrum mundi*, seeking for wrongs to be put right.

In a recent publication, media theorist Jonathan Crary has reflected upon the catastrophic tendency of twenty-first century screen life ruled by out-of-control algorithmic governmentality and 'sociocidal corporations', arguing that 'pathways to a different world will not be found by internet search engines. Rather, what is needed is exploration and creative receptivity to all the resources and practices developed over the long history of human societies for thousands of years' (2022: 122–3).

In my view, Crary's response to the catastrophic tendency in hypercapitalist milieus is half right. Pathways to a different world are needed to explore and utilize the creative potential of past ways not yet taken; however, these are to be found not by turning away from the utilities of the current digitized milieu but by turning otherwise within them. In light of Crary's proposal but with my turned position in mind, the figural hermeneutics proposed in this book sets us on track for the 'exploration and creative receptivity' of past resources from within film archives, to confront the catastrophe calling us into it. From this place, we give ourselves the chance of shifting from the future for which we are fated, to its anteriority projected otherwise, thereby putting ourselves on another path whose end we cannot predict.

By following the trace lines of past struggles calling for redress in a *methexis* – a poietic praxis of reshaping mnemotexts in care for the future – we give ourselves a chance to think otherwise in a new dimension of the sphere in which outlines of a different world appear with different values we ourselves have projected as *right*. By recognizing the values of this world as different *for us*, we are already on the right path to making it real – transforming our existing world from within the archive itself in this other world's image as radically new.

Notes

Introduction

1. In his essay 'Figura', Erich Auerbach speaks of the figure as an '*act* of making an image' (2014: 65), and as 'shape' (66). Figuring is the plasticity of sense which gives shape to ideas directed towards a future possibility, as 'something that could be perceived with the senses' (68).
2. The term 'neganthropic potential' has been drawn from the lexicon of Bernard Stiegler's 'organology' of the human relation to technology (2018), developed by him in thermodynamic terms while following Jacques Derrida's deconstruction of phenomenology to expose a trace system within it at the pre-conscious level. Stiegler's organological approach underlies the critical and analytic work undertaken in this book.
3. Oxford English Dictionary: forbear: 'to bear; to tolerate, endure'.
4. Vicky Kirby has made a compelling case for the quantum thought of entanglement, superposition and non-local interactivity to be adopted in the humanities as an explanatory tool for paradoxical phenomena experienced by humans in everyday life (2011: 9–10). Critiquing the nature/culture binary whereby the humanities disciplines have forbidden themselves from crossing the line between nature and culture, Kirby explores the relational force of 'spacetimemattering' as a retroactive process of 'intra-activity' between the observer and the observed: 'How we approach this phenomenon (which includes us), a phenomenon whose identifications entail constant morphogenesis, is to open the question of the human, and writing, as if for the first time' (21). Kirby's work follows Karen Barad's *Meeting the Universe Halfway: Quantum Physics and the Entanglement of Matter and Meaning* (2007), a groundbreaking publication bringing together the theory of quantum physics and the conceptual terrain of humanities disciplines to create new pathways for thinking, writing and research on the nature/culture divide.
5. My adoption of Laruelle here is in a limited sense insofar as his idea of radical immanence as 'vision-in-One' represses its trace – the after-effect of what remains on the screen – thereby overlooking its conditions of recommencement. However, this by no means discounts his insights into the quantum effect of non-local interaction as superposition developed in his later work (2013a) – a significant contribution to critically informed quantum thought from a humanities perspective.
6. Stiegler's proposal of the temporality of cinematic consciousness is drawn out of a critical engagement with Husserl's thesis on time consciousness (Husserl 1964), in

which '*consciousness of image*' (Stiegler 2011: 17) is excluded from primary and secondary processes (protentions and retentions). Stiegler shows how this exclusion means that Husserl cannot account for the novelty of repeated experiences of the same melody, carried by the slipping-in of tertiary retentions at work in the primary and secondary processes as a memory I did not experience but will have experienced each time the melody/film is repeated.

7 I have borrowed the term inexistence from Brentano's psychology of consciousness where it is employed to account for the directedness of mental phenomena to objects as qualitatively formed (Brentano 1973: 92). To in-exist is to not yet have being and, because of this, to be *directed* towards an object in preparation for judgemental action as a form of reality testing: 'in presentation something is presented, in judgement something is affirmed or denied' (93).

8 In his critique of Kant's transcendental unity of apperception in which the categories of thought arise independently of their objects, Fichte, who is following Maimon, argues the opposite: that 'the categories arise together with the objects, and in order to make them possible at all, they arise in the domain of the power of the imagination itself' (1988: 288). Fichte's imagination is primary projection, whereas for Kant, imagination is of a secondary kind. In other words, Fichte places the *noumena* – the 'thing in itself' – within the primary imagination as asymptotic: something to be striven for but never reached as 'the zero degree of representation' (Longo 2022: 143).

9 The transcendental field without a subject was proposed by Jean Hyppolite and Jacques Derrida as an abstraction from subjectification in worldly experience: a bracketed reality in the enquiry into the conditions of possibility for a rational subject in relation to a world in which this subject could possibly exist. As Stiegler points out, 'a subjectless transcendental field is one of the "conditions" of transcendental subjectivity' (2016: 315, note 53).

10 For the concept of infinite judgement in German Idealism see Longo (2022).

11 The *apeiron* is proposed by the ancient Greek philosopher Anaximander as the 'indistinct' – the primal flux of becoming (Rovelli 2017: 5–6).

12 Freud writes: 'To negate something in a judgement is, at bottom, to say: "this is something which I should prefer to repress." A negative judgement is the intellectual substitute for repression' (1984: 438).

Chapter 1

1 Fichte's *Tathandlung* – the free act of self-positing of an I seeking to complete itself – is a function of the mutual self-limiting of an *I–We* relation in the formation of a moral order based on 'the mutual influence of free rational beings upon one another

... according to the law of right' (Fichte 2000: 84), a 'perfectionist' theory of morality in which a moral order of human beings establishes itself by striving to realize the ideal of reason in agreements 'arrived at by free communication' (Ware 2018: 581).
2. For paraconsistency, see Introduction, section entitled 'Paraconsistency'. Paraconsistent logic can be applied to make sense of quantum entanglement in a general sense, not limited to 'sub-atomic particles but also between widely separated parts of the larger universe; ... the universe as a whole can be treated as a single immense quantum system bound together by conservation laws and thus by a multiplicity of quantum events' (Murphy 1999: 74).
3. Irreality refers to the condition in which something exists in a paradoxical state of being neither true nor false – a state of ontological undecidability (Goodman 1978: 19).
4. I have drawn the issue of being and non-being from Ó Maoilearca's discussion of paraconsistency in relation to Meinong's theory of impossible objects (2015: 121).
5. For the quasi-cause, see Gilles Deleuze, *The Logic of Sense* (1990: 148). A quasi-cause is a cause retrojected after the fact as an event of its 'having never happened'.
6. A *Kammerspielfilm* is a film set in the confined spaces of a self-restricting chamber. For the *Kammerspielfilm* in Weimar cinema, see Eisner (1969: 177).
7. Fichte describes view X as 'a synthetic concept X, which is genuinely present, and from the opposites disclosed by analysis we now have to infer what sort of concept the unknown X can be' (1982: 124).
8. For Irigaray, the paradigm case of mutual responsibility in sexuate belonging is Antigone's familial responsibility to have her brother's body properly buried against the patriarch Creon's orders in Sophocles' play (Irigaray 2013: 118).

Chapter 2

1. Benjamin undertakes the interpretive strategy of retroactive reading (reading backwards) on two drafts of a poem by Hölderlin, where the determinacy of the former – its invocation of mythic necessity in immortal life – is undermined by indeterminacy – the contingency of actions in mortal life – in the latter (1996: 22–23). Benjamin calls the procedure of retroactive reading *poetizing* as the freeing up of ossified states of being in interpretive textual procedures as the 'feeling of life, of life spread out and undefined' (24).
2. Murnau's *Entfesselte kamera* (unchained camera) is a camera apparatus freed from the restrictions of a stationary position on the set. Murnau writes of the *Entfesselte kamera* in terms of its capacity to enter into 'a symphony made up of a harmony of bodies and the rhythm of space; the play of pure movement, vigorous and abundant.

All this we shall be able to create when the camera has been dematerialized' (quoted in Eisner 1973: 84).

Chapter 3

1. Stiegler develops his concept of 'the *there*' by reworking Heidegger's notion of *Entschlossenheit*: the 'there being' of *Dasein* in the mode of resolute existence as refusal or resistance (Heidegger 1962: 343).

Chapter 4

1. In 'Little History of Photography', Benjamin reads old photographs from the turned position 'to find the inconspicuous spot where in the immediacy of that long-forgotten moment the future nests so eloquently that we, looking back, may rediscover it' (1999: 151).
2. In his book *Hegel: The Restlessness of the Negative*, Jean-Luc Nancy provides us with a way of thinking of non-indecisive action as a good that 'cannot be designated as given, presented, and qualified' (74); that is, as a *good in itself*.
3. For the distinction between *Zensur* and *Zensor* in Freud's theory of repression as disguise censorship, see Boag (2012: 148 ff.). Briefly, *Zensor* is conscious censoring, whereas *Zensur* is unconscious censoring.
4. Repressed suppression occurs when something in the unconscious *passes through* the preconscious where 'it is obliged to submit to modifications' (Freud 1976: 691).
5. For the 'regression' of the apparatus in the hallucination of dreaming, see Freud (1976: 692).

Chapter 5

1. I have drawn the concept of real connections from Marx's 'The German Ideology' in which real connections are defined as the practical connections 'with the material and intellectual production of the whole world' (1978: 163).
2. The idea of a planetarium perspective comes from Walter Benjamin's essay 'To the Planetarium', which proposes a cosmic view – an 'optical connection to the universe' (1979: 103) – seen across the dome of the planetarium looking up at its surface as phantasmagorical.

3 Simondon's ideas of moral act and moral law (2020: 378–9) correlate with Fichte's notion of 'moral law' set forth in *The Vocation of Man* (1987: 18).
4 For the relation of the *Kammerspielfilm* to Max Reinhardt's theatre see Eisner (1969: 177–8); Petro (1989: 174–5).
5 Balázs's reference to quasi-musical value is drawn from Bergson's notion of duration, in particular with reference to musical melody played on a phonograph like the 'relaxing of [a] spring' (Bergson 1911: 63). Balázs's film theory is a Marxist inflected version of Bergsonian image materialism.
6 The quoted phrase is from Marx's 'Economic and Philosophical Manuscripts' (1975: 356). The full sentence reads: 'A *being* sees himself as independent only when he stands on his own feet, and he only stands on his own feet when he owes his *existence* to himself.'
7 Marx derives his concepts of species-life and species-being from Feuerbach who 'sought to build his ontology on a generalization of the structures Fichte found in the mind' (Weekes 2016: 53).
8 Anthropic self-destruction correlates with 'the process of autoimmunization [which] consists for a living organism … of protecting itself against its self-protection by destroying its own immune system' (Derrida 1998, 73).

Bibliography

Anon. (1996), 'The Oldest Systematic Program of German Idealism', trans. Frederick Beiser, in Frederick Beiser (ed), *The Early Political Writings of the German Romantics*, Cambridge: Cambridge University Press, 3–5.

Antonioni, Michelangelo (1996), *The Architecture of Vision: Writings and Interviews on Cinema*, ed. M. Cotting-Jones, trans. various, Chicago: University of Chicago Press.

Aristotle (1941), *The Basic Works of Aristotle*, ed. Richard McKeon, New York: Random House.

Auerbach, Eric (2014), 'Figura', in *Time, History, and Literature: Selected Essays of Erich Auerbach*, trans. Jane O. Newman, Princeton: Princeton University Press, 65–113.

Aumont, Jacques (1997), *The Image*, trans. Claire Pajackowska, London: BFI Publishing.

Balázs, Béla (2010), *Early Film Theory: Visible Man and The Spirit of Film*, trans. Rodney Livingstone, Berghahn Books: New York.

Barad, Karen (2007), *Meeting the Universe Halfway: Quantum Physics and the Entanglement of Matter and Meaning*, Durham: Duke University Press.

Barthes, Roland (1993), *Camera Lucida: Reflections on Photography*, trans. Richard Howard, London: Vintage.

Beckett, Samuel (2010), *The Unnamable*, London: Faber and Faber.

Benjamin, Walter (1979), *One-Way Street and Other Writings*, trans. Edmund Jephcott and Kingsley Shorter, London: Verso.

Benjamin, Walter (1996), 'Two Poems by Friedrich Hölderlin', trans. Stanley Corngold, in Marcus Bullock and Michael W. Jennings (eds), *Walter Benjamin, Selected Writings, Volume 1, 1913-1926*, Cambridge, MA: The Belknap Press of Harvard University Press, 18–36.

Benjamin, Walter (1999), 'Little History of Photography', trans. Rodney Livingstone, in Michael W. Jennings, Howard Eiland, and Gary Smith (eds), *Walter Benjamin, Selected Writings, Volume 2, Part 2, 1931-1934*, Cambridge, MA: The Belknap Press of Harvard University Press, 507–30.

Benjamin, Walter (2002), 'The Work of Art in the Age of Its Technological Reproducibility', second version, in Eiland, Howard and Michael Jennings (eds), *Walter Benjamin, Selected Writings, Volume 3, 1935-1938*, Cambridge, MA: The Belknap Press of Harvard University Press, 101–33.

Bergson, Henri (1911), *Creative Evolution*, trans. Arthur Mitchell, Henry Holt and Company, Camelot Press, New York.

Bergson, Henri (1920), *Mind-Energy: Lectures and Essays*, trans. H. Wildon Carr, New York: Henry Holt and Company.

Bergson, Henri (1965), *Duration and Simultaneity: with Reference to Einstein's Theory*, trans. Leon Jacobson, Indianapolis: The Bobb's Merrill Company.

Bergson, Henri (1988), *Matter and Memory*, trans. Nancy Margaret Paul and W. Scott Palmer, New York: Zone Books.

Bergson, Henri (2007), *The Creative Mind: an Introduction to Metaphysics*, trans. Mabelle L. Andison, New York: Dover Publications.

Bergson, Henri (2019), *Time and Free Will: an Essay on the Immediate Data of Consciousness*, trans. F.L. Pogson, New York: Grey Rabbit Publications.

Blanchot, Maurice (1982), *The Space of Literature* trans. Ann Smock. Lincoln: University of Nebraska Press.

Blanchot, Maurice (1995), *The Writing of the Disaster*, trans. Anne Smock, Lincoln: University of Nebraska Press.

Boag, Simon (2012), *Freudian Repression: The Unconscious, and the Dynamics of Inhibition*, London: Karnac.

Bordwell, David (1977), 'Camera Movement and Cinematic Space', *Cine-Tracts*, 1, special issue, 19–25.

Breazeale, Daniel (1995), 'Check or Checkmate? On the Finitude of the Fichtean Self', in Karl Ameriks and Dieter Sturma (eds), *The Modern Subject: Concepts of the Self in Classical German Philosophy*, Albany: Albany State University Press, 87–114.

Brentano, Franz (1973), *Psychology from an Empirical Standpoint*, trans. Linda L. McAlister, London: Routledge.

Bresson, Robert (1986), *Notes on the Cinematographer*, trans. Jonathan Griffin, London: Quartet Books.

Breuer, Joseph and Sigmund Freud (1974), *Studies on Hysteria*, trans. James Strachey and Alix Strachey, Volume 3 of The Pelican Freud Library, Harmondsworth: Penguin.

Brown, William (2013), *Supercinema: Film-Philosophy for the Digital Age*, New York: Berghahn Books.

The Cabinet of Dr. Caligari (1920), [Film] Dir. Robert Wiene, Germany: Decla-Film.

Cavell, Stanley (1979), *The World Viewed: Reflections on the Ontology of Film, Enlarged Edition*, Cambridge, MA: Harvard University Press.

Colman, Felicity, et al. (2018), *Ethics of Coding: A Report on the Algorithmic Condition* [EoC]. H2020-EU.2.1.1 – INDUSTRIAL LEADERSHIP – Leadership in enabling and industrial technologies – Information and Communication Technologies. Brussels: European Commission. 732407, https://cordis.europa.eu/project/rcn/207025_en.html. pp.1–54.

Crary, Jonathan (2022), *Scorched Earth: Beyond the Digital Age to a Post-Capitalist World*, London: Verso.

Deleuze, Gilles (1986), *Cinema 1: The Movement-Image*, trans. Hugh Thomlinson and Barbara Habberjam, London: The Athlone Press.

Deleuze, Gilles (1989), *Cinema 2: The Time-Image*, trans. Hugh Tomlinson and Robert Galeta, Minneapolis: University of Minnesota Press.

Deleuze, Gilles (1990), *The Logic of Sense*, trans. Mark Lester with Charles Stivale, New York: Columbia University Press.

Deleuze, Gilles (1991), *Bergsonism*, trans. Hugh Tomlinson and Barbara Habberjam, New York: Zone Books.

Deleuze, Gilles (1995), 'Postscript on Control Societies', *Negotiations: 1972–1990*, trans. Martin Joughin, New York: Columbia University Press, 177–82.

Derrida, Jacques (1981), 'The Pharmakon', in *Dissemination*, trans. Barbara Johnson, Chicago: The University of Chicago Press, 95–117.

Derrida, Jacques (1990), 'Force De Loi: Le "Fondement Mystique De L'Autorité"', *Cardozo Law Review*, 11 (5–6): 920–1046.

Derrida, Jacques (1996), *Archive Fever: A Freudian Impression*, trans. Eric Prenowitz, Chicago: University of Chicago Press.

Derrida, Jacques (1998), 'Faith and Knowledge: the Two Sources of "Religion" at the Limits of Reason Alone', trans. Samuel Weber, in Jacques Derrida and Gianni Vattimo (eds), *Religion*, Cambridge: Polity Press, 42–101.

Derrida, Jacques (2002), 'Typewriter Ribbon', in *Without Alibi*, trans. Peggy Kamuf, Stanford: Stanford University Press, 71–160.

Derrida, Jacques (2011), *The Beast and the Sovereign, Volume II*, trans. Geoffrey Bennington, Chicago: University of Chicago Press.

Derrida, Jacques (2017), *Advances*, trans. Phillippe Lynes, Minneapolis: University of Minnesota Press.

Derrida, Jacques (2020), *Life Death: The Seminars of Jacques Derrida*, trans. Pascale-Anne Brault and Michael Naas, Chicago: University of Chicago Press.

Dunham, Jeremy, Iain Hamilton Grant and Sean Watson (2011), *Idealism: the History of a Philosophy*, Montreal: McGill-Queen's University Press.

Eisner, Lotte (1969), *The Haunted Screen: Expressionism in the German Cinema and the Influence of Max Reinhardt*, trans. Roger Greaves, Berkeley: University of California Press.

Eisner, Lotte (1973), *Murnau*, Berkeley: University of California Press.

The Father (2020), [Film] Dir. Florian Zeller, France UK: F comme Film, Trademark Films, Cine@, AG Studios Film4, Canal+, Cine+.

Fichte, Johann Gottlieb (1982), *The Science of Knowledge, with First and Second Introductions*, trans. Peter Heath and John Lachs, Cambridge: Cambridge University Press.

Fichte, Johann Gottlieb (1987), *The Vocation of Man*, trans. Peter Preuss, Indianapolis: Hackett Publishing.

Fichte, Johann Gottlieb (1988), *Early Philosophical Writings*, trans. Daniel Breazeale, Ithaca: Cornell University Press.

Fichte, Johann Gottlieb (1992), *Foundations of Transcendental Philosophy*, (Wissenschaftslehre) Novo Methodo *(1796/99)*, trans. Daniel Breazeale, Ithaca: Cornell University Press.

Fichte, Johann Gottlieb (2000), *Foundation of Natural Right: According to the Principles of the Wissenschaftslehre*, trans. Michael Baur, Cambridge: Cambridge University Press.

Film (1965), [Film] Dir. Alan Schneider, Script, Samuel Beckett, USA: Milestone Film and Video.

Flusser, Vilém (2000), *Towards a Philosophy of Photography*, trans. Anthony Matthews, London: Reaktion Books.

Foster, Clare (2015), '"Whose Theatre Is It Anyway?": Ancient Chorality versus Modern Drama' in *Anthropology, Development and Performance: Reflection on Political Transformations*, Alex Flynn and Jonas Tinius (eds), Houndmills: Palgrave Macmillan, 224–57.

Foster, Verna A. (2004), *The Name and Nature of Tragicomedy*, Ashgate: Aldershot.

A Fool There Was (1915), [Film] Dir. Frank Powell, USA: Box Office Attractions.

Freud, Sigmund (1976), *The Interpretation of Dreams*, Volume 4 of The Pelican Freud Library, trans. James Strachey, Harmondsworth: Penguin.

Freud, Sigmund (1984), *On Metapsychology: The Theory of Psychoanalysis*, Volume 11 of The Pelican Freud Library, trans. James Strachey, London: Penguin.

Gadamer, Hans-Georg (1975), *Truth and Method*, trans. Joel Weinsheimer and Donald G. Marshall, London: Sheed and Ward.

Gadamer, Hans-Georg (2007), *The Gadamer Reader: a Bouquet of the Later Writings*, ed. Richard E. Palmer, Evanston: Northwest University Press.

Goodman, Nelson (1978), *Ways of Worldmaking*, Indianapolis: Hackett Publishing Company.

Hegel, G.W.F. (1977), *Phenomenology of Spirit*, trans. A.V. Miller, Oxford: Oxford University.

Hegel, G.W.F. (1991), *Elements of the Philosophy of Right*, trans. H.B. Nisbet, Cambridge: Cambridge University Press.

Heidegger, Martin (1962), *Being and Time*, trans. John Macquarrie and Edward Robinson, Oxford: Basil Blackwell.

Heidegger, Martin (1997), *Plato's Sophist*, trans. Richard Rojcewicz and André Schuwer, Bloomington: Indiana State University Press.

Hintertreppe (1921), [Film] Dir. Leopold Jessner and Paul Leni, Germany: Gloria-Film.

Hui, Yuk (2019), *Recursivity and Contingency*, London: Rowman & Littlefield.

Husserl, Edmund (1964), *The Philosophy of Internal Time-Consciousness*, trans. James S. Churchill, Bloomington: Indiana University Press.

Ijsseling, Samuel (2001), 'Nietzsche's Yes and Amen', *Journal of Nietzsche Studies*, (22): 36–43.

Intervista (1987), [Film] Dir. Federico Fellini, Italy: Academy Pictures.

Irigaray, Luce (1985), *Speculum of the Other Woman*, trans. Gillian C. Gill, Ithaca: Cornell University Press.

Irigaray, Luce (2013), *In the Beginning, She Was*, London: Bloomsbury.

It's a Wonderful Life (1946), [Film] Dir. Frank Capra, USA: Liberty Films.

Johnston, Adrian (2005), *Time Driven: Metapsychology and the Splitting of the Drive*, Evanston: Northwest University Press.

Johnston, Adrian (2014), Adventures in *Transcendental Materialism, Dialogues with Contemporary Thinkers*, Edinburgh: Edinburgh University Press.

Kierkegaard, Soren (1957), *The Concept of Dread*, trans. Walter Lowrie, Princeton: Princeton University Press.

Kirby, Vicky (2011), *Quantum Anthropologies: Life at Large*, Durham: Duke University Press.

Kosch, Michelle (2021), 'Fichte on Summons and Self-Consciousness', *Mind*, 130 (517): 215–49.

Kovács, András Bálint (2007), *Screening Modernism: European Art Cinema, 1950–1980*, Chicago: The University of Chicago Press.

La Dolce Vita (1960), [Film] Dir. Federico Fellini, Italy: Riama.

Lacan, Jacques (1981), *The Seminar of Jacques Lacan, Book XI: The Four Fundamental Concepts of Psychoanalysis*, trans. Alan Sheridan, New York: W.W. Norton and Company.

The Lady from Shanghai (1947), [Film] Dir. Orson Welles, USA: Mercury Productions.

Langer, Susan K. (1953), *Feeling and Form: A Theory of Art Developed From Philosophy in a New Key*, London: Routledge.

Laruelle, François (2013), *Principles of Non-Philosophy*, trans. Nicola Rubczak and Anthony Paul Smith, London: Bloomsbury.

Laruelle, François (2013a), *Anti-Badiou: On the Introduction of Maoism into Philosophy*, trans. Robin Mackay, London: Bloomsbury.

The Last Laugh (1924), [Film] Dir. F.W. Murnau, Germany: UFA.

L'Eclisse (1962), [Film] Dir. Michelangelo Antonioni, Italy: Prod, Robert and Raymond Hakim. Dist. Cineriz.

Longo, Anna (2015), 'The Reality of the End of the World: Out-Science-Fiction and Horror Stories', in Sarah De Sanctis and Anna Longo (eds), *Breaking the Spell: Contemporary Realism under Discussion*, San Giovanni: Mimesis International, 31–48.

Longo, Anna (2022), 'Infinite Judgments: The Non-Being of the Idea', trans. Martijn Bujis, in *The Being of Negation in Post-Kantian Philosophy*, ed. Gregory S. Moss, Switzerland: Springer, 141–59.

Lotka, Alfred J. (1945), 'The Law of Evolution as a Maximal Principle', *Human Biology*, 17 (3): 167–94.

Lucretius (2007), *The Nature of Things*, trans. A. E. Stallings, London: Penguin.

Lumière, Louis (1936), 'The Lumière Cinematograph', *Journal of the SMPE*, 27, 49–50.

Lyotard, Jean-François (1986), 'Acinema', trans. Paisley N. Livingstone in collaboration with the author, in *Narrative, Apparatus, Ideology: a Film Theory Reader*, ed. Philip Rosen, New York: Columbia University Press, 349–59.

Lyotard, Jean-Francois (1991), *The Inhuman: Reflections on Time*, trans. Geoffrey Bennington and Rachel Bowlby, Cambridge: Polity Press.

Lyotard, Jean-François (2011), *Discourse, Figure*, trans. Anthony Hudek and Mary Lydon, Minneapolis: University of Minnesota Press.

Lyotard, Jean-François (2017), 'The Idea of a Sovereign Film,' trans. Peter W. Milne and Ashley Woodward, in Graham Jones and Ashley Woodward (eds), *Acinemas: Lyotard's Philosophy of Film*, Edinburgh: Edinburgh University Press, 61–70.

Martin, Adrian (2012), *Last Day Every Day: Figural Thinking from Auerbach and Kracauer to Agamben and Brenez*, Brooklyn: Punctum Books.

Martin, Adrian (2014), *Mise en Scène and Film Style: From Classical Hollywood to New Media Art*, Houndmills: Palgrave Macmillan.

Marx, Karl (1975), *Early Writings*, trans. Rodney Livingstone and Gregor Benton, London: Penguin.

Marx, Karl (1978), 'The German Ideology, Part 1', in Robert C. Tucker (ed), *The Marx-Engels Reader*, 2nd edition, New York: W.W. Norton & Company, 146–200.

Massumi, Brian (2011), *Semblance and Event: Activist Philosophy and the Occurrent Arts*, Cambridge, MA: The MIT Press.

Moore, Jason W. (2015), *Capitalism in the Web of Life: Ecology and the Accumulation of Capital*, Verso: London.

Mules, Warwick (2007), 'Media Sense: the Production of Sense at the Interface between New and Old Media Technologies', conference paper presented at Media in Transition Conference, MIT5, Cambridge, Mass., April 2007. https://www.academia.edu/24911455/Media_sense_the_production_of_sense_at_the_interface_between_new_and_old_media_technologies_1_Warwick_Mules, accessed 16 February 2023.

Mullarkey, John (2009), *Refractions of Reality: Philosophy and the Moving Image*, Houndmills: Palgrave Macmillan.

Murphy, Timothy S. (1999), 'Beneath Relativity: Bergson and Bohm on Absolute Time', in *The New Bergson*, John Mullarkey (ed), Manchester: Manchester University Press, 66–81.

Nancy, Jean-Luc (2002), *Hegel: The Restlessness of the Negative*, trans. Jason Smith and Steven Miller, Minneapolis: Minnesota University Press.

Nancy, Jean-Luc (2015), *After Fukushima: the Equivalence of Catastrophes*, trans. Charlotte Mandell, Fordham University Press: New York.

Nietzsche, Friedrich (1976), *The Portable Nietzsche*, trans. and ed. Walter Kaufmann, Harmondsworth: Penguin Books.

Ó Maoilearca, John (2015), *All Thoughts Are Equal: Laruelle and Nonhuman Philosophy*, Minneapolis: University of Minnesota Press.

Petro, Patrice (1989), *Joyless Streets: Women and Melodramatic Representation in Weimar Germany*, Princeton: Princeton University Press.

Priest, Graham (2000), 'Truth and Contradiction', *The Philosophical Quarterly*, 50 (200): 305–19.

Rear Window (1954), [film] Dir. Alfred Hitchcock, USA: Paramount Pictures.

Rodowick, D.N. (2001), *Reading the Figural, or, Philosophy After the New Media*, Durham: Duke University Press.

Ross, Daniel (2018), 'Introduction', in Bernard Stiegler, *The Neganthropocene*, trans. and ed. Daniel Ross, London: Open University Press.

Ross, Daniel (2021), *Psychopolitical Anaphylaxis: Steps Towards a Metacosmics*, London: Open Humanities Press.

Ross, Daniel and Man Ouyang, (2021), 'Towards a Metacosmics of Shame', in Ladson Hinton and Hessel Willemsen (eds), *Shame, Temporality and Social Change: Ominous Transitions*, London: Routledge, 103–23.

Rovelli, Carlo (2017), *Reality Is Not What It Seems: The Journey to Quantum Gravity*, trans. Simon Carnell and Erica Segre, London: Penguin Books.

Rovelli, Carlo (2021), *Helgoland: Making Sense of the Quantum Revolution*, trans. Erica Segre and Simon Carnell, New York: Riverhead Books.

Sallis, John (2018), *Elemental Discourses: The Collected Writings of John Sallis*, Volume 11/4, Bloomington: Indiana University Press.

Schrödinger, Erwin (1967), *What Is Life? The Physical Aspect of the Living Cell with Mind and Matter and Autobiographical Sketches*, Cambridge: Cambridge University Press.

Serres, Michel (2018), *The Birth of Physics*, trans. David Webb and William Ross, London: Rowman & Littlefield.

Simondon, Gilbert (1992), 'The Genesis of the Individual', in Jonathan Crary and Sanford Kwinter (eds), *Incorporations*, New York: Zone Books, 297–317.

Simondon, Gilbert (2020), *Individuation in Light of Notions of Form and Information*, trans. Taylor Adkins, Minneapolis: University of Minnesota Press.

Sloterdijk, Peter (1987), *Critique of Cynical Reason*, trans. Michael Eldred, Minneapolis: University of Minnesota Press.

Sloterdijk, Peter (2016), *Spheres, Volume 3, Foam: Plural Spherology*, trans. Wieland Hoban, South Pasadena: Semiotext(e).

Souriau, Étienne (2015), *The Different Modes of Experience*, trans. Erik Beranek and Tim Howles, Minneapolis: Univocal.

Stiegler, Bernard (1995), 'What Is Missing/What Makes Faults', trans. Daniel Ross, draft, first published as 'Ce qui fait defaut, *Cesure* 8 (1995): 231–78. https://www.academia.edu/54731473/Bernard_Stiegler_What_is_Missing_What_Makes_Faults_Ce_qui_fait_d%C3%A9faut_1995_, accessed 13 February 2023.

Stiegler, Bernard (1998), *Technics and Time, 1: The Faulty of Epimetheus*, trans. Richard Beardsworth and George Collins, Stanford: Stanford University Press.

Stiegler, Bernard (2002), 'The Discrete Image', in Jacques Derrida and Bernard Stiegler, *Echographies of Television*, trans. Jennifer Bajorek, Cambridge: Polity Press, 145–63.

Stiegler, Bernard (2009), *Technics and Time, 2: Disorientation*, trans. Stephen Barker, Stanford: Stanford University Press.

Stiegler, Bernard (2011), *Technics and Time, 3: Cinematic Time and the Question of Malaise*, trans. Stephen Barker, Stanford: Stanford University Press.

Stiegler, Bernard (2013), *What Makes Life Worth Living: On Pharmacology*, trans. Daniel Ross, Cambridge: Polity Press.

Stiegler, Bernard (2013a), 'The Theatre of Individuation: Phase-Shift and Resolution in Simondon and Heidegger', trans. Kristina Lebedeva, in Arne De Boever et al. (eds), *Gilbert Simondon: Being and Technology*, Edinburgh: Edinburgh University Press, 185–202.

Stiegler, Bernard (2014), *Symbolic Misery, Volume 1, The Hyperindustrial Epoch*, trans. Barnaby Norman, Cambridge: Polity Press.

Stiegler, Bernard (2014a), 'The Organology of Dreams and Arche-Cinema', trans. Daniel Ross, *The Nordic Journal of Aesthetics*, 47: 7–37.

Stiegler, Bernard (2015), *States of Shock: Stupidity and Knowledge in the 21st Century*, trans. Daniel Ross, Cambridge: Polity Press.

Stiegler, Bernard (2016), *Automatic Society, Volume 1, The Future of Work*, trans. Daniel Ross, Cambridge: Polity Press.

Stiegler, Bernard (2016a), 'The New Conflict of the Faculties and Functions: Quasi-Causality in the Anthropocene', trans. Daniel Ross, *Qui Parle*, 26 (1): 79–99.

Stiegler, Bernard (2018), *The Neganthropocene*, trans. and ed. Daniel Ross, London: Open University Press.

Stiegler, Bernard (2019), *The Age of Disruption: Technology and Madness in Computational Capitalism*, trans. Daniel Ross, Cambridge: Polity Press.

Stiegler, Bernard (2019a), 'For a Neganthropology of Automatic Society', trans. Daniel Ross, in Thomas Pringle, Gertrud Koch and Bernard Stiegler (eds.), *Machine*, 25–48, Lüneburg, Minneapolis: Meson Press and the University of Minnesota Press.

Stiegler, Bernard (2020), 'Noodiversity, Technodiversity: Elements of a New Economic Foundation Based on a New Foundation for Theoretical Computer Science', *Angelaki: Journal of the Theoretical Humanities*, 25 (4): 67–80.

Stiegler, Bernard (2021), 'Technics and Time, 4: Faculties and Functions of Noesis in the Post-Truth Age, a Posthumous Manuscript', trans. Daniel Ross. Unpublished manuscript.

Stiegler, Bernard (2021a), 'Afterword: On Positive Pharmacology', trans. Daniel Ross, in Daniel Ross, *Psychopolitical Anaphylaxis: Steps Towards a Metacosmics*, Open Humanities Press, London, 357–68.

Stiegler, Bernard (2022), 'The Ordeal of Truth: Causes and Quasi-Causes in the Entropocene', trans. Daniel Ross, *Foundations of Science*, 27, 271–80. doi:10.1007/s10699-020-09736-3.

The Third Man (1949), [Film] Dir. Carol Reed, UK: London Films.

Une Femme Douce (1969), [Film] Dir. Robert Bresson, France: Paramount.

Ware, Owen (2018), 'Fichte's Normative Ethics: Deontological or Teleological?' *Mind*, 127, 506, 565–84.

Weekes, Anderson (2016), 'Intersubjectivity, Species-Being, Actual Occasions: Social Ontology from Fichte to Whitehead', in Lukaszc Lamza and Jakub Dziadkowiec (eds), *Recent Advances in the Creation of a Process-Based Worldview: Human Life in Process*, Cambridge: Cambridge Scholars Publishing, 47–59.

Wood, Allen W. (2016), *Fichte's Ethical Thought*, Oxford: Oxford University Press.

Žižek, Slavoj (2012), *Less than Nothing: Hegel and the Shadow of Dialectical Materialism*, London: Verso.

Žižek, Slavoj (2022), *Surplus-Enjoyment: A Guide for the Non-Perplexed*, London: Bloomsbury.

Index

acinema 86–8, 90, 92, 102, 118
acting out 36, 60, 106, 111, 113, 118
action 2–3
    moral (see moral action)
    non-indecisive 101, 105, 110, 112, 162
    potential 4, 100
amor fati 73–4
    Nietzsche 73
anamnesis see Stiegler *hypomnesis/anamnesis*
Anstoß (Fichte)
    as check 27, 40–2
    as remainder 41
anthropy 24, 51, 58
    control societies 59
apeiron 21, 47–9, 53, 54
apparatus 101
    acinema 92
    dispositif 91–2
arche-cinema 13, 146–7, 149
archival future 15, 21, 26, 28–9, 46, 60
    Derrida 33–4
    idiotextual becoming 81
    memory trace 113
    promise 52
Antonioni, Michelangelo 2, 9, 23, 102
    style of direction 104–5
Aristotle 17, 21, 24
    primary imagination 17
art film 30, 75, 89–91, 93, 97, 102
    subversive potential 91
Auerbach, Erich
    figura 3, 70–1
automatization/dis-automatization 50

Balázs, Béla
    moral significance 134
    visual linkage 133–4
Barthes, Roland
    cut of the *real* 78
    photography and death 77

    punctum effect 10, 30, 77, 136
    this-has-been 77, 80
Beckett, Samuel
    amor fati 97
    life death 98, 145
    recommencement 55
    tragicomic structure 30
Benjamin, Walter
    optical unconscious 79, 105, 111
    poetizing 54–5, 60
Bergson, Henri
    cinematograph 15, 25
    crystalline flow 39, 63, 65
    crystalline sphere 15, 39, 55
    durational time and quantum thought 38
    memory cone 38, 55
    quantum field 63
Blanchot, Maurice
    death in the last instant 73
    distancing function of images 66
    power to begin 68
Bresson, Robert 87, 111
    blind camera 111–14
    optical unconscious 111, 114–17

The Cabinet of Dr. Caligari (Wiene) 134
camera apparatus 105, 107, 111, 112, 126
capitalism
    computational 24
    hyper- 24, 25, 28
    platform 59
Capra, Frank 82
care 1, 20, 21, 23, 58–9, 65
    neganthropy 22, 60, 81, 120, 125
    negative affectivity 23
    pharmacological 23
    right 23
    Stiegler 23, 83, 120
catastrophe, catastrophic 7, 9, 25, 27–8
    algorithmic governmentality 156
    death 74

eclipse 108
loss of the feeling of life 99
meaninglessness 103, 150
memory erasure 98, 102, 103, 146
photograph as 77
system failure 51
world collapse 147
chamber film (see *Kammerspielfilm*)
cinematograph 12, 15, 25, 33, 46, 128
   automaton 98
   disrupting technology 50
   film apparatus 111
   organon of perception 28
ciné-mnemotechnesis 34, 49
control
   algorithmic governance 24, 81, 120, 124, 156
   societies 59, 65
creative destruction
   hyper-capitalism 28
crystalline flow 60–3, 72
   quantum field 65
crystalline sphere 15, 48, 55, 60
   Gadamerian-Bergsonian 58
cut of the *real* 10
   punctum effect 78–9, 136
   relativity of views 125
   trauma 41

data code 24, 28
death-that-awaits 2, 8, 43, 94, 96, 113
   The Father 132–3, 137, 149, 151
death drive 8, 73
Deleuze, Gilles
   control societies 59
   The Lady from Shanghai 62
   power of the false 13
   pure crystal image 62, 96
   quasi-cause 3, 78
Derrida, Jacques
   archival future 29, 33
   life death 7, 30, 58
   moral obligation 19
   pharmakon 17, 20, 83
   quasi-machine 12
digital imaging 77
dispositif 8, 30, 87–8, 92
   as anti-system 113
   as counter-praxis 141–3, 146
   paraconsistency 130–1, 134
   paraconsistent logic 15
   spherology 123
   spiel 91, 102, 106
   as tactical avoidance mechanism 102
   visual linkage 134
drive 2, 9–10, 12, 24
   capitalism 59
   counter-resistance 11, 64, 149
   life death 83
   metastasis 89, 130
   resistance 9, 10, 92, 125
   self-destruction 45, 80
   technical systems 64

fabulation 23, 96, 132, 137
   cautionary tale-telling
face
   life and death 7–8, 68, 70, 71, 72, 73, 80
      as game of faces 139
   moral significance 134
The Father (Zeller) 129, 131–3, 135, 136–54
Fichte, Johann Gottlieb
   Anstoß 27, 40
   'free reciprocal efficacy' 41, 59, 130, 156
   I = I (self-positing) 7, 22, 25, 26, 41, 45
   power of the imagination 41
   right (*Recht*) 22
   Tathandlung 26, 41
figural, the 1–3, 27, 52, 123
   irreality of 7
   life death 7, 125
figural analysis 2, 12, 16, 71, 74, 118, 123
figures of resistance 3, 25, 102, 106, 155, 156
Film (Beckett, Schneider) 97–8
film noir
   dispositif 91–2
   voice-over 92
Flusser, Vilém
   acts of avoidance 112, 140
   photographic gesture 111
freedom, negative/positive 28

freedom, finite 59, 98, 103, 120, 130–1, 137
Freud, Sigmund
    blindness of the seeing eye 110, 114
    drive 9
    reality testing 25, 132
    repression 85, 89
    trauma 84
    unconscious/preconscious 110
    Verneinung 26, 107, 117, 132

Gadamer, Hans Georg
    field of views 20
    fusional hermeneutics 20, 54
    methexis 20–1, 53, 75, 81
    the right path 60
    spherical model 53, 55
    stoß (shock) 55, 67
game of faces 146
German Idealism 25
    split subject 27

Hegel, Georg
    ethical life (*Sittlichkeit*) 21, 29, 52
    I–We 21, 51–2
Heidegger, Martin
    Augenblick 57
    danger 112
    ennframing (*Gestell*) 25, 26, 112
    Ereignis 25, 89
    tool-being 50
hermeneutics
    figural 155
    fusional 20, 53
    turn 28, 81, 119
Hitchcock, Alfred
    MacGuffins 46
Hilbert space 38
Hintertreppe (Jessner and Leni) 133
hypomnesis see Stiegler
        hypomnesis/anamnesis

I–We 14, 21–2, 33–7, 51, 59, 124
idiotext 27, 34, 55–6, 58
    characteristics in film 91
    concretization 90
    leap 66
    this-has-been 79
    weave of mnesic traces 127

Intervista (Fellini) 81, 85–6, 88
interference 41, 146
Irigaray, Luce 45
    familial obligation 148
    sexuate difference 49
    speculum 47–9
irreal
    life death 8, 68, 71
    ontological ambiguity 39
    paraconsistency 40
    punctum effect 77
    quantum perspective 79
    true/false 39, 96
It's a Wonderful Life (Capra) 82–4, 85, 89

Johnston, Adrian
    drive 9
    transcendental materialism 16
judgement, infinite 19–20, 40

Kammerspielfilm 42, 66, 133–6, 152
    different from Expressionist film 134
    visual linkage 134
Kant, Immanuel
    transcendental unity of apperception 17
Kirby, Vicky
    quantum thought 5
Kovács, András
    modern art film 89–90
Kracauer, Siegfried 11, 14
Kuleshov effect 12–13, 123
    slipping-in 13, 79

Lacan, Jacques
    controlling master 119
    missed encounter 110, 138
La Dolce Vita (Fellini) 86,
The Lady from Shanghai (Welles) 62, 91–7
Langer, Susan K.
    tragicomic 71–2
Laruelle, François
    dyad couple 6–7, 102
    non-philosophy 6
The Last Laugh (Murnau) 66–70, 72, 73
L'Eclisse (Antonioni) 102–10

life death 7, 14, 15, 17, 23, 57
   Derrida 7, 30, 58
   irreal 71, 73, 81, 132
   pharmakon as 18 125
   propaedeutics 23
   punctum 78
   recommencement 151
   situations 22
   switching 75, 150
   tragicomic patterning 30, 71–2
light-life 8, 61, 63, 78, 123
   substance 124
   trace-data 55
Lyotard, Jean-François
   acinema 86, 92
   inhuman 64–5
   sovereignty of film 87–8, 90, 92
   thermodynamic systems 64
logic, paraconsistent 5

Maoilearca, John
   filmic substance 6
   paraconsistent logic 6
Martin, Adrian 8, 11–12, 14–15
   dispositif 91–2
   figural, the 12
memory, epiphylogenetic 146
methexis 20–1, 53–4, 55, 56, 57, 74
   ancient Greek dramaturgy 56, 60
   Gadamer 20, 53–4
   hermeneutics 20
   quantum superposition 81
mnemotechnesis 10, 127–8, 133, 156
   archival future 33
   film analysis 52
   film story-telling 57
   inhuman 64, 106
   paraconsistent logic 22
   quantum field 65–6
   technics of memorizing 14
   third memory 59
   transcendental materialism 16
missed encounter 137–9
Möbius strip 126
moral action 55, 130–1
   freedom 59, 119, 130
moral disposition
   of film 91–3, 97

moral right 19–21
Murnau, F.W.
   unchained camera 69–70

neganthropic resistance 92, 101, 103, 123–4, 125, 149
neganthropy 22, 51, 58, 98, 123–4
   as potential 3
   right 60
negative affectivity 23, 82, 131
negative entropy (negentropy) 8, 50
   drift 9
   self-destructive 51
   tendency towards degree zero 57
negentropic force 3, 6–7, 11, 155
noesis 17, 29, 56, 57, 123
   Aristotle 24
noetic freedom 16, 22, 24–5, 27, 28, 37, 52
   acinematic film 92
   erasure of 145
   judgement 57
   methexis 75
   moral consciousness 58–9

optical unconscious 113, 117, 141, 145
organic machine 12, 15, 16, 28, 61–2, 120
   cinematograph 15, 125

paraconsistency 5–7, 130
   quantum time 152
past
   absolute 39
   dead 9, 15, 34, 79, 90, 113
      recommencement 80–3
   Nachträglichkeit 127
pathways
   archival future 47
   circuitry of 56
   other 101, 140
   other pathways thinking 29, 81
   the right path 28, 60
phantasm 10, 28, 40, 61, 86, 117, 140–1
   Lacanian master 120
   as non-I 35
   as quasi-cause 79
   spectral world 145
pharmacological event 100

pharmakon 50, 97, 100, 151, 156
   bifurcating situation 83
   films as 19, 52
   as transitional object 117, 120
photographic index 77
planetarium perspective 133, 139
places of life 60, 85
Plato 17, 20, 29, 54
provocateur 130

quantum event(s) 30, 39, 75, 135, 136
   cascading 139, 144, 151
   paraconsistency 5–7, 127
   superposition, non-local interactivity, entanglement 5, 127
quantum field
   collapse 15, 108
   crystalline flow 65
   spherological view 126
quantum thought 5, 65
   fictionalizing 6
quasi-cause 3, 19, 98, 125, 129
   a posteriori reason 78
quasi-machine 12, 15
   mechanical creativity 12

real, the 10, 72, 16, 34, 38, 41
   archival future 34, 46, 52
   cut of 10, 41
   as remainder 65
   as resistive potential 66
Rear Window (Hitchcock) 42–7, 147
reason, sufficiency of 19, 91–2, 130–1, 133
   paraconsistent logic 134–5
recommencement 80, 100–1, 151–2, 154
   see also Blanchot's power to begin
remainder 7, 41, 107
resistance 4, 7–9, 87, 92
   acts of avoidance 112
   neganthropy 58, 92
   the will 101
resistive potential 3, 58–9, 65, 66
   creative 92
right
   contested situation 133
   German Idealism 19, 21
   moral obligation 19

   places of life 60, 85
   relations of right 22
   the right path 21, 28–9, 84, 93, 131, 154
Ross, Daniel 120
   anaphylactic collapse 51

Simondon, Gilbert
   crystalline flow 60
   moral act 37, 59, 130
   phase-shift 22, 36
   pre-individual field 22
   syncrystallization 27, 102
   transindividuation 27, 35, 59, 84
situation, pharmacological 21, 75, 83, 85, 88
   care 23
Sloterdijk, Peter
   cynical reason 24
   spatialized sphere 126
Stiegler, Bernard
   care 21, 23, 83
   doubly epokhal redoubling 50
   epiphylogenesis 84, 146
   hypomnesis/anamnesis 13, 46, 59, 128, 129, 131
   I–We 14, 21–2, 26
   Kuleshov effect 13
      as memory trace 85
      as supervening technical support 13
   moral consciousness 20, 59
   neganthropy 8, 22, 29, 51, 120
   noetic freedom 25, 99, 101
   organology 12
   pharmakon 20, 50
   punctum effect 10, 78
   reconstitutive technics 8
   tertiary retentions 10, 13, 78–9, 80
   traumatype 84–5, 87–9, 118–19, 111
Stimmung 53, 68, 90, 109, 131
   Kammerspielfilm 134
   quantum effect 127
   total truth effect 70
spiel
   acts of avoidance 112
   dispositif 102
   in situ praxis 112
   playing out 70, 91, 102, 103, 106
Spielraum (room to play) 111

summons (Fichte) 40
    Anstoß 41
syncrystallization
    desyncrystallization 102–3
    hyper-syncrystallization 36, 47, 113
    Simondon 27, 102

thermodynamics 15, 30, 50
    thermodynamic perspective 57
    second law of 58, 74
    thermodynamic system 64
The Third Man (Reed) 19–20, 23
time frame, definition 138–9
time frames (collapsing) 9, 129–30, 132, 133
    Kammerspielfilm 135
    quantum world 146
    recommencement 151–2
    visual linkage 136
trace-data 27, 30, 34, 55, 124, 126
tragicomic mode 73
transcendental field 17, 21–2
transcendental materialism 16–18
trap, pharmacological 88–9

traumatype 42
    return of the repressed 86, 88, 125, 133, 146
    stereotype 84–5
truth, ordeal of 117, 147

Une Femme Douce (Bresson) 114–19

view from nowhere 46, 56, 103, 106, 112, 124–5
    acts of avoidance 140
    time frames 139–40, 148

Welles, Orson 62, 90, 91–2
will, the
    neganthropic resistance 8, 101
    to nothingness 109
    unwilling the will 28, 101
        dis-automatization 59

Zeller, Florian
    as *provocateur* 130
Žižek, Slavoj
    Anstoß 40
    Lacanian master 120